Reprints of Economic Classics

ELEMENTS OF POLITICAL ECONOMY

ELEMENTS

OF

POLITICAL ECONOMY

BY

SAMUEL P. NEWMAN

[1835]

AUGUSTUS M. KELLEY • PUBLISHERS
CLIFTON 1973

First Edition 1835

(*Andover*: Gold and Newman, Publishers;
New York: H. Griffin & Company, 1835)

Reprinted 1973 by
AUGUSTUS M. KELLEY PUBLISHERS
Clifton New Jersey 07012

Library of Congress Cataloging in Publication Data

Newman, Samuel Phillips, 1797-1842.
Elements of political economy.

(Reprints of economic classics)
Reprint of the 1835 ed.
1. Economics. I. Title.
HB161.N56 1972 330 68-30535
ISBN 0-678-00691-1

PRINTED IN THE UNITED STATES OF AMERICA
by SENTRY PRESS, NEW YORK, N. Y. 10013

ELEMENTS

OF

POLITICAL ECONOMY.

BY SAMUEL P. NEWMAN,

LECTURER ON POLITICAL ECONOMY IN BOWDOIN COLLEGE.

"The best security for a free government, and generally for the public peace and morals is, that the whole community should be well informed upon its Political, as well as its other interests."—*Lord Brougham.*

ANDOVER:

GOULD AND NEWMAN, PUBLISHERS.

NEW YORK:

H. GRIFFIN AND COMPANY.

1835.

PREFACE.

It has been a leading object of the author of the following work, to prepare a text book, in which the more important principles of the science of Political Economy are developed in their application to the usages and institutions of our own country. The defect of the text books now in use in this particular, is acknowledged; and this circumstance has tended, in no small degree, to prevent the general and strong interest in the science, as a branch of education, which it may justly claim. For in a self-governing community, it is especially important, that the constitution of society should be studied, and "the reasons of things" well understood. Many unfounded prejudices are also thus removed, the public mind is enlightened, and led to adopt those measures, which are for the public good.

The author has not deemed it expedient to embrace the opinions of any school of Political Economists. It will be found, however, that he is more indebted to A. Smith's Inquiry into the Nature and Causes of the Wealth of Nations, than to any other work on this science. Many sentiments and opinions of this "Father of the science," are judged to be better founded and more valuable, than those of modern writers.

It is well known, that many principles of this science are yet unsettled. On this account, the author feels that he has a claim on the candor of the public, and he would respectfully request of all who may examine the following work, especially of those using it as a text book, that its defects, or any erroneous statements which it contains, may be pointed out to his notice.

Bowdoin College, July, 1835.

CONTENTS.

PART I.

PRODUCTION AND CIRCULATION OF WEALTH.

CHAPTER III.

Human Industry.

CHAPTER IV.

Natural aids to Production.

CHAPTER V.

Productive Capital.

CHAPTER VI.

Circulation of Wealth.

CHAPTER VII.

Price.

CHAPTER VIII.

Agriculture.

CHAPTER XII.

On the different classes of Productive laborers.

CHAPTER XIII.

On the different classes of unproductive laborers.

PART II.

DISTRIBUTION AND CONSUMPTION OF WEALTH.

CHAPTER I.

Distribution of Wealth.

CHAPTER II.

Wages.

CHAPTER III.

Interest, or profits of capital.

CHAPTER IV.

Rent, or profits of natural agency.

CHAPTER V.

Profits of the Undertaker.

CHAPTER VI.

Fees and Salaries.

CHAPTER VII.

Consumption of Wealth.

CHAPTER VIII.

National expenditure.

POLITICAL ECONOMY.

PART I.

ON THE PRODUCTION AND CIRCULATION OF WEALTH.

INTRODUCTION.

A nation as viewed by the Political Economist.

MEN are seen in their most improved condition, when associated together in large communities. The excitements of competition are then most strongly felt—enterprise and exertion are called forth and liberally rewarded. It is then that leisure and opportunity are found for the exercise and improvement of the mental powers; thus knowledge is increased and spread abroad, and the various arts and sciences cultivated and advanced towards perfection. In this state, too, the social affections are freely indulged, and the refined love of country, of family and friends, is awakened and cherished.

But what a family is here to be provided for! and how immense the amount of its daily consumption! How many bales of cloth must be furnished for its use! What toil and skill are required to construct habitations for its shelter! How many hands must be employed in fabricating the ten thousand little conveniences of life within and about these habitations!

But to supply the constantly returning animal wants of this national family, and to furnish what are esteemed the comforts and conveniences of civilized life, is but a part of what is to be accomplished. Measures must be adopted, which may ensure a defence both against foreign foes and internal aggression. A civil government must be established and supported; and, till the principles of peace become prevalent, armies and navies, with fortifications and implements of war, must be provided.

This numerous family must also be educated. When the grosser wants of our nature have been met, it is felt, that there are in man wants of a higher and more exalted kind, which ask gratification. Men of cultivated intellect and extended knowledge, must also be reared up to administer the concerns of a great nation. Such minds too are needed to devise and carry through the ten thousand projects and enterprises, and the complicated business transactions of a large and thriving community. Here then is a call for instruction, for books and the whole apparatus of learning. Schools, colleges and the different seminaries of learning, must be founded and endowed, and means used, by which the public mind generally may be enlightened and elevated.

An intelligent and reflecting people will also be mindful, that there are moral and religious relations and duties, in which men need to be instructed. They will come to the knowledge of civil and social rights, and will seek to be made secure in their enjoyment. Aware too of the evils which "flesh is heir to," they will be led to inquire what antidotes and remedies may give relief to the diseased and suffering body. Thus the calls for professional assistance will arise—the divine, the lawyer and the physician will be found, each rendering important service to the community.

A civilized community has also its imaginary wants to be supplied. Under this head is included all that pertains to the gratification of the taste—the refinements and elegancies of life. Such are the various productions of the fine arts. Such also are those articles of furniture, dress and equipage, which either are not necessary for the supply of the absolute wants of men, or might be furnished in more simple and less expensive forms.

There are two other particulars, in which the resemblance between a nation, as viewed by the political economist, and a numerous family, might be traced out. Both seek after an improvement of their condition, and both are called upon to make provision for the increase of their numbers. In neither case is it thought sufficient, to replace what has been consumed—that the close of the year should find the community, or the family, in circumstances equally favourable with those of its commencement. There is in both a constant struggle for advancement, for more enjoyment and greater independence. The numbers of both are also in ordinary circumstances increasing, and "for every new comer to the great feast of nature, a new cover must be provided."

Now for the supply of all these wants, what foresight, what planning, what complicated and extended arrangements, what patient, various and unremitted toil, are required!

Happily, there is found in the constitution of man provision for all that is thus demanded of him. He who in goodness formed man a social being, hath in wisdom adapted him to the social state. There is the desire of advancement, the strong, ever active disposition to improve our condition. There is the reasoning mind, which, instructed by the past, can extend forward its view to the future, can form plans and put measures in train for their accomplishment. There is the vigorous, enduring body, capable of strenuous and long continued effort, and of adapting itself with wonderful pliability to various circumstances and pursuits. Now it is by the exercise of what is thus natural to man, that the many and various wants of a large community are supplied. While each individual is following his own inclinations, and planning and laboring for himself, seeking his own aggrandisement, and obtaining a supply of his own wants, he is at the same time planning and laboring and accumulating for the whole community, and advancing the general welfare.

Objects of the science and plan of the work.

He who has thus looked upon man in a civilized community, and considered his wants, is prepared to understand what is meant by Political Economy. The leading object of this science is, to shew in what way the economical affairs of a nation may be so conducted, that its wants may be supplied and its prosperity promoted. It tells us, how the industry of a nation may be called forth and successfully directed, and how its resources, of every kind, may be developed and made efficient. It instructs us, how what is thus obtained is distributed among the different classes and members of a community, and points out to us the several ways, in which it may be judiciously and profitably consumed. It looks at the different employments and pursuits of men, and considers them in their relation to each other and to the general welfare.

It looks at the different classes of society, the rich and the poor, the capitalist and the laborer, and shows their connexion and mutual dependence. It extends its view to foreign nations, and, in opposition to generally received opinions, instructs men to rejoice in the prosperity of others. In fine, it inquires into all that pertains to the business concerns of a community, and investigates those subjects, which are in any way connected with the prosperity of the nation, and of its individual members, when considered as a part of the community.

It is not designed in the following text book, to exhibit any connected set of opinions on subjects pertaining to this science. Many of its principles yet remain unsettled, and while this is the case, error, if not embarrassment, may result from following a system. All that is here attempted, is to state and explain those principles of the science, which are of general interest, and admit of application to the business of life, and at the same time to answer some of the inquiries, which naturally arise in the mind of a reflecting man, when looking upon the economical arrangements of society. It is necessary, however, before instituting these inquiries, to give a brief explanation of the more common terms and phrases used in the science, and also to state with some minuteness, the arrangements of an economical kind, found in a well ordered community.

And here it may be expedient, very briefly to notice a prejudice against the study of this science, which exists in the minds of some. There are those who look upon all inquiries and discussions of this kind, as illiberal and degrading. They are associated in their minds with what pertains to the acquiring and hoarding of money.

But these prejudices arise from a limited and erroneous view of the science. Who would not wish to see all around him enjoying in decent competency, the comforts and conveniences of life? Who would not have each individual feel, that his own interests are deeply involved in the prosperity of others? Who would not have the different orders of society respect their mutual rights, and feel their mutual dependence? and what philanthropist does not desire, that the nations of the earth may understand and appreciate the advantages of peace and mutual intercourse? These are a part of the lessons taught by this science; and surely no one can justly pronounce a study low and degrading, whose instructions are thus practical and salutary.

CHAPTER I.

Definitions and explanations of terms and phrases used in the science.

The most important wants of man, in this state of being, are those of his animal nature. He must have food and clothing and shelter convenient for him. Should the inquiry be made, to what source are we to look for a supply of these wants? it is at once answered—to the earth on which we dwell. Its fruits, its herbs, its plants, its forests and its animals, are all made subject to man, and hence he is to find his daily food, the garments that cover him, the fuel that warms him, and the habitation by which he is sheltered. But what is thus spontaneously offered to man, is but a scanty supply, and in forms and under circumstances but ill adapted to his wants. The same power which appointed the earth to be for the use of man, hath also said, "of the sweat of thy brow shalt thou eat of the fruit thereof." It is to his own labor, in connexion with the fertility of the soil, and other natural advantages, that man is to look for the supply of his most urgent wants.

Human industry, then, is to be employed in the cultivation of the earth, and in adapting the supplies, thus obtained, to the wants of man. Hence arises the distinction of Agricultural, Manufacturing and Commercial labor. And as these terms, when thus used in the science of Political Economy, have a signification somewhat different from their popular use, a short explanation of them is here given.

By AGRICULTURE, in the popular use of the term, is meant the cultivation of the soil—that labor of man which is bestowed upon the earth to render it more fertile, and thus to increase the amount obtained from it for the supply of human wants. In its scientific use, the term is extended to all employments, by which these needed supplies are obtained from the earth. Thus fisheries, mining operations, the gathering of the wild fruits of the earth, the rearing of domestic animals, and the hunting of game, are all included under the head of agricultural labor.

From agricultural industry, using the term in this extended sense, are derived, not only food and other necessaries of life for immediate consumption, but all the materials used in the arts. Without agriculture, there could be neither manufactures, nor commerce. Hence, no doubt, the common impression, that agricultural labor is of more importance to a community, than manufacturing or commercial. Of the correctness of this impression, we may better judge, when definitions of these terms shall have been given.

Manufacturing industry is employed in adapting what is thus obtained from the earth to the wants of man. The process may consist in the mixture and union of different substances, thus forming a new substance, or compound, or it may be the altering of the form or texture of objects. In the former instance, it is a process in chemical; in the latter, in mechanical art. Thus all the arts of life, whether chemical or mechanical, and the common processes of domestic industry—the preparing of food, the making up of garments, are included under the term manufactures.

Commercial industry consists in buying and selling—in the transportation of commodities, and in placing them under such circumstances, as may suit the convenience of consumers. It includes navigation and internal transportation in all their different forms. It includes also the labors of the multitudes, who, as clerks, salesmen, porters, draymen, &c., are employed in large commercial establishments.

Production is the adapting of material objects to the wants of man. He by whom a process of production is carried on, is called a producer, and the result of the process, a product.

An analysis of the different forms of human industry which have just been explained, will shew the meaning and test the correctness of this definition. The wheat in the granary of the farmer, is an agricultural product. To obtain it, he prepared his grounds—he scattered his seed, and in due time he gathered in his harvest. And this agricultural laborer is said to be the producer of a crop of wheat. But what has he done? He has not brought into existence that which did not before exist. Availing himself of the fertility of the soil—of the warm influences of the sun and of the showers of heaven, by a process little understood by himself, he has caused these particles of matter, which now constitute the crop of wheat in his granary, to assume their present form, thus in part adapting them to the wants of himself and his fellow men.

Trace this same wheat, when by a manufacturing process it becomes bread. It is ground; it is mixed with other ingredients; these are kneaded together and subjected to the heat of fire. Thus the particles of matter in the wheat are made to undergo both a chemical and mechanical action. Their properties and their forms are changed. They exist now as a product in manufactures, and in this form are still further adapted to the supply of human wants.

These same material particles, now in the form of bread, are next conveyed from the work-shop of the baker to the residence of the consumer, and there given to him in exchange for money, or any other object of value, which the consumer is ready to give and the baker to receive, in exchange for his bread. Thus that, which, when in the form of wheat, was an agricultural product, and in the form of bread a manufactured product, becomes, as transported and sold by the baker, a commercial product. Its form and its properties remain the same; its location and its ownership only are changed. But this change of place and of ownership, is the process of commercial production, and obviously it is another step in adapting the products of agriculture and manufacture to the uses of man.

We now look at the product—bread in the hands of the consumer, and we say, that the whole process, to which the particles of matter in this loaf of bread have been subjected, from the time they existed in their dispersed state in the earth, or in the air, till thus given over to the consumer, is *production*—the adapting of what is found in the material world to the wants of man.

It will be noticed, that this definition of production limits its application to material objects. Some writers on Political Economy extend the meaning of the term, and speak of immaterial products. But it is thought, that the view now given is more simple, and better fitted to develope with clearness the principles of the science.

The inquiry respecting the superiority of agricultural over other forms of industry, may now be easily answered. It is true, there is a class of agricultural products—his daily food—which is absolutely essential to the existence of man. It is also true, that the agricultural laborer furnishes the materials, upon which the other forms of industry are employed. But we have seen, that agricultural production is in its nature the same, as the other forms of production. In each case, it is human labor, availing itself of such helps, as it can command. The result is also in each case the same—there is an adaptation of that which previously existed, to the wants of man. And in some climates, those particularly, where shelter is needed from the severity of cold and the inclemency of the sky, the products of manufacturing industry seem equally essential to existence, with those of agriculture.

Populous nations moreover could not long exist without the aids of commercial production. There does not then seem to be a good foundation for the impression, above referred to, of the superior importance of agricultural industry.

From the definition that has been given of production, the distinction between a productive and unproductive laborer may be readily made. The former is a producer, one employed in a productive process, assisting in some way in the adaptation of material objects to the wants of men. The latter, though a laborer, and though his labors may be highly profitable to himself, affording him competency and perhaps comparative wealth, is engaged in ministering to a different set of human wants. Professional men, statesmen and instructors, are unproductive laborers. So are those who furnish public amusements, when not employed in the creation of material products. A stage player and a musician, are unproductive laborers; a painter of portraits and a maker of fireworks are productive laborers. In the class of unproductive laborers, are also to be placed most of those employed as servants, and all those of every rank who constitute the standing armies and the marine force of a nation. In a wealthy and refined community, the number of unproductive laborers is great, and it will be inferred from the list of employments stated, that they constitute an important portion of the community.

According to the distinction now made, the natural philosopher, and the chemist, who are employed in the investigation of the properties and relations and laws of material objects, are productive laborers; and such are found in each of the three great departments of human industry. Sir Humphrey Davy, while employed in examining the nature of soils, that he might determine under what cultivation different tracts of land might be made most fertile, was an agricultural laborer. Watt, when engaged in making discoveries and improvements, pertaining to steam and steam engines, and the adaptation of this power to the arts, was a manufacturing laborer. Fulton, too, when investigating this same power and applying it to navigation, was an efficient commercial laborer. And this statement as to the nature of scientific labor, holds true, even though the philosopher himself make no application of his discoveries to any process of production, but leaves this part of the work to another. He is still to be ranked as a productive laborer.

Of natural agency, and other natural aids to production.

In the processes of production which have now been explained, human foresight and ingenuity are the guides, and, in most of them, human industry is the principal agent. But in different parts of these processes, much is effected by nature itself. Much also is to be ascribed to the increased efficiency of human labor, as aided by the properties of material objects and what are termed the laws of the material creation. To the former of these two classes of aids to production, I propose to apply the phrase *natural agency*, limiting what is often used to denote all natural aids of production, to those instances, in which the process, or an important part of it, is carried on by nature itself. Such, in raising a crop of wheat, is that process, which, in its several parts, we describe as the springing up, the growth and the ripening of the grain. Man prepares the ground, and scatters the seed, but nature makes the plant to germinate and grow. And thus it is, that nature itself becomes active in the work; and this aid, thus extended to man, is natural agency. So again, in the manufacturing of wheat into bread, the process of fermentation is a part of the work of production carried on by nature itself, and affords another example of natural agency.

The other class of natural aids to production, includes those instances, in which human labour is the efficient agent, but in doing the work, it avails itself to a greater or less extent in different instances, of the properties of material objects. In preparing his ground for a crop, the farmer makes use of his plough. But for this important implement in husbandry, man is indebted to certain properties of iron, its malleability and its hardness, and to the toughness and flexibility and strength of wood, of which materials the plough is constructed. So, in that most important aid to manufacturing and commercial production—the steam engine, it is to the properties of different metals, and of steam, or more properly of fire and water and air, that man is indebted for an assistant most efficient in itself, and admitting of various applications. And thus it is, that under the guidance of human ingenuity, the properties of material objects and the great laws of nature, such as gravitation, elasticity, galvanism, &c. which in fact are but properties of material objects, become aids to production.

And here it may be noticed, that the assistance derived from natural agency, using the phrase in the limited sense now stated, is, for the most part, confined to agricultural production. To some extent it is found in manufactures, chiefly in the chemical arts. In commercial production, it is unknown. The other class of natural aids, though found to the greatest extent in manufactures, is common to the three great divisions of human industry. The importance of this distinction will hereafter be seen.

Of the aids to production now described, man in a rude state of society, avails himself but to a limited extent. He gathers the spontaneous offerings of the earth, and makes some awkward and inefficient attempts to cultivate the soil; he has also his implements for securing his game, his canoe, his stone hatchet, and perhaps some rude agricultural tool. But of most of the natural aids to production around him, it may be said, that they are useless to him. He knows not of their existence, or, if he knows of them, he wants the ingenuity and patient toil, necessary to turn them to account. Of what avail to him are a fertile soil—the propelling force of the wind—the strong movement of the descending river, or the expansive power of steam. But in civilized communities, where science and art have taught men the importance of natural agency, and the properties of material objects around them, and further have instructed them in what ways these aids to production may be applied, important advantages are derived from this source. In almost every department of industry, these labor saving machines are found, and thus the efficiency of human labor is increased a hundred fold.

It has been stated, that the earth is the source, to which man is to look for the supply of his wants. And as different portions of the earth, or territories, offer these supplies, or the aids of nature by which they may be obtained, in varying degrees of amount and perfection, they are said to possess more or less of territorial advantages.

In the enumeration of territorial advantages, a fertile soil, offering in rich abundance nutritious fruits and plants for food, is of the first importance. Timber and other materials for building—forest trees or coal-mines for fuel—materials for the manufacture of cloth—mill privileges—metals and woods of different kinds, used in the construction of machinery and in the arts—fisheries and mines of the precious metals, may also be specified.

In judging of the relative importance of the territorial advantages of different countries, the two following principles should be regarded.

1. Of those commodities which are essential to the supply of a nation's wants, it is desirable, that a territory should furnish such as are with difficulty transported from a distance.

2. Of the territorial advantages which rank under the head of aids to production, those are more important which belong to the class of natural agents, than those which belong to aids of the second class.

From both of these principles, the superior advantages of a territory offering a full supply of agricultural products and facilities for agricultural production, might be inferred. In illustration of the former, I might refer to those extensive tracts of land in the Western States which are destitute of timber and other materials for building, and also of fuel. It is well known that though the soil of this region is favourable to the raising of grain, the absence of the agricultural products just mentioned, which are with difficulty transported from a distance, much diminishes the value of that portion of our country.

Productive Capital.

When men know how to avail themselves of the help of natural agency, and other natural aids to production, and thus to increase the amount of what is obtained by their labor, they find themselves in possession of larger supplies, than their immediate necessities require. Of the surplus thus obtained, the desire of improving their condition, leads them to lay aside a portion, as a provision for the future. Thus, by well directed industry and frugality, accumulations are made. A part of what is thus acquired and saved by individual producers, will be vested in such objects as will promote their comfort and enjoyment—in clothing, houses, furniture, &c. Another portion, and in a wealthy community this portion is large, is employed by its possessors to aid them in obtaining further supplies. It thus becomes an aid to production, and bears the name of *productive capital.*

The forms in which productive capital exists, are various. In agricultural nations, much is expended in the permanent improvements of lands, in cattle, in barns, granaries, and in different implements of husbandry. In manufacturing nations, a large amount exists in the form of machinery, in buildings, and in the materials used in different manufactures. So far as a nation is commercial in its habits, there will be investments in ware-houses, ships, and conveniences for internal transportation. And whatever be the prevailing form of industry, especially if it be manufacturing, a large outlay of capital must be made in giving support to laborers, who are engaged in processes of production.

The importance of capital as an aid to production, is

learned from the condition of those nations, in which, from any cause, there is a deficiency. Here is the source of many of those embarrassments and hindrances, to which newly settled countries are subjected. Many forms of industry, which are highly profitable, and to which from its territorial advantages the nation is adapted, cannot be pursued, and if they are attempted, it is at great disadvantage. It is indeed sometimes the case, that the industrious habits of a people—the strength and fertility of their soil, and the superiority of their other territorial advantages, will counterbalance in some good degree this deficiency. But even in such nations, if, from any cause —the coming in of new members of the community, who are men of wealth, or perhaps from prosperous returns to adventures in commerce—important accessions of capital are made, the salutary effects are at once seen.

Other instances, teaching the same lesson, are found in those nations, which from wasting wars, or other causes of desolation, are deprived of the capital they possessed. It is but slowly, that such nations recover from the reduced state, to which they have been brought. In all their attempts to regain their former wealth and prosperity, they are crippled and impeded from their want of capital, and perhaps are obliged to abandon many profitable forms of labor, in which they had before been engaged. The want of capital becomes the subject of common lamentation; and all are ready to acknowledge, that the proverb—the poor man's poverty is his ruin, is as applicable to communities as to individuals.

Wealth.

The word wealth, in our common application of the term to individuals, is used relatively. A man has wealth, who, compared with others around him, possesses a large share of those commodities, which, being adapted to the supply of human wants, whether these wants are real or imaginary, are esteemed of value. A fine painting, or a collection of shells, in a community where those are found who are willing to give for these objects money, or any other article generally esteemed valuable, may constitute wealth, as much so, as wheat, or money itself. Such is the meaning of the term wealth, when applied to individuals, and it is used in the same signification in the science of political economy, except that it loses its relative application.

If we further examine the use of the term, as applied to individuals, we find, that it is used to denote material objects only, and such material objects, as from their nature may be appropriated and transferred from one possessor to another. Air and water are essential to human existence, but, in ordinary circumstances, they cannot become the property of one individual, to the exclusion of others, and hence they are not objects of wealth. Sometimes, in a season of drought, or in a country where wells are few, water may be appropriated, and then it constitutes a part of the wealth of its possessor. Knowledge and mechanical skill are also esteemed valuable, but they are not wealth, for they are not material objects, neither can they be transferred from one possessor to another. Now those material objects which may be appropriated and transferred, and which are esteemed generally as valuable, are said to possess exchangeable value. Hence, wealth may be defined as a term used to denote those material objects, which bear an exchangeable value.

National wealth includes whatever material objects, bearing exchangeable value, are possessed by the individual members of a nation, whether in their private capacity, or as members of a corporation, or as members of a civil community. Every material object bearing exchangeable value, in the possession of the individual members of a nation, is a part of the wealth of that nation, and the whole amount of a nation's wealth, is the sum total of what is thus possessed by individuals.

Here perhaps it may be asked, how securities, both public and private, notes of hand, and other obligations of a like nature, are to be regarded. A large portion of the wealth of individuals, consists in well secured debts. Do these debts make up a part of national wealth? It may be said in reply, that objects bearing exchangeable value, alone constitute national wealth, and the obligation, which one member of the community is under to another, to convey a stated amount of these objects, cannot add to the amount in the nation. When, however, we look on nations in their commercial intercourse with each other, the excess of what is due by foreigners to the members of one nation, above what is due by the members of this nation to foreigners, if well secured, may be counted as a part of national wealth, for it gives a title to a certain amount of those objects, which bear exchangeable value.

CHAPTER II.

Economical Arrangements.

In here introducing the phrase "economical arrangements," I design to use it in the sense, in which it is applied to a family. If in domestic management, such plans are adopted, as promote the prosperity of the family, turning its resources to good account, supplying its wants at the least expense, and apportioning to each one according to his necessities and his claims, we might speak of these plans as economical arrangements. In the same manner, in the management of the concerns of the great national family, if territorial advantages, and other resources, are turned to the best account, so that the amount of products obtained is large, in proportion to the advantages for production possessed by the nation,—and if, further, there is a well ordered distribution of what is thus obtained, among the different members of the community, we might speak of the plans and course of things, which lead to these results, as economical arrangements. In the view here taken of this subject, an individual is supposed to look on a community, in an advanced state of its existence and in a prosperous and thriving condition, and to ask himself, what is the management, or what are the economical arrangements, by which these prosperous results have been secured? And in answering this inquiry, the attention is first directed to those arrangements which relate to the production of wealth. Those connected with its distribution will be found in the second part of the work.

Economical arrangements for the production of wealth.

In all nations in which civil government is established, and in which advances have been made in civilization and wealth, the rights of property are acknowledged and respected. However wealth may have been obtained by the members of such communities, whether by industry—by the use of natural aids to production, or of productive capital, or whether it has been received by inheritance, or gift, or in any other manner, in accordance with the principles of justice and honesty, it is secured to its rightful owner. It belongs not to the science of Political Economy, to investigate the principles on which the right of property is founded, or to state the methods, by which it is most fully and effectually secured. In all the reasonings of this science, it is supposed that this right exists and is respected.

One form of property thus secured to individuals, is land and other territorial advantages, and this appropriation of land and other natural aids for the production of wealth, is the first economical arrangement, which claims our attention.

Nations are said to possess the territories which they inhabit. This country once belonged to the aboriginal Indians. It is now the territory of the United States. In this sense of property, it is meant, that the authorities of a country exercise a jurisdiction over it, and have a right to appropriate to national uses whatever is required for public defence, and the administration of civil government. It is still further meant, that this territory is the portion of the earth's surface, where the members of this nation find a home, and to which they look as the source, whence a supply of their wants is to be obtained.

But there is another sense, in which a territory is the property of the people who inhabit it. The lands possessed by a nation, are divided into portions of different extent, and appropriated to individuals. Those who thus become proprietors of the soil, are permitted to use the tracts of land, which they possess, for their own benefit, being entitled to whatever products are obtained from them ; and further, they may, at pleasure, convey their title in the lands thus owned by them to others. The same arrangement exists in respect to all other territorial advantages, which from the nature of the case, can be appropriated. Such are water privileges, fisheries and mines.

It will be noticed, that this division of lands and other natural aids to production, among the inhabitants of a country, is far from being an equal distribution. Some possess extensive tracts of land—more than they can cultivate, and much more than is needed to furnish a supply of their wants. Others have no property in lands. So it is with respect to other territorial advantages ; they are unequally distributed. The members of a community, in which the rights of property are recognized, are not permitted to look on the bounties of nature, as a common stock, of which all are entitled to share alike ; neither can each one, without interfering with the rights of others, avail himself of the more important natural aids to production.

That this distribution and appropriation of land and other territorial advantages, is an economical arrangement, tending to increase the amount of products, may be easily seen. It is in this way, that the selfish principles in man are called into exercise, and thus a more careful and skilful cultivation of the soil, and a better improvement of other aids to production, are secured, than would otherwise be made. On the same principle, a profuse and wasteful use of the bounties and aids of nature is prevented. Experience has abundantly shewn, that these benefits result from the arrangement, we are considering. Men will not labor, unless they are permitted to reap the fruit of their labors ; neither will economy be practised in the use of those supplies or resources, which are not appropriated to individuals. Each one in his eagerness to supply his own wants, becomes reckless of the general good. In no instances, except where men have come under the influence of the Christian religion, or some equally strong pervading principle, and then only in small societies, has a community of goods been found practicable.

That this economical arrangement is highly important, and also that those who possess aids to production of any kind, should be made secure in what is thus appropriated to them, we may learn by looking at those countries, in which, either from the weakness, or the oppressive exactions of the government, this security is not enjoyed. The Ottoman dominions, are often referred to as examples of this kind.

Another economical arrangement, which is found in every prosperous and thriving community, is what, in this science, is called *division of labor.*

The wants of men become more numerous and various, as society advances in wealth and refinement. Hence we should anticipate a corresponding variety in the employments of each member of a community thus advanced. But directly the reverse is witnessed. As the wants of men are multiplied and become more varied, their employments become more limited and single. In the earliest state of society, each one is employed in supplying his own different wants. A part of his time is spent in obtaining food; another portion in providing clothing, another in supplying himself with a few simple articles of furniture; and so of other urgent wants. We look at a community more advanced, and we find its members engaged, each one in furnishing some one of these needed commodities, both for himself and for others, depending on the productive exertions of those around him, for the supply of other wants. A further progress is made in the condition of the community, its wants are increased and a large proportion of its members are employed, each one in contributing some minute fractional part only in the production of the commodities, by which these more numerous wants are supplied. Hardly any one seems to be exerting himself to obtain those commodities, which he himself needs, and many are employed in the production of articles, which they themselves are not accustomed to use. This statement exhibits to us, what is denoted by the phrase *division of labor*, and shews us, that the degree of minuteness, to which this arrangement is carried, corresponds to the progress of a community in refinement and wealth.

To learn more of the nature of this arrangement, it may be traced, as it is found in the three great departments of human industry. Indeed this division is itself the division of labor, and offers an illustration of the arrangement we are examining. But it is here proposed to look at the more minute divisions, or rather subdivisions of labor found in these departments.

It is in large manufacturing establishments, that the most striking examples of division of labor are seen. Adam Smith, in his Wealth of Nations, has stated the instance of a pin manufactory, and told us of some, the business of whose lives it is, to make the eighteenth part of a pin. The cotton manufactories of the present day, offer an example of the same minute division of labor. The process of making a yard of printed calico is divided into twenty five or thirty distinct parts ; each of these parts requiring one, and some of them two or more laborers. Looking then at the fractional part assigned to each laborer, it may be asserted in the same sense as before, that there are those, the business of whose lives it is, to fabricate the thirtieth part of a yard of calico. But it will be noticed, that such instances are more striking than others, because a greater number of the processes directed to the production of a single commodity, are conducted under the same roof, or in the same establishment. This however is not essential. The production of a manufactured commodity may be carried on in different places, at different times, and by different laborers, and thus offer an example of division of labor as minute, though not so obvious, as some that have been stated.

Commercial industry, next to manufacturing, offers examples of minute division of labor. This arrangement is seen in its fullest extent, in the retail business, as conducted in large commercial cities. Here are found extensive establishments for the sale of a single article of grocery, of tea, for instance, or of vinegar. And connected with each of these establishments, are many individuals, whose employments are entirely distinct from each other. One purchases the article of trade ; others are salesmen—others, clerks ; others are employed in weighing, measuring, &c. Estimating then the labor of an individual in the same manner as before, it may be said to be the business of his life, to do the tenth, or perhaps twentieth part of the process of retailing a gallon of vinegar, or a pound of tea.

Agricultural labor admits of division, far less than Manufactures and Commerce. So important is the aid of nature in this department of production ; or rather so large a proportion of the work in agricultural productive processes, is effected by natural agents, that man is obliged to accommodate his efforts to this agency of nature. Men can employ themselves in planting—in rearing the plants that nature sends forth, and in gathering the harvest, only at particular seasons. Hence the same laborer may conveniently perform different parts of the work, in furnishing any one agricultural product, and also be engaged at the same time in raising different products. Still, in circumstances which are favorable, division of labor is found to some extent even in agriculture. In populous countries, some are employed as gardeners, others as shepherds, and others again direct their efforts to the furnishing of some one agricultural product for the market. And if, in the enlarged use of the term agriculture, we include mining operations and fisheries, further illustrations are found in these departments of labor.

That the arrangement now exhibited, is to a high degree economical, may be inferred from the results, which are witnessed wherever it exists. On this topic, I take the liberty of introducing the following striking extract from the Wealth of Nations.

" It is the great multiplication of the productions of all the different arts in consequence of the division of labor, which occasions, in a well governed society, that universal opulence which extends itself to the lowest ranks of the people. Every workman has a great quantity of his own work to dispose of beyond what he himself has occasion for ; and every other workman being exactly in the same situation, he is enabled to exchange a great quantity of his own goods for a great quantity, or, what comes to the same thing, for the price of a great quantity of theirs. He supplies them abundantly with what they have occasion for, and they accommodate him as amply with what he has occasion for, and a general plenty diffuses itself through all the different ranks of the society.

Observe the accommodation of the most common artificer or day laborer in a civilized and thriving country, and you will perceive that the number of people of whose industry a part, though but a small part, has been employed in procuring him this accommodation, exceeds all computation.

The woollen coat for example, which covers the day laborer, as coarse and rough as it may appear, is the produce of the joint labor of a great multitude of workmen. The shepherd, the sorter of the wool, the wool-comber or carder, the dyer, the scribbler, the spinner, the weaver, the fuller, the dresser, with many others, must all join their different arts, in order to complete even this homely production. How many merchants and carriers, besides, must have been employed in transporting the materials from some of those workmen to others who often live in a very distant part of the country! how much commerce and navigation in particular, how many ship-builders, sailors, sail-makers, rope-makers, must have been employed in order to bring together the different things made use of by the dyer, which often come from the remotest corners of the world! What a variety of labor too is necessary in order to produce the tools of the meanest of those workmen! To say nothing of such complicated machines as the ship of the sailor, the mill of the fuller, or even the loom of the weaver, let us consider only what a variety of labor is requisite in order to form that very simple machine, the shears with which the shepherd clips the wool. The miner, the builder of the furnace for smelting the ore, the feller of the timber, the burner of the charcoal to be made use of in the smelting house, the brick-maker, the brick-layer, the workmen who attend the furnace, the mill-wright, the forger, the smith, must all of them join their different arts in order to produce them. Were we to examine in the same manner, all the different parts of his dress and household furniture, the coarse linen shirt which he wears next his skin, the shoes which cover his feet, the bed which he lies on, and all the different parts which compose it, the kitchen grate at which he prepares his victuals, the coals which he makes use of for that purpose, dug from the bowels of the earth, and brought to him perhaps by a long sea and long land carriage, all the other utensils of his kitchen, all the furniture of his table, the knives and forks, the earthen or pewter plates upon which he serves up and divides his victuals, the different hands employed in preparing his bread and his beer, the glass window which lets in the heat and the light and keeps out the wind and the rain, with all the knowledge and art requisite for preparing that beautiful and happy invention, without which these northern parts of the world could scarce have afforded a very comfortable habitation, together with the tools of all the different work-men employed in producing those different conveniences; if we examine, I say, all these things, and consider what a variety of labor is employed about each of them, we shall be sensible that without the assistance and co-operation of many thousands, the very meanest person in a civilized country could not be provided, even according to what we very falsely imagine, the easy and simple manner in which he is commonly accommodated. Compared, indeed with the more extravagant luxury of the great, his accommodation must no doubt appear extremely simple and easy; and yet it may be true, perhaps, that the accommodation of an European prince does not always so much exceed that of an industrious and frugal peasant, as the accommodation of the latter exceeds that of many an African king, the absolute master of the lives and liberties of ten thousand naked savages."

It is easy to assign the causes of the economical results brought to view in the preceding extract. Every one knows, that in manual labor a sleight of hand is acquired by the frequent repetition of the same process. Indeed, to all the labors, both of the mind and of the body, the maxim, "practice makes perfect,"may be applied. Hence, as the employments of laborers become more simple and limited, their skill and dexterity are greater. And as this principle is extended through the various departments of industry, the products which result are larger in amount and superior in their quality.

The saving of time, which would otherwise be lost in passing from one employment to another, is a further advantage connected with division of labor. This advantage, says A. Smith, "is much greater, than we should at first view be apt to imagine it. It is impossible to pass very quickly from one kind of work to another, which is carried on in a different place, and with quite different tools. A country weaver, who cultivates a small farm, must lose a great deal of time in passing from his loom to the field, and from the field to his loom. When the two trades can be carried on in the same work-house, the loss of time is no doubt less. It is even in this case, however, very considerable. A man commonly saunters a little in turning his hand from one sort of employment to another. When he first begins the new work, he is seldom very keen and hearty ; his mind, as they say, does not go to it, and for some time he rather trifles than applies to good purpose."

Division of labor, still further, leads to improved and abridged methods of performing different productive operations. When the attention of a laborer is directed to one simple process, he is very likely to hit on some improvement in the mode of performing it. In this way, important inventions in the arts are made, and the aids of nature variously applied in the different forms of labor-saving machines. The history of inventions tells us, that a large proportion of inventions in the different arts have been thus introduced. In connexion with this arrangement of division of labor, are also found classes of laborers, whose employment it is, to exert their ingenuity and their skill in contriving and constructing machinery of various kinds. There are those too, who, as natural philosophers, are engaged in the investigation of the laws of nature, discovering the properties of material objects, and unfolding to the view of men the mysterious agencies of the natural world.

These three causes then, the increased dexterity and skill of laborers—the saving of time and the discovery and invention of improved methods of conducting processes in production, account for the benefits which result from division of labor. But it may be asked, if there are not limits, to which this system may be carried, as an economical arrangement. There are limits, and obvious ones. Division of labor is profitable from the increased amount of products which attend it, no further than there is a demand, or vent, for these products. It would be a source of loss to those employed in the manufacture of calico, if by carrying division of labor to a great degree of minuteness, they should manufacture daily ten thousand yards of calico, when there is a sale for only half, or three fourths, of this amount. And here is one reason, why in the mechanical arts, and in commercial employments, division of labor is found to so small an extent in newly settled and thinly inhabited countries. There is not sufficient demand for one kind of labor, to give employment to a single laborer;—hence the same individual is often obliged to unite two or three kindred arts. Here also is a reason, why division of labor cannot be introduced to the same extent in agriculture, as in the other branches of production. Agricultural products are for the most part bulky and perishable. They are with difficulty transported to a distance, and can be kept on hand but for a short time; hence the market for them is limited. Manufactured products, on the contrary, are much more permanent in their existence, and can generally be transported with ease to any part of the world.

Another limit to division of labor as an economical arrangement, is found in the amount of capital required. In proportion to the degree of minuteness, to which division of labor is carried in any establishment, must the amount of capital be enlarged. This also is seen in manufactures more fully than in the other forms of industry. The greater the number of parts into which the process of manufacturing an article is divided, the more machinery must there be;—a larger amount of materials for manufacture must also be kept on hand, and more must be paid in the form of wages to laborers. These different items require productive capital for their supply; and as capital is in its nature limited, here also exists a limit to division of labor.

A third economical arrangement connected with production, remains to be exhibited. It is the system of *barter* or *exchange*.

Adam Smith says, that there is in man a "natural propensity to truck, barter and exchange one thing for another." The correctness of this opinion may perhaps be questioned, but it is certain, that men have strong desires to possess objects of value, and that, if they cannot obtain the objects of their desires in a more ready and direct way, they will resort to exchange or barter. "Give me that which I want, and you shall have this which you want," says the same author," is the meaning of every offer to bargain; and it is in this way, that we obtain from one another the far greater part of those good offices which we stand in need of. It is not from the benevolence of the butcher, the baker, or the brewer, that we expect our dinner, but from their regard to their own interest. We address ourselves, not to their humanity, but to their self-love; and never talk to them of our own necessities, but of their advantages."

This is a simple and natural explanation of barter, and if we look at a community in its advanced state, we find, that what may be called a system of barter, is in full operation. Every producer, to a greater or less degree, in determining his employment and pursuits, is looking at the market—he is preparing that which he may offer to others, to receive from them in return the commodities which he needs ; and it is in this way that a large proportion of the wants of men are supplied.

In thus speaking of a system of barter as existing in a community, it is simply meant, that there exists to all practical purposes an arrangement of this kind—a great extensive plan for the supply of the wants of the national family. To one looking on, it would seem, that one class of men had been appointed to furnish food for this great family—another to manufacture cloth of different textures—another to build houses, and still another to furnish these houses with different articles of convenience and comfort. But in truth no such settled arrangement exists ; all these results follow without any concert upon the subject, from the single principle of selfishness—because each one is seeking his own good. And it is found perfectly safe to calculate and rely on the operation of this principle. Does it ever happen, that on any day there is not found in our large cities what is necessary to feed their numerous inhabitants? But nobody sees to it, that this supply shall be brought to market. It is thought safe to leave the whole business to individual interest ; and there is nothing lacking.

That the arrangement here brought to view, is attended with important consequences, as it promotes production and increases the wealth of a nation, will now be shewn. It is so, as connected with division of labor, the advantages of which have just been stated. Were it not for this extended system of exchange, no vent could be found for the increased amount of products which result from that economical arrangement. But on this topic enough has been said, and there are other views, which may here be presented. By this system of exchange, existing as it does between individual members of the same neighborhood—between the country and the town—between one section of national territory and another, and between different nations of the earth, the various powers of production throughout the civilized world, wherever they may exist, or by whomsoever they may be possessed, are brought into advantageous action. And further, each individual member of the community, is thus enabled to participate in the advantages for production, found, not only in his own vicinity and in his own nation, but in any portion of the whole circle of civilized and commercial nations. To illustrate these positions, the view may first be limited to a neighborhood. Here are individuals possessing productive capital to a large amount—others are landholders, and many have no capital and no land, but they have strength and intelligence. Now that this neighborhood may thrive, there must be a joint action. The capitalists must bring forward their wealth to the work of production—the landholder must permit his fertile acres to be cultivated, and these laborers must engage readily in the work. But how is this result to be attained. It is by placing before each class motives addressed to its self interest; and this is effected by the system of barter we are considering. Give and I will give you in return, is the language addressed to each class. And it is language which is listened to,—all come forward with the resources at their disposal, to assist in the great work of production, being assured, that in proportion to what they contribute, will be the returns, which each shall receive. And when this joint action is thus effected, the laborer participates in the assistance, derived from the productive capital of the rich, and from the lands of the owner of territory; while both these classes derive important benefits from the laborer in return, and also mutual advantages from each other.

Extend now the view to the town and the surrounding country. Each has its advantages for production. One possesses a large amount of productive capital, and a commodious harbor, and is connected by commerce with remote countries, thus introducing a supply of various foreign commodities, at the lowest rates for which they can be furnished. The other has its fertile and highly cultivated soil, yielding rich returns to agricultural industry. The system of exchange is established, and each thrives, not at the expense of the other, but from the aid mutually given, and the stimulating influence exerted. Thus, too, each member of the crowded city participates in the benefit of the fertile territory around him, and, in return, each inhabitant of this surrounding territory, is enabled to avail himself of the large capital, and of the advantages for commerce, which the city possesses.

Look next at different sections of a country. Each has its peculiar advantages. Those of one section are favorable to the production of one kind of products; those of another section to the production of a different kind. But to develope these sectional advantages, there must be commercial intercourse between these two parts of the country. In the United States, for example, the South, from its climate and its soil, is adapted to the raising of cotton—the North, from its water privileges, the character and number of its laborers, and the large amount of its productive capital, can profitably engage in the manufacture of this cotton. Thus the basis for exchange exists, and as the arrangement is introduced, mutual benefits arise. The inhabitant of the Northern State has about him more comforts, his labor turns to better account, and his condition in life is improved, because in the Southern section of his country, facilities are found for the raising of cotton. And so, in return, the Southerner feels the benefit of the water privileges, the numerous and skilful laboring population, and the large productive capital of the North.

There remains one other view—the system of barter between different nations, to which the term foreign commerce is applied. The basis of exchange here, is the same, as is the foundation of commercial intercourse between different sections of the same country ; but the diversities of soil and climate and of other territorial advantages, are still more striking and important. Some products, which men are wont to look upon as among the necessaries of civilized life, can be raised only on particular portions of the earth's surface. Or if, by artificial means, a forced growth is attempted in other regions, the supply obtained is scanty in amount and inferior in its quality. This remark applies to the tea and coffee plants, the fruits of which are in so common use. Diversities in other aids to production—in capital and in labor, are also found to a greater extent between different nations, than between different sections of the same nation. Illustrations of these statements are familiar to all.

The advantages derived from foreign commerce are brought to view in another part of this work. It is unnecessary therefore to make an enumeration of them here. So far as they are connected with the production of wealth, they are the same in their nature, as those that arise from the intercourse between different sections of the same country. There is the same stimulating effect exerted upon the productive energies of different nations, and the same widening of the field, from which wealth may be obtained. It may here also be further added, that this arrangement is highly important to nations, as it supplies any deficiency in their facilities for production, whether this deficiency be temporary and accidental, or whether it be of a more permanent nature. A country may have been depopulated by some wasting sickness, or by war, or from the latter of these desolating and impoverishing causes, it may have become destitute to a great extent of productive capital, or its soil may be sterile, or it may to an unusual degree be destitute of water-power, and other advantages for manufactures. Now unless in some way these deficiencies can be supplied, such nations, though they may possess other advantages for production to an unusual degree, must suffer great inconveniences and privations, and can never attain to wealth and prosperity, until these causes of embarrassment, so far as they are temporary, are removed. The system of exchange between nations comes to their relief, and thus tends to equalize the condition of civilized man throughout the world.

The three great economical arrangements, that have now been brought to view, existing as they do together, and in joint operation, go far in accounting for the abundant supplies and the great amount of wealth, possessed by the civilized nations of the earth. Viewed as a whole, they may be said to constitute the management, under which nations grow up to greatness and wealth. There are indeed other minor arrangements ; but these will be found to be parts of the system, which has been exhibited, tending to the same result of national prosperity.

CHAPTER III.

Human Industry.

In preceding chapters, the great sources of national wealth, and the economical arrangements, by the aid of which the work of production is most advantageously conducted, have been brought to view. It is now proposed to look at human industry—at the aids to production furnished by nature, and at productive capital, separately, that we may learn, under what circumstances the highest benefits may be derived from each of these sources of national wealth. In this survey, opportunities will occur for the discussion of many questions of a practical nature, and for the developement of important principles in the science.

Few form any just conception of what is effected in a large and industrious community, by human labor. The products of labor are looked upon so much in detail, and as connected with the exertions and rewards of individual laborers, that no strong impression is made upon the mind. It would perhaps be surprising to some, who are wont to attach much importance to the aids of nature, and to capital, as they are seen in the imposing forms of large manufacturing and commercial establishments, to learn, that it has been estimated, that three fourths of the revenue of even manufacturing and commercial communities, are derived from human industry. But though it is difficult to make any just estimate, or to form any distinct conceptions of the results of human industry in a large and populous nation, we may make some approximation to a correct estimate, and aid our conception, by looking at a single town or village. Suppose a town to contain 1000 effective laborers of every kind, and that we allow fifty cents per day, as the average value of labor, computing 280 laboring days in the year. The revenue of these laborers then is $500 per day, and $140,000 per annum. No doubt there are many towns in our country of three or four thousand inhabitants, whose revenue from labor equals or exceeds this amount. It is true, that a large proportion of this revenue is consumed in supplying the daily wants of these laborers and their families, but this circumstance does not affect the correctness of our calculations as to the results of human industry. Now extend this view to our nation, in which are found two or three millions of productive laborers. How immense the revenue from all this labor! and how important is this source of national wealth!

Another view of human industry, which tends to impress the mind with a sense of its importance and extent, relates to the variety of forms, in which it appears. Mention has been made of the division of labor generally, and also of the three great branches of human industry, Agriculture, Manufactures and Commerce. But in each of these departments, especially in the two last, are found divisions and sub-divisions to an almost endless extent. There is also the labor of the mind, as well as the labor of the body—the thousands employed in planning, arranging and conducting the different processes of production, and the millions who carry these plans into execution. It is by dwelling on a view like this, that we obtain some, though a confused idea, of the variety of forms, which human industry assumes. And when we have followed out the division of labor to these minute divisions and sub-divisions and ramifications, we find bursting forth and attendant upon them, the unnumbered little rills of wealth, which, flowing together, form the larger streams, and empty themselves into the great ocean of national opulence.

Such then being the extent and importance of human industry as a source of wealth, whatever affects its developement, increasing or impairing its efficiency and amount, must be closely connected with the prosperity of a nation. Some causes thus affecting human industry, will now be stated.

1. Personal freedom, or that every man be permitted to labor for his own benefit, and in that way which he esteems most advantageous to himself, conduces much to the efficiency of human industry, as one of the sources of national wealth. The only limitation to this personal freedom which should exist, is, that an employment be not detrimental to the public good. So far, restraint is implied in the constitution of civil society.

To see the importance of personal freedom as it affects human labor, the industry of a slave population may be compared with that of a community of freemen. It is often said, that more work is done in the same time by ten New England farmers, than by twice that number of Southern slaves. Indeed it is sometimes acknowledged by Southern slave-holders themselves, that it would be for their interest, to hire free white laborers, and pay them liberal wages, rather than be at the expense of supporting their slaves, including childhood and age,—few and cheaply supplied as the wants of these slaves are. Now this difference does not arise wholly from a difference in the physical powers of slaves and freemen. The slave, being compelled to work for the benefit of another, and in that way which another prescribes, has no fondness for his employment, and no motive to exertion. The latter knows, that the amount to be received for his labor will be in direct proportion to his efforts ; or if he is laboring for another, to receive a stipulated reward, he still is conscious, that his reputation as a laborer, and connected with it, his success in life, are concerned. He puts forth therefore strenuous and unremitted efforts in his chosen employment. Free labor is also ordinarily performed with more skill than slave labor. It is a matter of public policy in free communities to enlighten the free laborer, and in slave communities, to keep the slave in ignorance. The former is generally a man of contrivance and reflection ; the latter is dull and stupid. Now every one knows, that even in the common employments of life—the simple operations of agricultural industry, for example, much advantage arises from skill and ingenuity. One man hoes a hill of corn in less time and in a better manner than another, simply because he has more skill, and labors to better advantage. Much more is this the case in the complicated processes of manufacturing labor. Hence, no doubt, the impression, which is probably correct, that slaves cannot be advantageously employed in manufactures.

But it is sometimes the case, that other restraints are placed on human industry, little less injurious than those of absolute slavery. In some nations, and those too accounted free, laws and regulations and institutions exist, which exert a similar influence. In English statute books, are found acts of Parliament, fixing the amount, which laborers of different trades and employments should receive for their labor. Especially have measures of this kind been resorted to, both in England and in other European nations, when, from famine or some wasting pestilence, the number of efficient laborers has been reduced, and the consequent demand for laborers has tended to raise the rates of wages. The effects of legislative enactments of this kind were soon seen. Laborers were unwilling to work, unless compelled by the authority of the State, or by absolute necessity. And when engaged in labor, they felt no motive leading them to constant and vigorous exertion, but made the amount of their labor to correspond to the pittance they received. Here then was a check to industry. Men were not permitted to labor for their own benefit without restraint, and as a necessary consequence less work was done—less wealth produced in the nation.

English history also tells us of chartered and privileged companies, under whose direction the different arts and trades were practised ; and all persons were forbidden to practise these arts and trades, unless they possessed, what was termed the freedom of the trade. These corporations also made by-laws and regulations, such as they saw fit to make—many of which were in the highest degree arbitrary and oppressive. The professed design of these regulations, was to prevent persons from practising a trade, with which they were not sufficiently acquainted. The real purpose was to prevent competition in manufacturing the articles of the trade, and thus to secure to the company higher prices.

One class of these regulations, which may serve as an example of the whole, are the laws of apprenticeship. No man was permitted to bind his son as an apprentice to any trade, who was not possessed of an income of twenty shillings a year from land. Masters also were limited as to the number of apprentices they might receive. Large sums were also demanded from parents as fees of apprenticeship, and a long term of service required. Obstacles were thus thrown in the way of those desirous of learning to practise the different arts, and, as a consequence, the number of useful laborers in the community was less.

That all regulations of this nature, with an exception hereafter to be stated, are unnecessary and injurious, being detrimental to the public good, and often oppressive to individuals, may easily be shewn. They are unnecessary. Their professed design, as already stated, is to secure the public against fraud and loss, arising from the want of fidelity and skill in those who practise the different trades and arts. But the public is not exposed to imposition and loss from this source, to an extent which requires such interference. In respect to those articles of production, which are submitted to the inspection and examination of consumers, and of the quality of which most men are fully capable of determining, it is safe, to leave it to those who purchase, to judge for themselves. If the work is executed in an awkward, bungling manner, the want of skill will at once be detected, and the producer will have his product left on his hands, being subjected to the loss, both of his labor and his materials. If there is designed deception, it will of course eventually be discovered, and the producer will lose both his character and his business. On the part of the consumer, also, there will be loss, but, in most instances, it will be small, and will lead him to be more cautious and wary. There are however some few instances, and these form the exception before referred to, in which some restraints, of the nature of those we are considering, may with advantage be imposed. Such instances relate to those commodities, of whose quality consumers are not capable of judging, and the testing of which might be attended with serious consequences to those making the experiment. The trade of the apothecary, in which it is required to compound and prepare different medicines, is an example of this kind. In such instances, the public may wisely require apprenticeship, or that in some other way, consumers be secured against injury and loss.

But it is not only the case, that the restraints on industry we are considering, are unnecessary and injurious to the public ; they are also oppressive to individuals.

It often happens, that from the original constitution of the mind, or from some early bias, connected with the circumstances in which individuals have been placed, there is a peculiar fondness and aptitude for some employment. Now should these individuals be permitted to engage in their favorite pursuits, they might highly benefit themselves, and do essential service to the public. But it may be, that the father of such an individual is a poor man, and possesses no land, from which a revenue of twenty shillings is derived, or it may not be convenient to serve a long apprenticeship, and to incur the expense required to obtain the freedom of the trade.

Another case may be stated. In the extent to which division of labor is carried in some of the arts, it often happens, that a laborer is engaged in performing one of the many parts of some process of production. But from some cause, there ceases to be a demand for the product, in the manufacturing of which he is engaged, and he is thrown out of employment. Now might he be permitted to engage in some kindred art, he might at once adapt himself to his new pursuit, and thus neither he, nor the public, would suffer loss from the suspension of his labors. But this the laws of trade corporations forbid.

In both these instances, certainly, and in others of a similar nature, the restraints imposed are injurious and oppressive.

The position to be maintained on this subject is the following: That with the exception which has been made, the practice of the different trades, should be open to all, with no other restriction or security for the public, than what a fair, and, as it will generally happen, a close competition, will produce. In this way, the interest and the rights, both of the public and of individuals, will best be secured.

Such is practically the course adopted in our own country. We have, it is true, laws pertaining to apprenticeships, but except in special cases, not requiring them. When engagements of this kind have been made, the law comes in for their regulation, to the mutual security and benefit of the master and apprentice ; and this is all that it does. Any man may offer his services to the public as a cabinet-maker, or as a carpenter, or a watchmaker, or in any of the common employments of life ; but in so doing he must enter the lists as a competitor with others, who are engaged in the same pursuit. If he is ignorant of his professed business and unskilful, the public will soon know it, and he himself will also learn the folly of his attempt to his cost.

The English system of poor laws furnishes another instance of restraint on human labor, injurious to the public and oppressive to individuals. As towns are bound to support their own paupers, each town endeavours to prevent individuals and families, that are not possessed of wealth, from gaining a residence within its limits. Hence many laws and regulations exist, which are designed to prevent the poor, however honest and industrious, from obtaining a settlement; and these laws are executed with great strictness and rigor. In our own country, if a man cannot find employment and a livelihood in one town, he removes to another, and again, if a more alluring prospect opens before him, he hesitates not to make a second removal. But to the poor in England, this is in effect forbidden. No matter how discouraging may be the circumstances in which a man may find himself, or what obstacles may oppose themselves to his enterprise and industry, if he is poor, it is not permitted to him to go where he may be surrounded by different circumstances—where his enterprise may be successful, and his industry meet its reward. He must drag out a miserable existence in the spot, which gave him birth. Such cruel and unjust regulations must be severe checks on human industry.

On the subject of personal freedom in connexion with labor, the following short, but sententious extract from the Wealth of Nations, contains a correct and important sentiment. "The property, which every man hath in his own labor, is most sacred and inviolable. The patrimony of a poor man lies in the strength and dexterity of his hands; and to hinder him from employing that strength and dexterity, in that manner which he thinks proper, without injury to his neighbor, is a plain violation of this most sacred property. The interposition of the lawgiver is impertinent and oppressive,"

2. Labor becomes more efficient in the production of wealth, when it receives a suitable reward.

Labor implies a sacrifice of ease, and wearisome and sometimes painful effort. To lead men to make this sacrifice, and put forth these efforts, some strong inducement must be placed before them. In the savage state, the obtaining of food and of shelter, is the motive to exertion, and when these urgent wants are supplied, the savage returns to a state of inaction. The same wants are to be supplied, and better supplied, in civilized life. But here other inducements to labor exist. In civilized communities, are different ranks—the distinctions of wealth and of power are known, and men are continually passing from one class in society to a higher. The hope then of bettering his condition, is before the laborer. He is prompted to continued and patient effort, that he may acquire property, and have around him an abundance of the comforts and conveniences of life, and thus be held in respect by others.

It will be seen, when we come to treat of the distribution of wealth, that the reward of the laborer is received by him under the form of wages, and the principles, on which the rate and value of wages depend, will then be brought to view. In the present connexion, it is enough to say, that the remuneration of the laborer should be ample, affording to him and to his family a generous support.

This is important, as it tends to increase the efficiency of the laborer. In most employments, the ability to work, must depend on the health and vigor of the body, and these circumstances are connected with a generous diet, and the enjoyment of the comforts and necessaries of life. A hardy, healthy, vigorous, laboring population, is an important contribution to the wealth of a nation, and such a population will be found in those countries only, where the style of living of this class of the community, is a style of comfort and abundance.

A liberal remuneration is still further important, as it tends to make willing laborers. Men usually exert themselves, in proportion to the reward, they are to receive. The operation of this principle has already been shewn, in the comparison instituted between the labor of slaves and of freemen.. But of those accounted free, many are so situated, that the only motive to exertion which they feel, is the strong, compulsive arm of necessity. Some, by their utmost efforts from day to day, are just able to obtain a supply of their daily returning wants. They struggle against a strong current, not daring for a moment to relax their efforts, lest they should be borne downwards to destruction. But the struggle is short, and the laborers, whose brief existence is thus a succession of hardships and privations, are soon lost to the community. Others gain a bare subsistence more easily ; but these, seeing no prospect before them of improving their condition, and that the most they can hope to effect by their labors, is to live, conclude that their wisest course is to live with as little labor as possible, and thus they become sluggish and indolent. Though members of a civilized community, in their habits of industry, they much resemble the savage, who labors only when roused by necessity to exertion. The contrast to these instances is striking, where laborers have brighter prospects opened before them. Not only is every hour improved, but all the operations of industry are performed with cheerfulness, and with greater skill and fidelity. An illustration of the strength and power of this principle, is found in the different manner, in which common day labor and job-work are performed. In the former case, the laborer does just work enough to satisfy his employer, and earn his daily wages ; in the latter, he toils till he is satisfied with himself—that is, generally, till his exhausted powers will enable him to work no longer. Now, when the situation of the whole laboring part of a community is such, that each one feels it for his own immediate interest to exert himself, turning every day and hour to some good account, the results will shew themselves in the increasing wealth and prosperity of the nation.

And in this connexion it may be remarked, that every nation, from a regard to its internal peace and quietness, is deeply interested in the style of living of its laboring population, and of course in the remuneration received for labor. When the condition of laborers is one of comfort and enjoyment, they are wont to become attached to the existing state of things, and to the institutions of the country—they feel a self respect, and a sense of individual importance and responsibility. Being able also to furnish themselves with the means of improvement, and to allow themselves time for the use of these means, they become intelligent and elevated in the scale of being. Thus they are enabled to form some opinion of the wisdom of public measures ; and being led to see that their own safety and prosperity are connected with the public welfare, they become valuable citizens, the friends and supporters of order and good government. But when the condition of laborers is one of hardships and privations, with no bright hopes to cheer and animate them, the reverse of what has been stated above is witnessed ; scenes of violence and commotion are often witnessed, and the materials for turmoil and revolution are ever found. To what other immediate cause than the degraded state of her laboring population, are we to ascribe the unsettled state of affairs, with which Ireland has been so long visited. In that unhappy country, from the concurrence of unfavorable causes, the rate of wages is low, while there is a scanty supply of the necessaries of life, in proportion to the wants of the community. Hence the style of living is reduced to the lowest point at which life can be sustained, and riot, and commotion, and idleness, and misery prevail. When too we look at England, where the state of the laborer is more elevated, and his wants far better supplied, there is also found in the subject of wages a source of complaint and inquietude. In manufacturing towns, a "strike," as it is there termed, or a turning out for higher wages, not unfrequently occurs, and such events are scenes of disorder, and sometimes of violence and bloodshed. They are evidence of dissatisfaction on the part of the laborer with the existing state of things, and are troublesome, if not dangerous to the public.

The reverse of all this is seen in the condition of the laboring population in our own country. Here the remuneration of labor is ample, and the style of living which prevails among the laboring classes, is one of comfort and abundance; and the happy effects are seen in the character and conduct of this part of the community.

3. The sentiments, habits, institutions, customs and morals of a nation, all exert an influence on labor, as a source of national wealth. A few instances will be specified.

In some countries, it is thought disreputable to labor. This impression is common in those nations, where a nobility, or any privileged orders, are found, or where slavery exists, or where, from any cause, the distinctions of rank are strongly marked. Hence in such nations, there are many who spend their days in absolute idleness—the drones of society. In other nations, it is thought honorable to labor, and the man who obtains by his own exertions a support for himself and his family, is on this account regarded with respect. The influence of these impressions will be seen in the gross amount of national products.

Nations also differ in their habits of industry. Some communities, either from constitutional temperament, or from customs, handed down from generation to generation, are an industrious people. There seems to exist in them a love of labor, and with much assiduity and toil, they carry forward and perfect the different processes of production, in which they engage. There are other nations, whose habits are the reverse ; they are indolent and inefficient.

The time spent by different nations as holidays—days, when labor is suspended throughout the community, is another circumstance of sufficient importance to be mentioned here. Without doubt, some seasons of this kind may advantageously be observed by every people, especially when they are of a nature fitted to cherish patriotic feelings, or to promote moral and religous improvement. But when, as in Catholic countries, this observance of holidays is carried to an extent, that a twelfth, or even a larger portion of the year, is thus spent in idleness and pageantry, the loss of so many days of labor becomes a source of impoverishment and evil.

An unwise system of poor laws, as it opens the way to

improvidence and idleness and vice, may also exert an injurious effect on the labor of a nation. And so of all immoral influences and habits, leading to profligacy and dissipation. But on these and other general considerations, it is unnecessary to dwell.

This view of the causes affecting labor as a source of national wealth, will now be concluded with a brief statement of the different ways, in which the government of a country may extend its assistance to this class of its citizens, and improve their condition.

1. It may extend to the laboring population full and complete security in the enjoyment of their rights of person and of property.

2. It may assist to enlighten and instruct them. These objects, it may effect by the dissemination of useful knowledge, and by affording encouragement and aid to education in its different departments. The common school system, as it exists at the present time in New England, sustained and supported by legislative enactments, is an example of the manner in which assistance of this kind may be given.

3. It can do much towards producing and sustaining a healthy moral condition of laborers.

No members of a community suffer more from the prevalence of vicious habits and practices, than laborers; especially is this the case, where there is a propensity to dissipation in any form, and to wasteful excess. It becomes then the duty of the public authorities of a nation, as guardians of the public welfare, to exert themselves in every way for the promotion of good morals. Something towards this important object, can be effected by direct legislative enactments for the prevention and suppression of vice, in some of its most prevailing forms; and so far as such acts of government are supported by public opinion, the strong arm of authority should ever be put forth in the cause of virtue. But there are indirect ways, in which the same results may be attained. The government of a country may give its sanction and aid to all judicious attempts to enlighten and influence the public mind, in what pertains to the moral, and, as intimately connected with it, to the religious welfare of the community. Above all, it should ever exert its commanding influence on the side of good order and sound morals.

CHAPTER IV.

Natural aids to Production.

In connexion with the explanation of natural agency and other natural aids to production, given in the introductory chapter, it was remarked, that man in a civilized community avails himself of these aids to a far greater extent, than when in a savage state. Indeed the difference between these two states of society as to the comforts and enjoyments of life, is in no small degree to be traced to this source. Civilized man, it is true, works more constantly; but this is not all—he works to better advantage.

Every one knows, that the returns of the soil under skilful cultivation, are increased many fold. Tracts of land in this country, which once afforded a scanty subsistence to a wandering tribe of Indians, now yield a rich harvest for the support of a dense population. But this increased supply does not arise from any new gifts of nature. There existed in this territory the same natural agency when in possession of its former inhabitants, as at present; but this natural agency needed the assistance and guidance of man to develope it and make it efficient.

These untaught Indians, also, had around them material objects, with the same properties which they now possess—the same woods in the forest, the same ores in the earth. But they knew not of the existence of these objects, or, if they knew of their existence, they were ignorant of their useful properties and how to avail themselves of their assistance. Hence, so far as they made attempts to avail themselves of natural assistants, such attempts were rude and inefficient. An Indian would furnish himself with that useful implement—an axe. He selects a hard stone, and by long continued and laborious friction, he gives to it a rude form and an imperfect edge. He then selects some sapling tree, cuts off the top of it, cleaves the trunk and inserts his axe. The parts of the divided trunk are then brought together, and after they have again united the tree is cut off below, and thus a handle of convenient length and firmly attached to the axe is obtained. How much shorter and more skilful is the process, by which the intelligent mechanic furnishes the same tool! and how much better also is the implement adapted to its destined use!

Another striking illustration is found in the aid derived from those properties of water, which adapt it to bear heavy burdens on its bosom and to give them an easy passage along its surface, thus assisting man in the work of transportation. To avail himself of this aid of nature, the savage hollows out with great labor, the trunk of a large tree, or constructs his frail canoe of bark, and then with his simple paddle forces it on the water from one bank of the river to its opposite, or along the margin of the sea. Contrast this little canoe, frail in its materials and structure, and limited in its uses, with the stately ship, whose ribs are of oak, and whose sinews are iron, and which, under the guidance of the magnetic needle, dares traverse the pathless ocean, bearing in its bosom rich stores of wealth.

On the benefits derived from the improved use of natural agency—especially from the fertility of the soil, it is unnecessary to enlarge. Every one knows what these advantages are, both as to their extent and importance. Food is thus furnished in greater quantity and of superior quality. Materials are also obtained, which being subjected to the fashioning power of art, supply in abundance other wants of the human family.

The benefits derived from other natural aids to production, as this assistance is rendered in the form of tools and implements of industry, are also sufficiently obvious. There is hardly any kind of labor, in which men do not in this way avail themselves of the aids of nature, and where too this assistance is not in the highest degree important. But when we come to see these aids of nature in the form of machinery, and to trace out the consequences of the introduction of this machinery in a community, where, from the economical arrangements that exist, the pursuits and interests of different classes and individuals are closely interwoven, mutually affecting each other, the advantages derived from the natural aids to production, are not so obvious. And further, to the introduction of the aids of nature in the form of machinery, objections are made, which require a distinct consideration. I propose therefore to shew, why what are called labor-saving machines are so termed, and also, how the introduction and use of them affect the different interests of the community.

Suppose a colony of one hundred families, emigrating from a nation in the enjoyment of the comforts and conveniences of civilized life, to be located in some remote territory, and compelled in the early years of their existence, to look to their own efforts and resources for a supply of their wants. They carry with them of course a knowledge of the arts and institutions of civilized life, and the most common and important implements of labor. Their first efforts in their new settlement are directed to furnishing themselves with habitations and food, and then, as far as is practicable, with other conveniences and comforts, to which they have been accustomed. We look in upon this colony the third or fourth year after its establishment, and we find its members are industriously employed in different ways, supplying the wants of the community. The whole number of laborers we will suppose to be one hundred and fifty. Of this number, seventy five are engaged as agricultural laborers, and twenty five are mechanics, twenty five are manufacturers, and twenty five are either professional men or domestic servants. While labor is thus proportioned out, the economical concerns of the colony are so arranged and conducted, that the wants of its members are supplied and provision made for its gradual increase. Let us now suppose, that some important machine is invented—a power-loom for example. What are the effects of its introduction. It is soon found, that of manufacturers employed in weaving cloth a less number is needed. It had before required ten laborers to manufacture the cloth used in the community; but now, by the assistance of the power-loom, two can perform the work before accomplished by ten. But of the eight laborers thus set at liberty, two must be added to the list of mechanics, to be employed in making power-looms and keeping them in repair; the remaining six are set at liberty, to engage in some other department of labor. Here then is one immediate and direct effect of the introduction of this machine—the same amount of products is obtained by less labor; hence the machine is called a labor-saving machine. But let us look at other consequences.

The price of cloth, depending principally in this early state of the colony on the cost of its production, was such when ten laborers were engaged in its manufacture, that all the industrious families in the colony could afford to clothe themselves, and for this purpose a certain part of their annual revenue was set aside. But now that the use of a labor-saving machine has diminished the cost of production, the price of this commodity is diminished;—cloth of the same quality has become cheaper. It follows, that should the same amount be expended annually in the purchase of cloth, more will be obtained and probably of a better quality. Hence there arises a demand for more cloth, corresponding to the diminution of its price. Another power-loom therefore must be made and put into operation, and a larger amount of materials used in the manufacture of cloth, must also be provided. Two consequences then result; 1. The colony is better supplied with the commodity, in the production of which the newly invented machine is employed. 2. Employment is provided, either in furnishing an additional amount of materials for the manufacture of the commodity, or in constructing a new machine and working it, for as many laborers as were before engaged in furnishing the same commodity, or for even a larger number. Other more remote effects might be traced out; but, at present, the attention may be confined to these two.

It will now happen, that in consequence of the introduction of another power-loom, the amount of cloth manufactured will be greater than before, while its price will be in a corresponding degree still further reduced. But the families in the colony are not desirous of obtaining a larger amount of cloth. They prefer to expend a smaller proportion of their income in the purchase of this article, and to employ the surplus thus left to them, in the gratification of some other desire.

Let us first suppose, that this surplus is devoted to obtaining a larger supply of some home product—of wheat, for example. The demand for this agricultural product is at once increased; more land must be cultivated, more labor and more capital employed in this branch of industry. Thus, in consequence of the introduction of a labor-saving machine into a branch of manufactures, a new stimulus is given to another department of industry, additional employment is furnished to laborers, and a further investment of productive capital is made. Thus too the different classes of society feel the benefit of the aids of nature, as they are brought to their assistance in the form of labor-saving machines; and the prosperity of the whole community is promoted.

But now let us suppose, that a different disposal is made of what is saved from the diminished price of cloth. Our colonists, who in their new settlement have been deprived of some of those articles of comfort and convenience, to which they had been accustomed before their removal, having a surplus on hand, are led to think of their former enjoyments. But these desired commodities are not to be obtained within the limits of the colony—they are the products of a foreign soil. Soon however it is ascertained, that in some foreign country, where these desired articles are produced, there is a demand for cloth, and that by the aid of power-looms cloth may be manufactured and sent to this foreign market, for a sum not exceeding the current price in that market. Instead then of expending their surplus income in the purchase of a home product, they send it abroad in the form of cloth, to be exchanged for some foreign commodity. Thus, as the result of machinery, foreign commerce is introduced, with all the benefits resulting from it, both as it offers a more abundant and varied supply to the wants of the community, opens a new form of industry, and stimulates to increased efforts in every department of production.

If now we look back on the statement that has been made, we find, that the following consequences result from the introduction and use of labor-saving machines:

1. From the same labor a greater amount of the commodity, in the production of which the machine is employed, is obtained; and as the price falls in proportion to this increased amount, each consumer is enabled to obtain by the same expenditure a larger supply.

2. Should the newly invented machine be used to an extent, which increases the supply of the article beyond the demand of the community, its price still further falls; and as a less expenditure will suffice for obtaining this commodity, a surplus will be saved from the revenue of consumers. This surplus may be expended, either in

the purchase of a larger amount of some home product, or it may be sent abroad in exchange for some commodity of foreign production. In either case, an addition is made to the wealth of the community, and a stimulus given to other departments of production.

3. Laborers thrown out of employment by the introduction of machinery, eventually find employment in the same, or some other branch of production, to which a stimulus is given. They will also, as consumers, share in the benefit of a diminished price and an increased supply of the comforts and conveniences of life, resulting from this source. And here, in connexion with this last inference, the principal objection to machinery offers itself to our consideration. It is said, that though it be allowed, that laborers, with others in the community, eventually derive important benefits from the use of machinery, still, its introduction is attended with so great inconvenience and distress to those thrown out of employment, that these advantages are more than balanced. To shew the extent of these evils and inconveniences, an appeal is made to the history of the past, and to the sufferings and attendant tumults and riots of later times. We are told, that in the last century, the introduction of a machine for wool-combing into England, threw out of employ 30,000 laborers. Similar consequences attended the invention of power-looms and calico-printing. When such multitudes, it is said, are thus deprived of their accustomed labor, the evils suffered by them are great, and much time must elapse before the remedies, which have been referred to, will come to their relief.

It is common for laborers, when thus thrown out of employment by the introduction of machinery, to apply to the government of the country for relief. Their first petition usually is, that the government would interfere to prevent the use of the newly invented machine. But this petition, it is evidently not the policy of the government to grant. On the contrary, the public good requires the promotion of whatever tends to increase the amount of products in a country, developing its resources and augmenting its wealth. Besides, it would be prevented from thus interfering, on the principle of competition. The invention, if important, might, and probably would be adopted by some other nation ; and as the effect of its adoption is to diminish the cost of production, the nation thus adopting it, would compete advantageously with other nations in foreign markets. On this account, therefore, the government of the country, where the invention is made, would prefer to encourage it, and thus secure to its own citizens the advantage of a lower cost of production.

Another way, in which it is asked, that government would give relief, is by providing employment for those thus deprived of their accustomed labor. This is sometimes done, when a portion of the public revenue is expended in public works, or internal improvements. Relief of this kind, however, is but partial and temporary, and from the difference in the kind of labor, is after all not very acceptable. But there is another measure adopted by most governments, which, by securing the gradual introduction of machinery, gives important relief to the laborer, and at the same time offers encouragement for the invention of labor-saving machines. I refer to what are termed patent rights.

The immediate object of patent rights is remuneration for useful discoveries and inventions. This is effected in the following manner: While the use of a newly invented machine is confined to the inventor, and those to whom he may sell the right of using it, the saving made in the cost of production, should the former price of the commodity be continued, goes to increase the profits of the producers. But should the price be lowered in proportion to the diminished cost of the commodity, this diminution of the price gives a command of the market; and thus from larger sales the same amount of profits is secured. In either case, the inventor receives the benefit of his invention. But while the inventor is thus remunerated, the gradual introduction of the newly invented machine, and, of course, relief to the laborer, is secured as effectually, as if a law were enacted and enforced with this specific object in view. Before there is a reduction in price, and even after that reduction has commenced, those employed in the old mode of producing will still continue their labors. And as they will generally know of the improvements, they will thus have time to look about them and find some new employment. Besides, it is thus effected, that before laborers are driven from their accustomed pursuits, one of the most efficient remedies for their relief is brought into operation. I refer to the increased demand for the product, arising from the diminution of its price.

In what has now been brought forward on the subject of labor-saving machines, particular reference has been had to manufactures. But most of the principles stated, apply to inventions of this kind in the mechanical arts, and in the common occupations of life. In these instances, however, the number of laborers, whose interests are affected, is small, and change of employment, so far as it is necessary, is attended with little inconvenience. Here too the law of patent rights comes in with important relief; for as the demand for the kind of labor to which the invention pertains, is limited, the inventor finds it for his advantage, to keep up the price of the product nearly or quite to its former rate. Of course, the old laborers are very gradually supplanted.

Circumstances favorable to the developement of natural aids to production.

Natural agents and other aids to production which arise from the properties of material objects and the laws of nature, are said to be developed, when they are made known and turned to the best account. It is the object of this section to state some circumstances, favorable to the developement of the aids of nature, in this use of the term.

1. The cultivation of the natural sciences.

It has been stated, that it is the appropriate business of the chymist and natural philosopher, to investigate the properties of material objects and the laws of the natural world. Wherever, then, there is a class of men thus engaged, making inquiries of this kind their study, it may reasonably be expected, that important discoveries and inventions will be made. It is true, that some of the aids of nature are so obvious, and so profusely offered to man, that the most careless cannot but notice them, and the most indolent avail themselves of their use. But even in these instances, much is often effected by the guidance and assistance of science. Thus a fertile soil is a natural agent, of which all may know, and of which also, as it offers its spontaneous fruits, all may avail themselves; yet this soil becomes far more productive, when its cultivation is directed by the scientific agriculturalist. It also often happens, that important discoveries and inventions seem to be accidental, or they are made by those who are employed as laborers, and who are unacquainted with the principles of science. But most frequently, even in these cases, such discoveries and inventions are not turned to the best account, till the guiding assistance of science has been given.

But the history of inventions tells us, that the instances are not few, in which most useful and important discoveries and inventions have resulted directly from the patient research, the able reasonings, and the often repeated experiments of scientific men. The miner's safety-lamp is a striking example. Before this highly important aid to the miner was brought to its present degree of perfection, Sir H. Davy devoted more than a year to laborious investigations and experiments. It is in this way, also, that, in the manufacture of cloths, the business of colouring has been brought to its present improved state.

And in this connexion it may be remarked, that the habits of mind, which are formed by scientific researches and reasonings, are in themselves of great advantage in the developement of the aids of nature. Much that is included under the head of invention, is but the new combination and application of the properties of material objects—of natural and mechanical powers; and for work of this kind, ingenuity, which is but another term for quickness of discernment, combined with skill and strength in reasoning, is required. Hence all those employments, which tend to sharpen the discerning faculties of the mind, and to quicken its powers of analysis and combination, are indirect aids to the developement of the productive powers of nature.

2. Minute division of labor.

In the chapter on economical arrangements, the connexion between division of labor and the invention of machinery was brought to view. I add here, that as this division becomes more minute, the probability that such inventions will be made, is in a corresponding degree increased. The reasons of this statement are obvious. Just in proportion as division of labor becomes more minute, each single process becomes more simple, and consequently more easily admits of the use of machinery. It would be beyond the powers of human invention, to contrive a machine, which receiving the raw cotton, should turn it out printed calico; but when the making of this calico is divided into twenty or thirty distinct processes, machinery is with little difficulty introduced into many of these processes. And further, the probability of its being invented is increased from the circumstance, that the whole attention of the laborer is directed to some single process, and he will very naturally be led to inquire, in what way this process may be performed with the least amount of labor to himself. Some highly important improvements in machinery have in this manner been introduced.

The same principle is also illustrated in the improvements, which are made in some branches of agricultural industry. Individuals, who confine their attention to the raising of some particular vegetable, or any one agricultural product, often obtain an unusual degree of skill, which is seen, both in the largeness of their crops and the superior quality of their products.

3. Whatever causes tend to increase the demand for products, are favorable to the developement of the aids of nature.

The stimulating effect of an enlarged demand upon production, was to some extent brought to view in the chapter on economical arrangements; but it may be looked at in connexion with our present topic of inquiry. It is the object of labor-saving machines, to increase the amount of products obtained from the same or less labor. Hence an enlarged demand for products acts as a stimulus upon study and invention; and thus, indirectly, whatever causes tend to increase the demand for products, lead to the developement of natural aids to production. These causes are the opening of foreign markets, and the stimulating effects of different branches of production upon each other in a prosperous and thriving community. In England, natural aids to production have been developed to an extent unequalled in any other country, which is without doubt to be ascribed in part to the great amount of her domestic consumption, but principally to the stimulating influence of her extensive foreign commerce.

It is from these views, that the governments of different countries are led to the adoption of measures, designed for the encouragement of home products. In this way they seek to develope the productive resources of a country of every kind,—those pertaining to labor and capital and natural aids. It is the latter, however, which are more especially had in view. And whatever may be thought of the wisdom of such measures, the principles on which they rest, are a corroboration of the statement that has here been made. It is by enlarging the demand, that this encouragement is given.

The supposition is sometimes made, that machinery is introduced, so as entirely to supersede the labors of man; and it is asked, whether, in this case, the resulting effects would be advantageous.

I answer, that the supposition is an impossibility. The making of machinery must of itself give employment to many. And further, the object of machinery is not so much to supplant human labor, as it is to render that labor more efficient and productive. Machinery has in this respect been well compared to a fertile soil. Suppose, that by the exertion of a miraculous power, the fertility of the soil throughout the world should be increased four-fold, so that for the coming year the returns of agricultural industry should be greater in this proportion. There would of course be a great increase of food and of other agricultural products, for the supply of human wants. The price of these products would also fall, but the larger amount obtained by the agriculturalist would make up for this diminution of price, especially as he, in common with others, would, as a consumer, share in the benefits of the greater abundance. It is true, also, that another year some of those, who had been engaged as agricultural producers, would find it necessary to change their employments, and to engage in some branch of manufacturing, or commercial industry. But now suppose, that a like increase of productive power should take place in manufactures and commerce, and that thus the amount of labor, required to supply the great family of man, should in a corresponding degree be diminished. It does not follow, that men need be idle, or that their condition would not be improved. Should men be relieved from the necessity of toil to supply the wants of the body, there are other and higher occupations in which they might engage; for there is to man the labor of the mind, and the accumulation of stores of knowledge, more valuable than those of material things. Here indeed is one argument in favor of the unlimited introduction of machinery; its introduction is connected with the progress of the human race in knowledge and intellectual advancement. For it may be anticipated, that in proportion as men are set free from the necessity of toil in the supply of their animal wants, they will have both leisure and inclination to engage in the labors of the mind.

CHAPTER V.

Productive Capital.

An explanation of the phrase, productive capital, has been given, and its accumulation shewn to be the result of industry and frugality. A general statement has also been made of the different forms it assumes, and of the aid which it gives in the work of production. I propose in the present chapter still further to consider it as a productive agent, and to bring to view circumstances favorable to its accumulation and efficiency.

Transformations to which capital is subjected in the work of production.

Capital, to become productive, must be consumed. Of the grain of wheat, it is literally true, and figuratively so of productive capital, in whatever form it may be vested, that, except it die, it bringeth forth no fruit.

And here, I propose to trace the transformations, to which capital is subjected in the different processes of production. In agriculture, at the commencement of the economic cycle,* the capital of the farmer, who is we will suppose the owner of his farm, is in his barns, his granaries, his fencing and other permanent improvements of his farm—in his wagons, carts and other implements of husbandry, in his cattle, his seed, his dressings, which are to be applied to the land—in his stock of provisions for the support of himself, of his laborers and of his cattle, and in his money for meeting incidental expenses and the payment of the wages of laborers. Now of the capital thus vested, a part is said to be fixed capital, and a part, circulating. Of this distinction, the real ground is, that during every economic cycle, a part is partially and another part totally consumed. The improvements on the farm, and what are called the fixtures, will last for a certain number of years—suppose twenty as the average,—one twentieth part of their value is then annually consumed. The average consumption of the implements of husbandry is shorter—perhaps five years. Then comes the capital of which the consumption is total, that vested in seed stuff, in dressings, in provisions and in money. This then, so far as capital is concerned, is the process of production; during the economic cycle all this value—that is, a twentieth part of the improvements of the farm and of the fixtures upon it, a fifth part of the value of the implements of husbandry,

* This phrase conveniently expresses the whole course of production, from the time that outlays are made, till returns are received. In agriculture, seed-time is its commencement, and harvesting its ending.

used in the cultivation of the farm, and the whole amount used as circulating capital, disappear. Then again, at the end of the cycle, which in this case is the time of harvesting, this same value reappears in the form of the annual proceeds of the farm, and, if the process is a profitable one, it returns with an increase of its amount to the farmer.

Similar in all respects are the transformations of capital in manufacturing production. At the commencement of the economical cycle, the capital of the manufacturer is vested in his buildings, his machinery, the raw materials to be manufactured, and the wages of laborers. As the process goes forward, the capital thus vested is in part or wholly consumed, and reappears in the manufactured products. Here then, as the result of the process, is the same value under another form, and in connexion with it the profits of the manufacturer.

So in commercial production, the capital of the merchant is in his ship, in the cargo with which she is freighted, in the wages of seamen and other laborers, as clerks, porters, stevedores, &c. So too, when the process is concluded, though the principal part of the investment may have been changed in its form many times, its value is retained, and the whole reappears with the profits of the adventure.

Thus it is, that capital, to be productive, must be consumed—that is, it disappears in one form, to reappear in another.

Capital as directed to different employments.

Nations differ from each other as to the proportional amount of capital, which is employed in the three great branches of production. Thus from the prevailing mode of investment, some nations are called agricultural nations, some manufacturing, and others, commercial. In the same nation, changes in the mode of investing capital are not unfrequently made, not perhaps general changes, but individuals are withdrawing their capital from one form of production and giving it a new direction. Our inquiry relates to the moving cause, by which capital is thus directed to different branches of production.

The general answer to our inquiry is—the rate of profits. Capitalists are ever asking, from what investments the largest revenues are received, and the variations of profits, that occur in different branches of production, are followed by corresponding changes in the modes of investing capital. The causes, which thus affect the rate of profits, are numerous. The discovery of some new territorial advantages—the invention, or new application of machinery—the opening of a new market, or the loss of an old one; or any of those changes in the wants of a community, to which we give the name of fashion, are the most prominent of these causes. Other causes also arise of a more limited nature, affecting the interests of individuals only, or of some one department of production. As soon then as capitalists find out, that the rate of profits obtained by others is greater than their own, they have before them a motive to change the investment of their capital, and this motive will prevail, unless other considerations of paramount importance come in to prevent.

Thus it is, that capital is directed to different employments by the rate of profits. But the considerations which modify this general principle, need to be stated. They are as follows;

1. The difficulties connected with a change of investment.

A capitalist, whose property is productively invested, will generally find a change attended with inconvenience and loss. Such changes are usually effected by the aid of a circulating medium. The property now in possession, must be turned into money, and this money must be expended in the purchase of property of a different kind; and it not unfrequently happens, that this double transfer is attended with loss. He will also take into the account the knowledge and skill, which he is capable of bringing to the management of his property in its new form, compared with what he has been accustomed to exercise, and also the personal inconvenience and trouble, to which from a change of business he must be subjected. The man, for instance, who from his early years has been familiar with the management of property as vested in a farm, may know, that the same amount of capital would yield him a larger revenue, if employed in navigation; but it might not be wise in him, on this account, to sell his farm and vest his property in shipping.

2. The risk, which attends different investments.

It is well known, that capital in some employments, is much more exposed to injury and loss, than when differently situated. And since the practice of insurance has become common, this difference of exposure is generally estimated, and taken into the account, in determining the profits of different investments. Our farmer would without doubt regard this as an important consideration, when inquiring, whether he might advantageously exchange his paternal acres, for the floating, perishing ships of commerce. But there is another kind of risk, which is not always so carefully considered—the risk of success. The revenue of capital vested in some branches of production, often appears to be unusually large, when the attention is confined to the income of some prosperous individuals, and thus many are led to form erroneous conclusions, and in the end are subjected to losses and disappointment. In such instances, a more just estimate is made, by taking the average rate of income of all those thus employing their capital, and when this is done, the result will often be found to differ essentially from individual cases. Some merchants, in the course of a few years, acquire large estates, and in looking at these successful adventurers in commerce, we may be led to the conclusion, that the rate of profits on mercantile capital, is much larger than on agricultural. But should we take into the account the many losses sustained by the community of merchants, the number of failures, as well as the instances of uncommon success, it would be found, that the average rate of profits in commerce, does not differ from that of capital, when vested in other branches of production.

Other considerations of less extent in their influence, and which need only to be mentioned, are the following; the pleasantness of the business, in which it is proposed to engage, and its reputation in the community—its moral bearings, and the associates with whom it will require intercourse, &c. We may add also other views of a more private and personal nature.

From the princi le, that the rate of profits determines the manner of investing capital, which is brought to view in this section, the important inference may be drawn, that the government of a country should abstain from interfering, directly or indirectly, with the mode of investing productive capital in the possession of individuals. So many are the circumstances to be taken into the account, in determining the question of investment, that neither an individual ruler, nor a public body of legislators, can advantageously judge. It is therefore wiser and safer, to leave the whole subject to those, who are more immediately interested. The motive to seek after the most profitable mode of investment, is sufficiently strong in every breast; and where the minds of men are in some good degree enlightened, and knowledge is generally diffused, there will be no want of enterprise, or sagacity. It is true, there will be instances of rash and foolish investment, and losses will be sustained; still the general welfare will on the whole be promoted by the course here recommended.

Why is the amount of productive capital in modern nations, greater than in former periods of the world?

It will be readily allowed, that the amount of capital in modern nations is much greater, than was possessed by the nations of the world a century ago, and further, that it was greater at that time, than at the commencement of the preceding century—in other words, that, excepting perhaps some powerful nations which became for a time conquerors of the world, and by violence and extortion collected together its riches, there has been a regular progress in national wealth. It is true, that, if in the history of most nations, we look at particular periods, we shall find, that causes have been at work to impoverish and weaken them. Such are the exactions and wrong-headed measures of oppressive and unwise governments—the profusion and extravagance, both of rulers and of private individuals, and more than all other causes, the enormous expenditures and the ruinous losses of protracted wars. But these causes, though while they last they are highly injurious, and their consequences are severely felt, are temporary, and there is in thriving communities, as in the human system, when subjected to the power of disease, a restorative principle, which makes its elastic and healing power to be felt. Hence, if our comparisons are instituted between remote periods, the influence of these temporary causes will be lost, and it will be found, that, notwithstanding the hindrances that have arisen, there has been in the community of nations a steady and decided advance in wealth.

Now our question looks at this fact, and is designed to call forth an explanation of it. And it will be noticed, that the answer to this inquiry brings to view the circumstances, which are favorable to the accumulation and increased efficiency of productive capital.

Whether there is more industry in the world now, than there was a century ago, in proportion to its population, is a question, which it might be difficult to decide. It is certain, however, that in civilized nations the amount of annual products is much increased. As nations have become more populous, and the style of living has been raised, there are more wants to be supplied, and not only is a supply to these more numerous wants furnished, but it is more generous in amount and better in quality than at former periods. There must then either be more labor in proportion to population, or this labor must be more productive. That the latter is the case, all must see, and what has been said in a preceding chapter on the aids of nature, fully accounts for this enlarged production. Here then, without doubt, is the principal cause of the larger amount of productive capital found in modern nations. Owing to the more extensive and improved use of natural assistants, human industry has become far more efficient—man, if he does not work more, works to better advantage. Hence the surplus left to producers, after supplying their wants, is greater, and here is one source of those accumulations, which constitute productive capital. To corroborate this statement, we might look at those nations, in which the aids of nature have been thus developed—to England, for example. To every one, the increase of her productive power, arising from the extent, to which she has availed herself of natural aids, especially in the form of machinery, is obvious and striking, and the accumulation of her productive capital has fully corresponded. A second source of this enlarged amount of productive capital in modern nations, is closely connected with the statement just made. From the more extensive and improved use of natural assistants, and the consequent lessened cost of production, the price of most articles in common use has fallen. Hence, though men do not consume less than in former times, but on the contrary though they consume more, there is still a diminution in the cost of living. Many articles also now in use, are not only cheaper, but in every respect far better, than those formerly used for the same purposes. Modern paper-hangings compared with ancient tapestry, is an example. Thus it is, that the diminished price of commodities, leads to the same result, as would be attained by a greater degree of frugality,—men have around them more of the comforts and conveniences of life, but they spend less. Thus also the two causes—the greater productiveness of human industry, and the diminished price of the necessaries of life, conspire to swell the amount of productive capital in modern nations.

The habits of modern communities compared with those of ancient times, tend to the same result. Formerly, rich men kept about them a great multitude of attendants. It was in this way that their wealth was displayed, and their pride gratified. But this portion of the community, whose maintenance exhausted the revenues of the rich, was supported in indolence, or if any service was rendered, it was of an unproductive kind. Now, also, the revenues of the rich are distributed for the support of numerous dependents ; but those thus maintained by them are in the workshop and the manufactory, and the fruits of the service which they render, are seen in the comforts and luxuries of life. Thus the crowd of retainers, instead of lounging about the castles of the great and the affluent, has become a crowd of productive laborers ; and the effects of this change of national habits are seen in the increased accumulation of capital.

The greater security of capital in modern times, is another reason, why more is accumulated. Formerly, in many parts of the world, men were afraid to be known to possess wealth, as it invited to oppression and violence, either from the government of the country, or from robbers and plunderers. In most modern nations it is otherwise. Individuals are found, whose capital and revenues are estimated by millions, and who yet hold their immense possessions in perfect security.

At the same time that greater security is afforded to capitalists, the revenue derived from the use of capital and the more liberal views which prevail on the subject of usury, have placed before men strong motives to exert themselves for its attainment. With many, the end at which they aim in their daily toil, is to acquire, and vest in some profitable manner, a sufficient amount of capital, to make them independent—that is, to derive a revenue from their capital, sufficient to support them in the style of living, to which they have been accustomed.

Thus the fact, that the amount of capital is larger among modern nations than at former periods, has been accounted for, and at the same time some of the circumstances favorable to the accumulation of capital, and its efficiency as an agent in production, have been stated.

How ought capitalists to be regarded in the community?

Among some classes of society, there not unfrequently exists a prejudice against men of wealth—a feeling, that such have got more than their share of the common stock, and that on this account, or for some other similar reason, they are just objects of suspicion and dislike. At least, the impression is not uncommon, that the interests of the rich are in some way opposed to those of the less wealthy.

Correct views on the subject of capital, both as to the manner in which it is obtained, and the uses which are made of it, are well fitted to shew, that such prejudices are without foundation. If a man acquires wealth by extortion, by oppressing and grinding the poor, or by any unfair and dishonest practices, no matter how strong the prejudices which are felt against him, nor how openly they are manifested. But the fact that there are rich men who are dishonest men, is no good reason, why men of wealth, as a class of the community, should be regarded with suspicion and dislike. There are poor men who are dishonest, still we are to hold in respect the honest poor.

In most instances, the rich man's wealth is the fruit of his own industry and frugality, or a portion of it may have been received by inheritance from others who were industrious and frugal. Or it may be, that a part of this accumulated wealth is rent, received for lands that have been cultivated and made to yield a supply of agricultural products; another part may be interest for the loan of capital productively vested. In either case, there is no ground for prejudice against the capitalist, whose wealth has been thus acquired. For in a well ordered community, it is permitted to every man, in fair competition with others, to obtain whatever he can acquire by the exertion of his powers of mind and body, and by the employment of his resources in the work of production. The road to wealth is alike open to all. And neither he who supinely sits down and does nothing, nor he who fails in his attempts to make progress in this path, should murmur and complain, because others go on prosperously. Further, he who has thus acquired wealth, and is thus acquiring it, is a public benefactor. A capitalist cannot employ his wealth productively, without benefitting the community in which he lives. He helps to develope the territorial resources of the country—he also gives profitable employment to its laborers, and he assists in bringing into successful action those productive powers, and sustaining those economical arrangements, with which the public prosperity is closely connected. Do not the same individuals who cherish these prejudices against the rich, complain, and with much more reason too, if capital is hoarded up, or sent abroad to be expended in foreign countries?

Neither is there ground for prejudice against the rich, because a portion of their income is expended in what are called the luxuries of life. It is obviously for the benefit of the whole community, that its members should be permitted to gratify their taste, and indulge their imaginary, no less than their real wants. The prospect of this indulgence is to most men the exciting motive to enterprise and exertion, and until some higher and purer motive shall be substituted in its place, it is important that the full power of self interest be felt.

Inequalities in wealth are found in every nation; and so long as men differ from each other in habits of industry and frugality—in forethought and skill and prudence, there must be inequalities of this kind, wherever the rights of property are respected. And every reflecting man knows, that it is best that such inequalities should exist. It is not indeed necessary, or desirable, to do any thing to create or increase them. On the contrary, the institutions and laws of a civil community, should place every man in this respect, as in others, on a perfect equality. There should be no privileged orders, no favorites of power. So far as inequalities of property exist, they should be those, which arise necessarily from the nature of man and the primary essential principles of civil society.

But while the distinctions of rich and poor are found in every civilized nation, it is also the case, that no member of a civil community, is, in the strict sense of the word, independent. If the poor must look to the rich for capital, by whose aid their industry becomes more advantageous both to themselves and to the community, the rich are no less dependent on the poor that their capital may be employed and be made productive. Of what avail also to the rich man is his wealth, were there no laborers to furnish a supply of those commodities, for the attainment of which wealth is desired and expended? If there is any one truth, taught more clearly than all others in the science of Political Economy, it is the mutual dependence and close connexion of the different members and different classes of a civil community upon each other. "The eye cannot say to the hand, I have no need of thee; nor again the head to the feet, I have no need of you."

From the principles stated in this and the two preceding chapters, we are led to the conclusion—that the wealth and prosperity of nations are intimately connected with simple habits of life, pure morals and widely-diffused intelligence. Indeed so far as improvements are made in the condition of nations, they are ultimately to be traced to these causes; and the highest improvements are witnessed, where these causes are in combined and joint action. Unfortunately, however, this combination is rarely found. Advances in knowledge are often connected with declension in morals, and with departures from simple habits of life.

1. That a nation may become great and powerful, its members must be simple in their habits of life. The strength of a nation is in its laboring population. Here is the true basis of national greatness. But a laboring population to be efficient, must be healthy; and health is closely connected with simplicity of diet and of other habits of life.

A healthy climate is often enumerated among the territorial advantages, possessed by a nation. And from its connexion with the efficiency of human industry, it deserves to be thus regarded; where miasmata, or other causes of disease, prevail, the region is highly unfavorable to labor. But far more injurious and withering to the strength of a nation, is intemperance, or excess in any form. On this point, we are not left to depend on inferences made from the principles of Political Economy, or of any other science. The voice of history is loud and full in the testimony which it bears. If we look to the early settlers of most countries, we find them to be men of simple habits of life; necessity may have first led them into this course, but duty and self interest have confirmed them in it. We find also, that while these simple habits remained, the amount of labor accomplished, was greater, in proportion to the number of laborers, than at any subsequent period. In the language of poetry, this portion of a nation's history is sometimes called the iron age—the age, whose most striking features are hardihood and strength and vigor and enterprise. Perhaps the world has rarely exhibited a better example of this iron age, than was seen among the Puritans of New England.

But a simple style of living is also connected with national advancement in another way. Frugality, we have seen, is one source of those accumulations, which constitute the productive capital of a nation; and in proportion as a simple style of living prevails, these savings and accumulations will be greater. For facts illustrative of this statement, I might again refer to the early history of this country, especially as contrasted with what has since been witnessed. It is generally supposed, that the amount of products consumed in the daily support of the laboring population of this country, is greater, in proportion to the number of inhabitants, than in any other, and recent investigations have shewn, that the amount annually wasted in ruinous excesses, is immense. There can be no doubt, then, that were the simple habits of the early settlers found among their descendants, and the wasteful excesses of intemperance stayed, the salutary consequences of reform would soon be seen in the advancing wealth and prosperity of the nation. Indeed, within a few years, much conducive to national welfare has in this way been accomplished; and those engaged in the promotion of this object, should be regarded as the benefactors of their country. Neither is it improbable, that retrenchment and reform in other habits of life, may yet be made, which shall be attended with like beneficial results to the community.

2. A nation, to become prosperous and great, must be a virtuous nation. This proposition is often laid down, and its truth is more generally allowed than felt. At least, many probably are not careful to trace the connexion between pure morals and national welfare. What has just been said on simple habits of living, is one way, in which this connexion is exhibited; since most departures from simplicity of style in the habits of life, are vicious indulgences. Another way in which this connexion may be traced out, is in the effect of the state of morals prevailing in a community, on the habits of industry. A common proverb tells us, that indolence opens the door for vice, and it is equally true, that the same office is in return done by vice for indolence. On the contrary, a moral people will be almost uniformly an industrious people. Men labor most patiently and strenuously, when the motives to exertion are most strongly and constantly

felt; and no motives are of stronger and more uniform power, than those of moral obligation. Purity of morals is also closely connected with that security and quiet—that well ordered and peaceful state of society, which invites to enterprise and to the accumulation and use of capital. It is true, the strong arm of government must be extended for the protection of the rights of person and of property, but the strength of this protecting arm is in the good morals of the community. There is also found in a healthy moral atmosphere, something that invigorates—that calls forth enterprise and effort. Those who dwell in the midst of the impurities of vice, must feel the enervating and destructive influences around them.

It would be easy to enlarge on the different statements here made, but their correctness may be inferred from the principles found in the preceding chapters. They are also abundantly illustrated and confirmed by what is seen in different communities. Every reflecting and observing man knows, that the tendencies of virtue are all favorable both to individuals and to nations.

3. A nation to become great, must be intelligent.

I mean by this proposition, that there should be found in every nation men of science, capable of investigating and exhibiting to others, the laws and properties of material objects around them, and of applying what is thus discovered to the practical purposes of life; and also that intelligence should be generally diffused among the various classes of society.

The importance of scientific attainments to a nation, is directly inferred from the tendency of these attainments, to develope and bring into advantageous action the natural aids to production which exist in a nation. This is one sense, in which knowledge is power. But on this topic enough has already been said.

The general diffusion of intelligence among all classes of society, is equally important to national prosperity. Labor under the guidance of intelligence, becomes more efficient and profitable. A reading, reflecting people, capable of understanding the relations of society, and of discerning the different ways in which their own interests may be affected, capable also of arranging and planning their business transactions, in that way, which may turn to the best account the resources at their command, will always be in advance of those, who are characterised by their ignorance and stupidity.

The importance of education, both in its higher departments, and in what in this country is termed the common school system, is here seen in a strong light. But it belongs not to an elementary work, to dwell on the practical bearings of the principles it unfolds. Political Economy enjoins it upon every nation, to diffuse the light of knowledge through all classes of society. It teaches, that whatever is thus expended, is capital well employed, yielding a large and highly profitable revenue to the public.

CHAPTER VI.

Circulation of Wealth.

It has been stated, that few members of a community advanced in wealth and civilization, labor directly for the supply of their own wants. Each productive laborer confines his efforts to the furnishing of some one product, and looks to the system of exchange, as the method by which he is to obtain a supply of the various commodities which he needs. Of this system of exchange as connected with the business of production, something has already been said in the chapter on economical arrangements. It is here proposed, to take a more extended view of the circulation of wealth, and to shew by what methods and upon what principles it is conducted. This will require an explanation of the phrases—*a medium of exchange* and *a measure of value*. It will lead also to inquiries connected with the basis and the variations of price. Thus the way will be prepared for further views on the subject of production, and for the statement of those principles, which are connected with the distribution and consumption of wealth.

A medium of exchange.

In the early stages of society, the few exchanges which are made, are effected by barter—that is, one commodity is exchanged directly for another. But in a more advanced state—when the economical arrangements connected with production are established, this direct exchange of commodities is attended with much embarrassment and difficulty. The farmer may have on hand a surplus amount of the products of his farm, and he may wish to exchange a portion of this surplus with some other producer—the cabinet maker, for example, for articles of furniture. But the cabinet maker has already perhaps a sufficient supply of the produce offered by the farmer, and he himself wishes to exchange his furniture for some articles of grocery in possession of the merchant. And thus the business of exchange becomes embarrassed. But, in the progress of society, a remedy has been provided for these inconveniences. There is a commodity in common use, which every one is ready to receive in return for what he would exchange, and with which he is enabled to obtain from others those articles which he wants, and which others are willing to give away in exchange. Thus, in the case supposed, the farmer exchanges his wheat for this commodity which all are willing to receive. With this commodity he goes to the cabinet maker, and obtains from him the articles of furniture he wants. And then again the cabinet maker, by the aid of the same commodity, effects an exchange for the groceries of the merchant. Thus it is, that this commodity, which all are willing to receive for what they are disposed to exchange, and by the aid of which all can obtain the supplies which they want, when these supplies are in the market, becomes *a medium of exchange* or, as it is sometimes called, a *circulating medium.*

We learn from history, that many different commodities have been used for this purpose. In some nations, especially those but in part civilized, or which have made but small advances in wealth, whatever commodity constitutes the larger share of the wealth of the community, or from any cause becomes more frequently than others an object of exchange, is wont to be used as a circulating medium.. Hence, among pastoral tribes, cattle is the common medium of exchange. Thus Homer speaks of the armour of Diomede, which cost nine oxen, while that o Glaucus cost one hundred oxen. And so, in later times, dried fish in Newfoundland, sugar in the West Indies andf tobacco in Virginia, are said to have been used for the purposes of exchange. But of all the commodities, that at different periods and in different parts of the world, have been used as a circulating medium, no one has fulfilled this office so extensively and for so long a time, as the precious metals in the form of money. We read of the shekels of silver, as current money with the merchant in the times of Abraham. We know also, that in Greece and Rome, the metals were coined and used for the same purpose. And in later times, this use has become general among all civilized nations. I propose then to state some reasons, why this preference is given to the precious metals as a medium of exchange.

1. They have a sameness of quality in all parts of the world. One grain of pure gold is exactly similar to another, whether brought from the mines of Europe or America, or gathered from the sands of Africa. Neither is its quality liable to be altered by those causes, which affect most other commodities. It is not injured by time—it does not become spoiled or decay. Hence the value of pure gold depends on the quantity alone. We know that two grains are always worth exactly twice as much as one.

2. The precious metals admit of minute division and exact apportionment. This is effected by fusion, and in this process nothing is lost; the several parts are equal to the whole and have a ratio to each other in exact proportion to their weight. The importance of this property of the precious metals, in adapting them to the purposes of exchange, will be readily seen.

3. Another circumstance, which adapts the precious metals to be used as money, is their rarity and the consequent difficulty of their attainment. If either salt, as in Abyssinia, or iron, as in Sparta, were in general use at the

present time as a circulating medium, we see at once, that the quantity required in a commercial community, would be inconvenient, both from bulk and weight. It would be possible also to increase the amount of these commodities with a suddenness and to a degree, which would at once essentially affect their value, and derange the business transactions of the whole community. All these inconveniences are prevented by the rareness of the precious metals and the difficulty of their attainment. On the other hand, the precious metals are not so rare, that the portion of them required in the common transactions of business, are too minute for convenient use. This might to some extent be the case, if gold only were used.

It will be readily inferred from this statement, that the continuance of the use of gold and silver as a medium of exchange, must depend in part on their rareness. Should the supply of them become much more abundant than at present, it may be necessary to resort to the use of platina, or of some object less common than the precious metals.

4. The precious metals admit of coinage.

The value of a piece of gold or silver is determined by its fineness and its weight. It is necessary therefore, whenever any portion of the precious metals is used as money, that its purity and its quantity should be determined. But to assay and weigh in every instance, what is given and received in the numerous exchanges constantly made in a commercial community, would cause much trouble and delay. To prevent this inconvenience, the coinage of the precious metals has been introduced. At first, this process consisted only in impressing a stamp on a piece of metal to indicate its fineness, leaving the quantity in each case to be determined by weight. Afterwards, the impression was made to cover the whole piece, and indicated not only the purity of the metal, but its amount; and then payments were made by tale. This process of coinage is usually conducted by the national government, or by some body of men, in whom public confidence is placed.

In the process of coining, it is usual to mix with the pure gold or silver, some portion of alloy. This increases the hardness of the coins and prevents their injury by wear. This amount of alloy is so small, that in estimating the weight and value of the coins, regard is had only to the pure gold and silver they contain.

Such are the properties of the precious metals, by which they become adapted, in the form of money, to the business of exchange. But in communities where a circulating medium is in constant use, and where too the amount of value thus exchanged is frequently large, and remittances are sometimes to be made to distant places, it has been found necessary to resort to another expedient. Representatives of the precious metals and of other objects of value, in the form of bank notes and bills of exchange, have been introduced, and made to do the same office, as the precious metals themselves. In this way, remittances of large amount may be made to any distance, and since the materials of which these representatives are made, are light and cheap, the transportation of them is attended with little expense or risk, and the wear of them is too inconsiderable to be calculated as a loss. The nature of these representatives of coined money will now be explained.

1. *Bills of exchange.* A bill of exchange is a demand

on some individual, or (individuals in) company, for a definite sum of money, and gives to its possessor a claim to receive the specified amount at a future time or a distant place.

A., who is a merchant in Boston, sends a cargo of grain to Liverpool, and consigns it to a commercial house in that port. He then draws a bill of exchange on the consignee for the amount of the grain. This bill of exchange, payable at sight, or in a certain number of days after it is presented, is sold to another merchant, or to a banker in Boston, and sent by the purchaser to Liverpool in payment of some debt due in that city. Thus, by the aid of this bill of exchange, the exporter of grain from this country has received payment for his grain, and the foreign merchant, who had exported manufactured products and sent them to this country, has received the amount due him for his manufactures; and the whole transaction, on both sides, has been conducted without the expense or risk attendant on the transportation of specie.

When commercial intercourse is carried on between two countries to a large amount, many of these bills of exchange will be found in both, which will be brought into frequent use, in making remittances from one country to the other; and the saving of the expense and risk of the transportation of specie, will give to these bills a small additional value. If B., a merchant in Boston, is bound to the payment of a debt of $ 10,000 in Liverpool, and can be saved the trouble and risk of sending specie to this amount from Boston to Liverpool, he can afford to pay a small premium for a bill of exchange.

But besides this additional value, which a bill of exchange acquires from its utility as a convenient mode of remittance, its value is often affected by other considerations. Sometimes the state of the currency in one country is less sound than in another; the specie part of it may be more worn, or there may be an undue proportion of a depreciated paper currency. A bill of exchange drawn on a country whose currency is thus depreciated, unless other and stronger reasons prevent, will be *below par*, or worth less than the face of it. And when the circumstances are changed, a contrary effect is produced, and the exchange will be *above par*.

But the cause, which more than any other affects the value of bills of exchange, is the relative supply and demand of them, or the state of the exchange market. This requires therefore a more particular statement.

Suppose the amount of bills drawn on England, during the past year, by merchants in the United States, to be twelve millions, while the amount drawn by English merchants on this country, does not exceed ten millions. Now, in adjusting accounts, the ten millions drawn on one nation will obviously meet the same amount drawn on the other, leaving a balance of two millions to be paid in specie, or in some other way. The English merchant, then, finding that there is a deficiency of bills of exchange drawn on this country, will be desirous of obtaining a sufficient amount with which to make his own remittances; and the same being the case in respect to others, competition commences; and thus, on the principle of supply and demand, the value of these bills is increased. But while the exchange with England is in favor of this country, the exchange between the United States and France will perhaps be against the former; and at the same time, in the commercial transactions between France and England, the exchange may be in favor of England. In this case, some of the surplus bills on France in England, might be sent by the English merchant to the United States, in payment of debts due, and then again be remitted, for the same purpose, from the United States to France; and thus an equilibrium would be restored.

From this statement, it is seen, that bills of exchange are highly useful for the circulation of wealth. But this utility is in practice closely connected with the banking system, in the account of which some further views of the nature of bills of exchange will be given.

2. Bank notes, or, as they are usually termed in this country, bank bills, are promissory notes, issued by private bankers, or by banking companies, to pay on demand a sum specified on the face of the note. They are used in the home trade, for making remittances to different sections of the same country, and in the smaller and more common business transactions of the community. Thus, in many countries, they constitute an important part of the national currency.

Rightly to understand the nature of this portion of a circulating medium, some knowledge of banks is required. I shall therefore here introduce a brief account of these institutions, exhibiting the manner in which they are constituted, and the advantages resulting from them to the community.

The oldest banking institutions of which we have knowledge, were *banks of deposit*. Of these, especially of that established at Amsterdam, A. Smith has given a detailed account.* A shorter statement is here offered.

---

* Wealth of Nations, Book 4, Chap 3.

The principal design, in the establishment of banks of deposit, was to counteract the effects arising from a depreciated specie currency. The larger nations of Europe were wont to issue from their own mints a large proportion of their specie currency, and as any portion of this currency became worn, it was withdrawn and replaced by a new coinage. But in smaller States, especially in those extensively engaged in commerce, a large proportion of the circulating medium was in foreign coins, which, not being subjected to a new coinage, became much worn and depreciated in value. Hence bills of exchange drawn on merchants in these States, and payable in a depreciated currency, were of less value in the exchange market. To meet therefore these bills of exchange with a better currency, the merchants of these States made deposits in a Bank, established under the authority of the State, and which made payment of all demands upon it in a currency of the full standard value.

Another advantage more closely connected with the circulation of wealth, was also derived from these banks of deposit. Merchants and capitalists in their business transactions, made and received payments by transfers of stock on the books of the bank, and thus the trouble of weighing or counting specie, and of removing it from one place to another, was prevented.

Banks of deposit were founded as early as 1609, and some institutions of this kind continued in operation till near the close of the last century. Their expenses were defrayed by a small per centage on the transfers of stock, and by the higher value of bank currency. But the advantages offered by these banks were of a limited kind, and they have since been supplanted by banks of discount.

Banks of Discount.

These institutions are so called from the circumstance, that a leading object in their establishment is the loan of capital, for which interest is received under the name of discount. For the establishment of a bank of discount, a large amount of capital is required, which is usually furnished by individuals, who being themselves either unable, or from some cause indisposed, to employ their property in a productive manner, prefer to intrust it to the care and management of others. Property thus vested, is bank-stock—those thus contributing and owning it, are stockholders—those to whom it is intrusted, are directors.* I propose to look at these banks principally as facilitating the circulation of wealth, and in this view I remark,

1. Banks of discount, by the issue of bills, increase the circulating medium of a country.

When a bank is first established, a portion of its capital is paid by stockholders in specie, and the whole of this specie, or such part of it as the business of the bank requires, is kept as a deposit in the vaults of the bank. Thus, by the establishment of a bank of discount, a portion of the specie currency is withdrawn from circulation.

---

* Banks in the United States are private institutions, incorporated for the more convenient conducting of their concerns, in the same manner, and on the same principles, as manufacturing Companies, and other similar establishments receive acts of incorporation. The right to circulate printed notes, payable to bearer, is incidental, and conferred by express Statute, the Bank paying an equivalent, either in the form of tax, or bonus, to the Government.

To supply the deficiency thus occasioned, notes, or bills, are issued by the bank, and supposing this issue of bills to be limited to the amount of specie withdrawn, the advantage gained would be the substitution of representatives of coined money, more convenient in their form for some of the purposes of exchange. But this is far from being the case. The bills issued by a bank of discount, usually exceed the specie in its vaults by many times the amount of this specie. Thus, then, an addition is made to the circulating medium of a country.

Here perhaps the inquiry will arise, how this amount of bankbills is introduced into the currency of the nation? And to answer this inquiry, it may be necessary to make a brief statement of the manner, in which the business of loaning is conducted in these institutions. This may most conveniently be done by the aid of an example. Suppose a wholesale merchant to sell goods to a retailer, to the amount of $ 2,000, on three months credit, and to receive his note, payable at that time. This note, which is called commercial paper, is then presented to the bank with added securities for its payment, and there discounted— that is, the bank advances to the wholesale merchant the present worth of the note, which is the face of it, deducting the discount. After the time of credit has expired, the full amount of the note is paid by the retailer, or his securities, to the bank. Now it is in connexion with these transactions that the bills of the bank are put into circulation; for of the $ 2,000 advanced by the bank to the wholesale merchant, a large proportion, or the whole amount, is in its own bills, while but a small proportion, and perhaps none, of the return payment, made by the retail merchant, is in the bills of the bank. And thus as commercial paper is continually received and advances made upon it, opportunity is offered to a bank to put in circulation any amount of its own bills it may deem safe and for its interest.

But bank bills have been spoken of as the representatives of specie and other objects of intrinsic value. What values then, it may be asked, are represented by that portion of these notes, which are in excess of the specie in the vaults of the bank. Suppose, for example, a bank, whose capital is $100,000, has on hand specie to the amount of $20,000, and bills in circulation to twice the amount of its capital. The inquiry is, what values are represented by the $180,000 of excess. I answer, the values, which, in the form of commercial paper, are pledged to the bank in payment of sums advanced by it. These values thus pledged, and thus represented, are the real and personal estates of all those individuals, whose names, as principals, or securities, are found on the commercial paper, for the time being, in possession of the bank. Hence, then, should the bills of the bank be returned upon it, with a demand of promised payment, every solvent and well regulated institution will be able to meet this demand, if not immediately, within a short period—that is, when its commercial paper becomes due. And it may here be remarked that the basis, on which the operations of a bank of discount are conducted, is a calculation of probabilities. Those conducting its affairs, know the amount of specie on hand. They know also the amount of funds deposited in the bank, and are able to form an opinion as to the continuance of these deposits, and of their probable increase or diminution. They know also the amount of commercial paper, becoming due at different periods, and from their acquaintance with the course of trade, they can judge to what extent demands for the discount of commercial paper will be made. And from these several premises, most of which, it will be noticed, are of the nature of probabilities, the directors of a bank are able to determine, what amount of specie it is necessary to keep on hand, and also what amount of bills it is safe to keep in circulation, and generally, in what manner the affairs of the institution should be conducted.

2. Banks of discount offer facilities for the circulation of wealth, in the forms of bank-credits, drafts, checks and other expedients of a similar nature.

The remittance of large amounts of specie from one section of a country to another, is attended with expense and risk; neither is the trouble and labor small, of weighing, or counting, and delivering into the possession of another, large quantities of specie, when not transported to a distant place. Now in communities where a well established system of banking is found, consisting either of local banks, or a national bank and its branches, or of both, this trouble and expense and risk, are saved. And this is effected, not by bank bills merely, or principally, but by other expedients, more or less connected with the banking system. Such are transfers of credit on the books of a bank, bank-checks, drafts, &c. To these we may add notes of hand and bills of exchange, which become part of the circulating, or rather commercial medium of a country principally through the instrumentality of banks. The amount of values, whose ownership is daily transferred by these expedients in a large commercial nation, exceeds, many times, the exchanges effected by the circulating medium of the nation, both in the form of specie and bills. In this way, then, banks offer further facilities for the circulation of wealth.

The question may here arise, how far banks are essential as a part of a system of exchange? Some have supposed them unnecessary, and that transfers of value might be made by notes of hand, bills of exchange, drafts on individuals, &c. without any assistance from banks. And this opinion is probably correct. The basis of the whole system of credit currency is mutual confidence. So long as men put this confidence in notes of hand, bills of exchange &c. they may form a part of this currency, and no longer. And the same is true of bank bills; so long as there is confidence reposed in them as the representatives of value, they are current, and when this confidence ceases to be felt, they will no longer form a part of the circulating medium. At least, this will be the case with that part of the bank bill currency, which is in excess of specie in the vaults of the bank. Hence, then, a paper credit currency might exist without banks or bank bills, so long as it has this mutual confidence, on which to rest. But a system of exchange thus conducted, would be attended with far less convenience to the public. At least the offices now rendered by banks, in connexion with a commercial medium of the kind stated above, must then be rendered by individuals, or by companies established for these purposes.

To form a just estimate of the service rendered to the community by banks, so far as they aid in the circulation of wealth, the necessity of an increasing currency, corresponding to the progress of a nation in wealth and commercial business, should be taken into the account. Were the circulating medium of a nation restricted to specie, it would be necessary, that as the amount of wealth to be circulated increases, either the value, or the amount, of this currency should in a corresponding degree become greater. Suppose the amount of specie in this country to be no greater than it was fifty years ago, and no paper currency to be in use. In that case, the value of a dollar would be perhaps tenfold greater, than at the present time, that is, it would exchange for ten times the amount of commodities in the market, and other coins, both of gold and silver, would increase in value in like proportion. This, it is easily seen, would be attended with inconvenience, especially in the circulation of the smaller denominations of coin. Or if, to prevent this increased value of specie currency, it were attempted to furnish a supply, corresponding to the greater demand, the attempt would require a large amount of capital and labor, now productively employed in other ways; and even then the attempt perhaps might prove unsuccessful. Banks then, as they furnish the additional currency needed, with little expense to the community, are of important service.

So far I have spoken of banks of discount, as connected with the circulation of wealth. There are other advantages arising from them, to some of which I shall now briefly refer.

1. They present a profitable and safe opportunity for investing capital.

Men of large capital often wish to be relieved in whole, or in part, from the trouble and care of employing this capital, or of loaning to others. There is also in every community, a class of capitalists, who need the assistance of others in making their property productive. Such are those, who from age, or any disability, have retired from business—minors, whose support is to be derived from funded property, and eleemosynary institutions. To all such, a bank investment is the most favorable that can be found. If the institution is properly managed, property, thus vested, is safe, and yields a revenue, equal to the usual interest of money, and sometimes exceeding it. It is also easily transferable. Bank-stock is generally *at par*, and often above.

2. They increase the amount of productive capital in a nation.

This result, to some extent, follows from the preceding. From the opportunity offered by banks for the convenient and safe investment of capital, a much larger amount of individual revenues is saved, and becomes a part of the national productive capital, than would otherwise have been the case. Especially is this amount large, where Savings Banks are established, whose funds are usually placed under the management of banks of discount. Many millions of dollars have in this way been added to the capital of the United States within a few years, which otherwise would probably have been unproductively spent.

3. Banks render the capital of a nation more productive.

This results from the circumstance, that Banks are a medium of communication between the wealthy classes of society and the industrious and enterprising, enabling those who can offer good securities, to avail themselves of capital for processes of production. The capital of a nation is also rendered more productive, by the quick returns obtained for products through their instrumentality. The manufacturer, for example, who disposes of his wares on a credit of sixty or ninety days, might find himself embarrassed, if obliged to wait this time for the return of his capital. He might even find it necessary to suspend the operations of his manufactory and to dismiss his workmen. Or to prevent this, he might be obliged to apportion his capital differently, and to conduct his business on a smaller scale. To free himself from these inconveniences, he offers his notes to the Bank, and receives at once their present worth, and thus is enabled to make all necessary advances for conducting his business.

It may be further added, in this connexion, that the prompt and punctual habits of business, which are found wherever banks are in operation, are highly favorable to the productive powers of a community. At least, where these institutions exist, payments are more promptly made, and the productive capital of the community is turned to better account.

These statements, shewing the different ways, in which banks of discount aid in economising capital, should be accompanied with the remark, that though they may economise, they cannot create capital, where it does not already exist. Neither is it wise to attempt the establishment of a bank in a part of the country, where the amount of business is not sufficient to give employment to the capital thus funded ; for it should ever be remembered, that capital, to yield a revenue, must be productively employed. The unsuccessful attempts sometimes made, to establish banks in sections of the country where they are not needed, shew that these considerations do not always receive the attention they merit.

It will be noticed, that the view here taken of banks of discount relates to their direct influence on the economical interests of the community. The objection is sometimes brought against these institutions, that they are dangerous to the liberties of a nation, especially as they are found in free States. Money, it is said, is power; and if this power be in the hands of a banking company distinct from the government of the country, it may, for sinister ends, oppose and thwart those measures, which are required by the public good. If, on the contrary, this power is exercised by the government itself, it may be used to oppress and injure its subjects. In either case then it is liable to be abused. In reply it may be said, that it is obvious that these abuses of the power conferred by money, are not in their nature necessarily connected with banking companies; money might still be accumulated and these abuses exist, where banks are not found. Still, if there is connected with banking institutions a peculiar liability to abuses of this nature, so far there is an objection to their establishment in a free state. At least, this consideration should lead to peculiar watchfulness and care.

Measure of value.

Objects have value attached to them, either because they are adapted to the supply of human wants, or because they may be used in obtaining a supply of these wants. A distinction is made between value in use and value in exchange. Whatever a man possesses which is useful to him, may be said to have a value in use, but of the objects thus possessed, those only have a value in exchange, for which others are willing to give objects which are accounted valuable, in return. Water is highly useful; it has therefore a value in use. But where, as is the case in most parts of the world, an unlimited supply of it may be obtained with little or no trouble, it has no value in exchange—no one will give any thing in return for it. But change the circumstances in which it is found,—let the supply of water become limited, or let its attainment be attended with difficulty, or require labor, and it begins at once to have a value in exchange. Now it is with those commodities only which have exchangeable value, that our inquiries are concerned. And here the different circumstances which are requisite, that objects may have exchangeable value, may be noticed. 1. There must be a limitation in the supply of them; nobody will give value in exchange for that of which there is an unlimited supply. 2. Their attainment must be attended with some sacrifice, or labor; otherwise, no one will be willing to give in exchange for them commodities, which have cost labor or some sacrifice. 3. There must be a demand for them; a commodity, of which there is a limited supply, may have been acquired by its possessor with much labor, and he may value it as highly useful to himself, but if there is no demand for it—if no one else wants it, or is willing to give that which is valuable in exchange for it, this commodity will have no value in exchange.

Another point may here be noticed—that the exchangeable value attached to any object, will depend on the amount of other objects, for which it may be exchanged—in other words, that this exchangeable value is altogether a relative value. B. has a piece of broadcloth. This broadcloth has to its owner a value in use—but the amount of this value in use no one can estimate. The broadcloth has also a value in exchange. It may be exchanged for thirty bushels of wheat,—for forty yards of flannel,—for six hats, &c. And should it be asked, what is the exchangeable value of this piece of broadcloth? the only way to answer this inquiry, is thus to make an enumeration of the different objects, with the amount of each, for which the broadcloth might be exchanged. This to be sure is attended with some trouble, and might not give any very definite view of the exchangeable value of the article, but it is the only way in which this value is to be determined. When however we come to make frequent exchanges of commodities, the necessity of something more definite, and which may enable us to institute a comparison between different commodities, as to their exchangeable value, is felt. We want a measure of value—something, which in respect to the comparative value of objects, shall answer the same purpose, that a yard-stick, or a foot-rule, does in comparing the length of bodies.

To meet this want—that is, to find some commodity, which shall be a perfect measure of value, has ever been a perplexing problem to political economists. Adam Smith proposes, that human labor should be taken as a measure of value. Others have proposed wheat; others, money. It is unnecessary to examine in detail the statements and arguments of writers, in support of their different proposed measures of value. One insuperable objection exists to these objects, and to all that have ever been proposed. They are in themselves variable, and this can never be true of any accurate measure of value. The exchangeable value of wheat is not only liable to be affected annually, as the season is more or less favorable to its production; but improved methods of cultivation and many other causes may affect it. Human labor, also, is worth more or less, according to the circumstances under which it is performed, or the skill which is put forth. It feels too all the modifying influences of relative supply and demand. Money is perhaps less subject to these variations of value than the other objects proposed, and being, from several circumstances, which will hereafter be stated, better fitted to become a measure of value, is practically in use for this purpose. But that money in the form of the precious metals, or of their representatives—bank-notes or bills of exchange, is not a perfect measure of value, may be learnt from the following statements, which, though they anticipate in part what is afterwards said on the subject of price, are here introduced, as showing more fully the nature and uses of money.

1. The value of money will vary with the labor and expense required to obtain it, that is, with the cost of its production. As this remark relates to the material of money, it can apply only to a specie currency.

2. The value of money will vary with variations in the proportion of the amount found at any time in a nation to the amount required for the purposes of a circulating medium, or, as it is more commonly expressed, with the relative variations of supply and demand.

3. Money is subject to nominal variations.

It might be sufficient, in support of the first and second proposition, to say, that money is subject to the same influences as affect the value of other commodities, and to refer to what is afterwards said upon the subject of price. But I prefer to improve the opportunity, to offer some historical illustrations, with which it is important to become acquainted.

When the mines of South America were first known to the inhabitants of Europe, and large amounts of gold and silver were received from them, there was an immediate depreciation in the value of these metals. The cost of their production was less, and the supply in proportion to the demand, became more abundant; from both these causes therefore their value became less. This depreciation, in the case of silver, has been usually estimated as tenfold, so that an ounce of silver, after the discovery of these mines, would exchange for only one tenth of the commodities, for which it had been previously exchanged. But while this increased supply at a diminished cost, tended to diminish in the proportion above stated, the value of silver, another cause came into operation, which tended to raise its value. This cause was a demand for a larger circulating medium. The discovery of America and of the passage around the Cape of Good Hope, made about the same time, by exciting the enterprise of the nations of Europe, and opening new and advantageous fields for the employment of their capital and labor, increased to an important extent, the business transactions of the old world. The wealth of the different European nations became greater, and as there was more value to be transferred from one individual to another, and transfers were more frequently made, it became necessary, that the circulating medium of these nations should be enlarged. And thus a portion of the larger supply, furnished by the new mines, was absorbed by the demand for a larger circulating medium. Hence it is, that the depreciation in the value of silver, which occurred at this period, instead of being tenfold, as before stated, was only threefold, that is, an ounce of silver, instead of being estimated at one tenth of its former value, was reckoned at one third of this value; and this allowance is usually made, in estimating the value of sums stated in silver currency before the year 1520. When the currency is gold, the depreciation is estimated at one fourth.

The state of the circulating medium in England, from the year 1797 till 1819, during which interval the bills of the bank of England were not redeemed in specie, but were made a legal tender by act of Parliament, offers further illustration and proof of these propositions. At the period to which I refer, the circulating medium of England consisted of a small proportion of gold and silver, of the notes of the country banks, which were redeemable, and of the notes of the bank of England, which were not redeemable. But so great was the demand for a circulating medium arising from the immense amount of the business transactions of that country, that so long as the bank of England restricted itself to a moderate issue of its notes, the value of the whole currency was sustained, and this too, even when the subsidising of foreign troops had drained the country of its gold and silver coins. In this case, then, the notes of the bank of England had a value, not as the representatives of specie, nor as the representatives of other values, pledged for their redemption. They had an intrinsic value of their own, arising from their utility, and dependent, as to its intenseness, on demand and supply.

From these statements, the inference is made, that the value of money depends on the same causes, as the value of other commodities, and of course is fluctuating.

The same inference is also to be drawn from the fact, that money is imported and exported by merchants, on the same principles, and in the same manner, as other articles of merchandise. When the precious metals are more abundant, and on that account cheaper, in a foreign country, than in his own, the exporter, who has carried abroad a cargo of the staple commodities of his own country, brings back in return gold and silver, either coined, or in bullion. He does so, because it is the most profitable importation he can make. And so, if specie is more abundant in his own country, in proportion to the demand for it, than in foreign countries, and on this account cheaper, he sends it abroad, just as he would any other commodity, of which there is a surplus in the market.

I now proceed to consider my third proposition, that money is subject to nominal variations of value.

By nominal variations, I mean those variations, which result from changes in the denominations of coined money. The governments of different countries, supposing that the credit and currency of the circulating medium are dependent on their acts of authority, and not upon its own intrinsic value, have taken it upon themselves at different times, to alter, or as they were wont to term it, to raise this standard of value. In doing this, they have sometimes diminished the size and weight of coins, causing them still to retain the same name. In other instances, they have introduced a larger portion of alloy; and then again they have altered the denomination of the coin, calling that a dollar, for example, which before had been denominated a half dollar. In these several cases, it is at once seen, the result was the same—a less amount of gold or silver was found under the same denomination. The object to be attained by making these changes, has also, in most instances, been the same. The governments by whom they have been made, have in this way paid their debts at reduced rates, thus defrauding their creditors of their just dues. Such variations in the nominal value of coins, which are evidently acts of fraud and injustice, are soon known, and the discovery is followed by corresponding changes in the price of all commodities in the community. In a short time, the depreciated coins are found passing only for their real worth, which is determined by the amount of gold and silver which they contain. Unless, however, these variations are known, and a due allowance made for them, the reader of history, or whoever may attempt to compare values at different periods, will be liable to mistake. On this point I take the liberty to introduce the following instructive paragraph from Smith's Wealth of Nations.

"The denominations of coins seem originally to have expressed the weight or quantity of metal contained in them. In the time of Servius Tullius, who first coined money at Rome, the Roman As or Pondo contained a Roman pound of good copper. It was divided in the same manner as our Troyes pound, into twelve ounces, each of which contained a real ounce of good copper. The English pound sterling in the time of Edward I. contained a pound Tower weight, of silver of a known fineness. The Tower pound seems to have been something more than the Roman pound, and something less than the Troyes pound. This last was not introduced into the Mint of England till the 18th of Henry VIII. The French livre contained in the time of Charlemagne a pound, Troyes weight, of silver of a known fineness. The fair of Troyes in Champaign was at that time frequented by all the nations of Europe, and the weights and measures of so famous a market were generally known and esteemed. The Scots money pound contained from the time of Alexander the

First to that of Robert Bruce, a pound of silver of the same weight and fineness with the English pound sterling. English, French, and Scots pennies too, contained all of them originally a real pennyweight of silver, the twentieth part of an ounce, and the two hundred-and-fortieth part of a pound. The shilling too, seems originally to have been the denomination of a weight. *When wheat is at twelve shillings the quarter,* says an ancient statute of Henry III. *then wastel bread of a farthing shall weigh eleven shillings and four pence.* The proportion, however, between the shilling and either the penny on the one hand, or the pound on the other, seems not to have been so constant and uniform as that between the penny and the pound. During the first race of the kings of France, the French sou or shilling appears upon different occasions to have contained five, twelve, twenty, and forty pennies. Among the ancient Saxons a shilling appears at one time to have contained only five pennies, and it is not improbable that it may have been as variable among them as among their neighbours the ancient Franks. From the time of Charlemagne among the French, and from that of William the conqueror among the English, the proportion between the pound, the shilling, and the penny, seems to have been uniformly the same as at present, though the value of each has been very different. For in every country of the world, I believe, the avarice and injustice of princes and sovereign states, abusing the confidence of their subjects, have by degrees diminished the real quantity of metal, which had been originally contained in their coins. The Roman As, in the latter ages of the Republic, was reduced to the twenty-fourth part of its original value ; and, instead of weighing a pound, came to weigh only half an ounce. The English pound and penny contain at present about a third only; the Scots pound and penny about a thirty-sixth; and the French pound and penny about a sixty-sixth part of their original value. By means of those operations the princes and sovereign states which performed them, were enabled, in appearance, to pay their debts and fulfil their engagements with a smaller quantity of silver than would otherwise have been requisite. It was indeed in appearance only; for their creditors were really defrauded of a part of what was due to them. All other debtors in the state were allowed the same privilege, and might pay with the same nominal sum of the new and debased coin whatever they had borrowed in the old. Such operations, therefore, have always proved favourable to the debtor, and ruinous to the creditor; and have sometimes produced a greater and more universal revolution in the fortunes of private persons, than could have been occasioned by a very great public calamity."

It has now been fully shewn, that money, being itself fluctuating as to its own value, can never become an invariable standard of value. Still, as before intimated, it answers this purpose in the common transactions of business. If at the same time and place, I wish to institute a comparison between two different commodities, I am enabled to do this, by stating the price of each. And since we are accustomed to express the value of commodities in money, this is easily and readily done. But if I knew the price of a commodity in England five hundred years ago, and also its present price, or if, at the present time, I knew the value of one commodity in this country, and of another in China, I should not thus be enabled, in either case, without other data, and other calculations, to form a comparison of the value of these commodities. In these instances, money is not a measure of value.

CHAPTER VII.

Price.

Having thus explained what is meant by a circulating medium, and by a measure of value, and having also stated the expedients in use for these purposes, our next inquiry relates to price, or the current value of objects as rated in money. It has been said, that exchangeable value is relative in its nature—in respect to a particular commodity, it is determined from comparisons instituted between this commodity and many others in the market. But in making these comparisons, we resort to the use of money as a measure of value ; hence it is common to express exchangeable value in money. We say that an article is worth so many dollars, or so many shillings, according to the currency in use. But here the inquiry arises ; In affixing current prices to objects, what is to be our guide? We say that a bushel of wheat is worth $2,00 ; a yard of broadcloth of certain quality $7,00 ; a cwt. of sugar $10, 00. What leads us to these results in respect to the price of these different commodities? To obtain an answer to these inquiries, suppose that we go into the market, and see what are the views which there prevail upon this subject. We ask the price of some article,—a hat, for example. We are told, that it is $7,00. We object to this price perhaps, as too high. But the manufacturer assures us, that a hat of this quality cannot be afforded for a less sum. It costs that to make it. Perhaps he then goes into particulars. He tells us that furs are high, and that the materials of which the hat is composed cost him a certain amount. He then tells us how long a time, or the amount of labor, it takes to make a hat. Perhaps he has something to say about shop-rent, or the other expenses of his establishment; and then he adds, "A man must live," by which he means, that a manufacturer of hats, as well as other producers, must obtain the usual profits on his business. But perhaps the purchaser replies, I bought last year a hat of the same quality for five dollars. True, you did so, says the other, but that was because the market was overstocked with hats. Too many were engaged in this branch of business, and it became a losing concern to us all. We could not sell our hats for what it cost us to make them. Hence many hat manufacturers failed, and others were compelled to leave the business for want of employment. The result has been that the supply has become proportioned to the demand, and hats now bring a fair price.

Now here, as I conceive, stated in the common language of the market, is the whole theory of price. The basis of it is the cost of production. Its temporary variations, or rather its oscillations about the same point—now higher and now lower, are the relative influences of supply and demand. There are it is true other causes of variation—the value of the different items which make up the cost of production varies, or the measure of value varies. In either case, there is a correspondent variation in price.

But here it is necessary to look more narrowly into the subject of the cost of production. In the case just supposed, which is that of a product in manufactures, these items are, 1. The amount paid for materials—this comes under the head of productive capital. 2. The labor employed in manufacturing the article. 3. The expenses of the establisment—buildings, tools &c. This also is included under the head of productive capital. To these items we must add the profits of the manufacturer, or what is paid him as the undertaker and conducter of the business, distinct from the wages of his labor as a manufacturer. Capital, labor and profits, then, make up the cost of production of this, as they do of most manufactured articles.

Suppose next, that the commodity, into the cost of whose production we inquire, is an agricultural product—a load of hay. This is sold perhaps for $12,00 per ton, and the producer who brings it to market, tells us that it cannot be afforded for a less sum. What items make up the cost of production of this commodity? One portion, as before, is labor. A second is capital, including what is expended in improvements on the farm—in farming utensils—cattle &c. A third is rent, or an equivalent for the use of the natural agency employed—that is for the use of land. A fourth item is profits, as before.

Suppose the cost of production of a commercial product is next to be determined—a cwt. of coffee, whose price is $12,00. The items which here make up the cost of production, are, 1. The interest on the capital vested in the coffee offered for sale—also of that expended in the establishments for commercial production—shipping, warehouses, both for the wholesale and retail trade &c. 2. The wages of those employed as laborers in transportation, and in buying and selling the commodity. 3. The profits of business.

It will be noticed, that in these statements, I look at the cost of production to the manufacturer, to the agriculturist, and to the merchant, severally, without going into an analysis of the original cost of the product in each instance. We learn from them, that the cost of production is made up of the interest on capital, of wages, of profits, and in some instances of rent, for the use of natural agency. Whatever then affects one of these items, either as to its amount, or its value, will cause a variation in the cost of production. If from the invention of a labor-saving machine, or from any cause, the amount of labor required in the manufacture of hats is diminished, there will be a diminution in the cost of production. The same result will follow, if from any cause the exchangeable value of labor, or the rate of wages, becomes less. So too of capital; if some method of production is invented, which requires a less amount of capital, or if the rate of interest paid for the use of capital become less, in either case, the cost of production is affected. The same holds true of natural agency. And in respect to profits, if, from any cause, there is a variation in the general rate of profits, or if the rate of profits in any particular branch of production should be affected in any way, there will be a correspondent variation in the cost of production. It will indeed often happen, that these influences on the cost of production, thus arising from different sources, will counteract each other. Thus the application of a larger amount of machinery in the raising of a commodity, will diminish the charge for labor, and increase that for capital In other instances, there may be a diminution of the amount of capital required, but this may be balanced by a rise in the interest paid for the use of capital.

Thus, without taking into the account the variations resulting from relative supply and demand, we see that important and frequent variations may arise, in connexion with the cost of production itself. I do not here stop to state the causes, which at different times affect the value of the different items in the cost of production. These are brought to view in another place, and the statement of them is not necessary to the investigation of the subject of price.

On supply and demand.

We come now to the examination of what is justly regarded as the great disturbing cause of price,—the influence of supply and demand. And here an explanation of these terms, as used in the science, is required. Demand, in its widest sense, is another expression for the wants of men. To the extent of these wants, there may be said to be a demand for that which will supply them. But as the term is here used, another important circumstance comes into the account. It implies both the willingness and the ability to give, in return for what is thus wanted, an equivalent in value. In respect then to any commodity, so far as there is in a community an ability and a willingness to give for it that which has exchangeable value, to the same extent there may be said to be in this community a demand for this commodity.

Supply, on the other hand, means, not only that an object is in existence, but that it is in the market—that is, those possessing it are willing to part with it upon receiving an equivalent, as determined by the same principles, which determine the price of other commodities of a like nature.

And here, incidentally, in connexion with this explanation of the terms supply and demand, we may see what constitutes a market. It is production itself, which opens a vent, or creates a demand for products. He who is successfully engaged as a producer of that which has exchangeable value, is acquiring the ability to supply his own wants, which, it has just been said, is essential to constitute demand. Hence the greater the number of such producers in a community, and the greater the variety of products, the greater will be the demand for different products, or, in other words, the better the market. And thus it is, that every one becomes interested in the prosperity of those around him. Hence also it is more desirable to be the citizen of a thriving, advancing community, than of one which is stationary, or whose movement is retrograde.

But to return to the subject of supply and demand as affecting price. When the current price of an article is the same as its cost price, by which I mean the cost of its production, it is an indication, that the supply of this article corresponds to the demand for it. In this case, then, supply and demand exert no influence upon price. But if from any cause the demand exceeds the supply, there follows at once a rise of the exchangeable price above the cost price. It is so, since there are more who wish to obtain the article than can be supplied with it, and this produces a competition among purchasers. On the contrary, if, from any cause, the supply exceeds the demand, the exchangeable price falls below the cost price. Here the competition is on the part of those who have the article to dispose of; for since there is a larger amount in the market than can find purchasers, each seller is desirous of sustaining as little loss as possible. He endeavors therefore to undersell others, and is willing to sell at a rate below cost. Thus it is that the relative variations of demand and supply are continually affecting the exchangeable price of commodities, at one time raising it above, and at another sinking it below, the cost of production.

From the statements which have now been made, it may be inferred, that the causes which affect the current prices of commodities, may be traced to three different sources; 1. To variations in the measure of value. 2. To an increase or diminution of the cost of production. 3. To the state of the market, or the relative influence of supply and demand. I propose to consider, separately, each class of these disturbing causes of current price.

Price as affected by variations in money or the measure of value.

We have seen that the precious metals, the materials of coined money, are subject to variations in their value. In this respect, they differ not from other commodities. The cost of their production varies, and they feel, in its full power, the influence of supply and demand.

It has also been stated, that money varies in its exchangeable value from alterations, made by the governments of different countries, in the coins and denominations of the standard currency. The gold, or silver, in the same coin, is greater in amount and purer in its quality at one time, than at another; or by some act of authority, the relative value of different denominations of coined money is changed. Now whatever be the nature of the cause thus affecting the measure of value, whether connected with the cost of production of the materials of this measure, or with authoritative alterations of the standard currency, no sooner is this variation in the measure of value known to exist, than its disturbing influence on the current prices of all objects in the market, will be felt. If there are more dollars in the country than are needed as a circulating medium, or if the amount of silver in a dollar is less, or the proportion of alloy greater, in each case, the exchangeable value of a dollar becomes less. And since money is used as a measure of value, the current price of all commodities in the market, will be affected by this variation in the value of money. The article of furniture, which before was estimated at $20, is now valued at $22; and so of other commodities.

In modern times, since the monetary systems of different countries have become well established, the influence of this disturbing cause on current price is slight, and gradual in its operation. Hence the business classes of the community suffer but little inconvenience from this source. The same man is both buyer and seller, and usually about to the same amount; so that he gains as much on one score, as he loses on another. When however it produces a depreciation in the value of the currency, the effect will at once be felt by those, whose income is a fixed or a stipulated amount. They will find, that though their revenue be nominally the same, its value is diminished. This will be the case with all those, whose income is derived from rents, or from money at interest,

The same is true of those whose support is received in the form of salary. Thus it has often happened in this country, that the salary of an office, which a half-century ago was considered a good living, has ceased to furnish a support to the incumbent; and the depreciation in the exchangeable value of money, is a principal cause of this difference. So too, and from the same cause, it is found, that the revenues of some ancient eleemosynary institutions, which are paid in money, have depreciated in value, while those paid in wheat, or other agricultural products, have from the same and other causes become far more valuable.

And here may be mentioned another disturbing cause of price, the effects of which are often great loss and inconvenience to all classes of the community. I refer to the partial and sometimes total depreciation in the value of bank notes—the representatives of coined money. Banking institutions often have a large amount of their notes, or, as they are usually called, bills, in circulation, in the hands of many different individuals, when, from some cause, they become unable to redeem their bills, and thus those holding them suffer a partial or total loss. For the notes of a broken bank, if current at all, are circulated at a large discount, perhaps for half or one third, of their nominal value. But the evils which result from occurrences of this kind, are not confined to the actual losses of the holders of notes, or the embarrassments of business transactions from a depreciation of a part of the currency. A shock is given to confidence in the representative part of the circulating medium generally, which is often attended with much inconvenience and loss. Hence the breaking of one bank often leads to the insolvency of others.

The inference to be made from this statement is, that the government of a country, as the guardian of the public welfare, ought to exercise much caution and wisdom in the establishment of banking institutions, and to watch narrowly over the manner in which their concerns are conducted.

In connexion with the subject of variations in the measure of value, the inquiry may arise, In what way may the reader of history be enabled to form a correct estimate of the value of objects, whose price is stated in ancient histories? This cannot be done with perfect accuracy, but an approximation to this result may be made in the following manner.

Suppose we read that some commodity was worth in Athens, at the time of Pericles, a certain number of talents of silver, and we wish to know the value of this commodity in our own currency. We first ascertain what was the amount of pure silver at Athens in the talent, at that time. For this information, we must rely upon historical statements. We then, from the same source, find out the value of silver in some staple commodities of that time, particularly in the commodities used as bread stuff. Having thus ascertained how much wheat, or other staple commodities, an ounce, or any amount of silver was exchanged for at that time, we in the same manner institute a comparison between the same amount of silver and the same, or like commodities, in our own times. We thus obtain what is needed for determining the value of silver in the two periods compared. It only remains for us, to express this amount of silver in our own currency. It will be noticed, that the larger the number of articles, of which a comparison between their value and that of silver is instituted, the more accurate will be the conclusion which is drawn.

Price as affected by the fluctuations of the market.

So great is the influence of supply and demand upon the price of commodities, that it may be likened to the pendulum of the clock. It is the regulator—that which secures the steady movement of the whole machine. I design in this section, to bring forward some instances, in which its power is felt, and thus to shew both the causes and the consequences of variations of price, so far as they arise from this source.

It sometimes happens, that the crops of wheat are less than in other years, by one third, or one half, of their usual amount. And though it may not be an unfavorable season in every part of the world, the transportation of so bulky a commodity from one country to another, is attended with so much labor and expense, that little relief can be expected from this source. Such a deficiency occurred in this country in 1816. Now it is usually the case, that the amount of wheat raised in a country, as of all annual products, is nearly proportioned to the usual demand. When, therefore, there is a deficiency in the crop to the extent stated, the supply in the market must fall far short of the demand. The cause is obvious;—that natural agent, which assists man in the production of wheat, has been less efficient than usual. What then are the consequences, when, in respect to so important a commodity, the supply falls far short of the demand?

And first, how are the interests of the producers affected? The farmer, who has usually raised five hundred bushels of wheat, this year, from the same land, and the same outlay of capital and labor, has obtained but half that amount. But in former years, the price of wheat was $1,00 per bushel; it is now $2,00. He may now, then, should he sell the whole crop, receive as much money in exchange for it, as in former years; and even save something, since the expense of harvesting and of transportation to the market may be less. But the farmer is himself a consumer of wheat, and it is only the surplus part of his crop that he sells. And though in a year of scarcity he may consume much less wheat in his family, his profits from his wheat crop, will probably fall far short of what he is accustomed to obtain. Even then, if we suppose that, counting what is consumed in his family at the rate of $2,00 per bushel, he receives a sufficient amount to meet the expenses of production,—that is, if the exchangeable price of the whole crop equals the cost price, still he makes no larger profits than usual, and as a consumer of wheat, he suffers loss, in the same manner as other members of the community. Thus it appears, that the usual impression, that the gains of the farmer are greater in years of scarcity, is incorrect. He may obtain a higher price for his wheat, but he has less to sell, and in common with others, he may be considered as paying a higher price for what he consumes in his own family.

We look next at the consequences which result to the community. It is evident, that as there is less wheat to be consumed by one half, than in common years, economy must be practised by consumers generally. A part of the crop in years of plenty, may have been used perhaps in making whiskey, or for some other purposes, than bread stuff for man. It must no longer be used for these purposes. Some portion also may have been sent abroad in exchange for foreign commodities. This portion must now be kept for home consumption. And further, more wheat may have been consumed in families generally, through the country, than is necessary. Domestic retrenchment must then be put in practice—less wheat must be used, and some other agricultural products, as potatoes, or garden vegetables, must be substituted in its place. Should the government of a country undertake, in a year of scarcity, to pass laws, regulating the consumption of wheat, so that the deficient crop might hold out till another harvest comes round, it would probably enact, that in these several ways, the consumption of wheat should be lessened. But the same result is effected, and without any act of authority, by the rise of price, consequent on the diminished supply. As wheat has become dearer, those possessing it find it foı their interest to use it only for bread-stuff; they will for the same reason keep it at home, rather than send it abroad. And each family will use it with as little waste as possible, substituting for it, so far as is practicable, some other and cheaper commodity.

And here we may incidentally notice the importance of having the style of living of the mass of the community sufficiently high to allow of its being reduced. In Ireland, where the prevailing food is potatoes, if a failure of the potatoe crop occurs, there is no cheaper commodity, which can be substituted in its place, and great suffering and turmoil are the consequences which ensue. But where, as in England, wheat, and, in this country, meats, are in general use, there is an important resource to the nation against seasons of scarcity.

Thus it is, that in a year of scarcity, the deficient crop is husbanded by means of the increased price, with the least possible inconvenience and loss, both to producers and consumers. And now, if we continue our view, we find, that when the season for a new crop has come round, the advanced price of wheat will lead more to engage in its production,—more land will be cultivated, and the outlay of labor and capital in this branch of production will be larger. And perhaps, as it often happens, the next season is one of unusual plenty—the supply exceeds that of common years, as much as it had fallen short of it the year before. Now, then, the supply exceeds the demand, and if we look at the consequences, both to producers and consumers, we find, that they are the reverse of those before stated. The price immediately falls, even below what is wont to be obtained in common years; but as the surplus of the farmer is larger than usual, in proportion to his outlay of capital and labor, he obtains his average profits on the whole crop. It is not then as a producer, but as a consumer of wheat, that the farmer himself is benefitted by a year of plenty, in common with other members of the community. And it is here to be noticed, that in respect to a product of prime necessity, as wheat, just in proportion as the price is diminished, the demand will increase. In common years, many families might consume more wheat, than they do, could they afford to purchase it. And the diminution of the price, consequent upon the excess of supply, puts it within the power of such families, to enlarge their consumption. Hence, through the whole community, the increase of demand from this source, will be considerable. Further, as the price of wheat is reduced, it is used for other purposes than breadstuff, and exporters will perhaps find it for their advantage to purchase it and send it to foreign markets.

Thus, in respect to agricultural products of prime necessity, and of general consumption, the variations of price, consequent upon the fluctuations of the market, tend to prevent the inconveniences and losses, which would otherwise be felt both by consumers and producers. When the supply falls short of the demand, the high price which results, enables the producer to obtain from a less amount of wheat, which he has to dispose of, what repays him for the cost of production ; and at the same time husbands the crop, so that less inconvenience is felt from the scarcity by consumers generally. On the other hand, when the supply exceeds the demand, the reduction of price brings the commodity within the ability of greater numbers to purchase it, and enables those before using it, to use it in larger quantities. Thus again the community is benefitted, and the exchangeable price is kept from falling below the cost of production.

I will now state a different case. England, before the late war with this country, was accustomed to supply our markets with various manufactured products; and to furnish this supply, many laborers and a large amount of capital were employed. When the war broke out, this vent for her manufactures ceased. And as her home consumption, and that of other foreign markets, could not furnish a demand, in proportion to the supply of these commodities, there was a glut of them, which was attended with a great reduction of their price.

This case differs from that which has been stated, both as to its cause and the nature of the commodities concerned. In the former case, the excess of supply arose from the uncommon fruitfulness of the season, added to an over effort in production, which had been caused by the scarcity of the preceding year. In this case it resulted from the loss of a foreign market by war. The product too, in the former case, was one of prime necessity, the demand for which always keeps pace, in some good degree, with the increased supply and consequent diminution of price. In the latter, the products, though in general use, are of a class, not absolutely essential to human subsistence, and though their consumption may be enlarged by a reduction of their price, still this enlargement of demand is limited, and by no means in proportion to the excess of supply.

To those then engaged as producers of manufactured products, a glut of the market, such as that referred to, must be attended with great loss and embarrassment. No enlargement of demand comes in, of sufficient extent to take off their excess of products, even at reduced prices. Neither, as in the case of agricultural products, is a larger amount received from the same outlay, so that, though the price for any definite quantity falls, the increased amount of products sold, makes up the deficiency of profits. And besides the loss on products sold for less than the cost of production, the investments of capital in buildings and machinery, must either be permitted to remain inactive, or be sold at an immense sacrifice.

But let us now see in what manner the interests of the community in this case are affected. From the reduction in the price of manufactures, those who wish to obtain a supply of articles of this kind, can purchase them at a much lower rate, than usual—a rate below the cost of their production. But few families can afford to expend a larger proportion of their income in the purchase of manufactures, than they are accustomed to devote to this purpose. They will then generally rest satisfied with obtaining from the same expenditure, a larger supply. Besides, the home consumers of these commodities, are themselves producers, and they soon find their own prosperity affected by the depression of other productive classes around them. Their own revenues fall short of the usual amount, and they find, that they have less to expend in the purchase of manufactures, than in seasons of more general prosperity. And then, too, if remote consequences are taken into the account, it is found, that the reduction of prices, which results from an excess of supply, is followed by an advance, to the same, or a greater amount. For no sooner do those engaged in this business find that it is a losing concern, than they cease to manufacture, and endeavor, so far as they can, to withdraw their capital from this mode of investment, and to direct it to some other branch of production. At least, they will permit it to remain unemployed, until better times open to them the prospect of receiving their usual profits. In the mean time, the products in the market are consumed, and a demand arises, to meet which, no adequate supply exists. Perhaps, too, the war is at an end, and the old markets, and, it may be, new ones are opened. Now then, the demand greatly exceeds the supply, and those who would obtain these products, must pay a price, as much beyond the cost of production, as before it had fallen short of it. Thus too, for a while, producers make large profits, and on the principles stated in the chapter on capital, a larger amount of productive capital is directed to this branch of production.

There are numerous other causes, in addition to those now mentioned, which produce fluctuations in the market and other attendant consequences. Such fluctuations are indeed, to some degree, continually occurring in most branches of production; and it conduces much to the prosperity of a nation, that they should be slight. In proportion to their importance, their disturbing influence is felt by all classes of the community, and though for a time some few may be benefitted, the general results are embarrassment and loss.

Price as affected by variations in the cost of production.

The falling of prices from a diminished cost of production, is the only variation, which can occur with profit both to producers and consumers. It is also permanent. When the cost of production of any commodity in general use is reduced, and its price in the market falls, every member of the community, ever afterwards, finds it necessary to appropriate a smaller portion of his revenue to the obtaining of that commodity, or, if he continue to appropriate the same sum, he receives in return a larger amount of the same commodity and perhaps of improved quality. Others too, who have been unable to obtain this commodity, because of its high price, can now afford to purchase it; and thus the comforts and conveniences of life are extended to a larger number of individuals. Among many instances of this kind, which have occurred within the last century, the invention of the stocking loom may be referred to, as affording a striking illustration. Since the invention and general use of this machine, the price of a pair of stockings has fallen to one third of its for me amount. He then, who was accustomed to spend ten or twelve dollars annually for this article, supplies himself for one third of this sum, and many, who at the former price could not afford to wear stockings, can now furnish themselves with this article of comfort.

It is unnecessary here to trace out the effects of variations in price, resulting from this source. This has already been done in the chapter on machinery. I will here only add, that the consequences, there ascribed to the introduction of labor-saving machines, are applicable, so far as price is concerned, to a diminution in either of the items, which make up the cost of production, from whatever source it may arise.

In applying the principles that have been brought to view in this chapter, to different classes of commodities, it will be found, that these classes will essentially differ in the extent to which they are subject to variations of price. Agricultural products which are in general use and of prime necessity, such as the common articles of food, though their price may vary from year to year as affected by the fertility of the season, will be found less subject to permanent alterations of price than other commodities. The reason is obvious ;—there is always a tendency to equalization between the supply and demand of this class of products, that is, between population and the means of subsistence. It is also the case, that labor-saving inventions, and other improvements, which affect the cost of production, are less frequently made in agriculture than in other branches of production. Hence it is, that in our attempts to ascertain the value of the precious metals at former periods of the world, we refer to wheat as a commodity, whose price has been more uniform than that of any other. Manufactured products in general use, next to agricultural products, will be less subject to variations of price. I refer here to the common articles of clothing and of furniture in our domestic establishments. Such commodities, though their price may be affected by changes in the cost of their production, are less subject to fluctuations of the market, the demand generally equalling the supply. The class of commodities, which more than all others feels the effect of the different causes which lead to variations of price, consists of those manufactured products which are articles of luxury. It is here especially, that the influences of fashion are felt, as they affect supply and demand, thus leading to variations of price. Hence it is, that the profits made on the more common products of manufactures in domestic use, are more sure, and in the end usually much greater, than what are received on the more expensive articles of luxury.

Another remark, which is also here suggested, relates to the importance of uniformity of price. Variations in the prices of the common articles of consumption, are ever sources of inconvenience and not unfrequently of positive injury to the public, especially to the less wealthy portions of the community. If the prices of such commodities fall below the average rate, the poorer classes are thus enabled to enlarge their consumption, and raise their style of living, but in a short time, perhaps, the cause which had led to a reduction of prices, ceases to operate,—the former prices are restored, or perhaps there is an advance upon them. It then becomes necessary that the style of living should also be reduced, which is usually attended with mortification and painful privations. And this mortification and want of customary enjoyments must also be endured to some extent, where depression of price occurs without any previous elevation. Other classes of the community, also, when variations of price are often occurring, become less enterprising, and less ready to engage in the processes of production; since they know not, but some unexpected change of price may defeat all their plans and calculations. It will be noticed, that I here refer to those variations of price, which arise either from alterations in the medium of circulation, or from the fluctuations of the market as connected with supply and demand. Those variations which result from a diminished cost of production, are permanent, and as they are gradually introduced, no injurious consequences result.

The different economical arrangements, and the several agents, concerned in the production of wealth, have now been brought to view, and the principles stated, by which its circulation is regulated. It now remains, to look at these arrangements and agents as they exist together, and are brought into joint and combined action in the different departments of human industry. Opportunity will thus be presented, to state the circumstances favorable to the introduction and advancement of the different branches of production, and to shew the influence of measures, adopted by the governments of different countries, and of other adventitious causes, on the economical interests of communities.

CHAPTER VIII.

Agriculture.

Of the three great branches of industry, Agriculture is that, to which, in the progress of nations, their productive powers are first directed. It is so, since it meets the most urgent of human wants—it furnishes the daily food of man. The common labors of agriculture are also simple in their nature, requiring no lengthened apprenticeship to become familiar with their performance. Neither, in its early state, is a large amount of capital needed to conduct successfully its simple processes. And further, it is in its nature antecedent to Manufactures and Commerce, since it furnishes the materials and objects, on which these branches of industry are employed.

But agriculture, even in its early and most simple state, cannot exist to any extent without the aid of manufactures. It must look to this source for its ploughs and carts and the various implements of husbandry. So abundant also are the returns of agricultural industry, that it soon leads to commerce in its more common forms. The agricultural producer soon finds, that he has a large surplus, which it is for his advantage to exchange for other products. He finds also, that he has wants which his farm cannot supply.

As nations become more populous, and make progress in wealth, and other branches of industry are introduced, the demand for agricultural products increases, and consequently more labor and a larger amount of capital, are directed to this branch of human industry. The farmer finds it necessary to enlarge his establishment. He must be able to avail himself of the improvements made in husbandry;—division of labor to some extent must be introduced, and his whole business conducted on a larger and more extensive scale. It is not necessary, however, to trace the progress of agriculture, or to state its different divisions. The statements and inquiries here made are simply designed to bring to view those circumstances, which are favorable to its advancement and prosperity.

How may agriculture be improved and advanced?

Most of our farmers cultivate their farms as their fathers have done before them. The same crops are raised—the same tools used and the same methods of cultivation are practised, year after year. Compared with other branches of industry, few innovations are made, and little enterprise is manifested. Still, if we compare the state of agriculture a half-century ago and at the present time, we find, that in most countries some progress has been witnessed. Though the common farmer has been content to go on in the old way, others have been studying and contriving and trying experiments and making improvements of which he has availed himself.

To this work of improvement, the different sciences, especially the science of chemistry, have contributed. Men of wealth have also amused themselves, and done good service to the country, in the experiments, which they have made on what may be called model forms. And further, agricultural societies, and in some instances the governments of different countries, have adopted measures, leading to the same results. The improvements, thus introduced, may be classified as follows ;

1. New modes of cultivation are discovered, resulting from a better knowledge of the properties of different soils, and of their adaptation to the raising of different fruits and grains and other agricultural products.

2. Improvements are made in the breeds of domestic animals used upon a farm—horses, oxen, sheep, &c.

3. New tools and implements of husbandry,—or those of an improved form, are introduced. In some departments of agricultural industry, labor-saving machines are invented.

It is unnecessary to enlarge on these different heads. Something has already been said on the first, when treating on the developement of natural aids to production. Of the second, the introduction of the merino breed of sheep into this country is an example. Of the third, the patent office at Washington shews many striking instances. More probably has been done in this way for the improvement of agriculture, in the United States, than in all other countries.

Another class of improvements, in which the farmer is much interested, relates to facilities for transportation. Such are railways, canals and well made common roads. Agricultural products are bulky. Much of their value therefore, must depend on their proximity to a market. A bushel of corn, which in the cities on our sea-board is sold readily for one dollar, in the remote interior of the country, will command only one half or even one fourth of that sum. Now should a railway or canal be opened to this remote interior, so as to connect it with a market, the price of corn is immediately affected ;—it is doubled, or perhaps tripled ; and so of other agricultural products.

The inquiry is sometimes made, whether it be more advantageous to a nation, that its territory should be divided into small farms, of five or ten acres, in possession of numerous proprietors, or into larger tracts of two or three hundred acres ? In this connexion, we are led to answer this inquiry in favor of large farms. Every farmer must be provided to some extent, with an apparatus for his business. He must have his tools, wagons, working cattle, barns, granaries, &c. Now, if a territory be divided into small farms, either the amount of capital vested in this manner, will be much greater than is required where farms are larger or agricultural business will not be well conducted for the want of this capital. Besides, the progress of science is pointing out new methods of cultivation, and the inventions of art are offering new implements of husbandry to the farmer. Of these, he, who has a large capital and a farm of some extent, can afford to avail himself, and it is important to the interests of agriculture in the country, that this should be done.

The government of a country may cherish and encourage agricultural industry in various ways.

It may aid and excite scientific men, to make those discoveries, which lead to improvements in agricultural industry. Discoveries of this kind are sometimes made at great expense, and it seems reasonable, that as the public generally are to derive benefit from them, this expense should be paid from the public purse.

It may grant patent rights to those who make inventions in agricultural tools and implements.

It may either directly, or through the medium of agricultural societies, offer bounties, or rewards, to those farmers who excel in the management of their farms, and in raising superior products from the soil.

It may assist in diffusing information on subjects, which relate to improvements in agriculture, whether the result of scientific investigations and reasonings, or of practical farming.

By a system of internal improvements, it may do much to facilitate the transportation of agricultural products, and thus open new markets to the farmer.

At present, much is done in our own country for the last mentioned object, by joint stock companies, who receive an act of incorporation, and look to collections in the form of tolls, for a remuneration of what is advanced by them. But such tolls are a tax, which is burdensome to the agricultural part of the community ; and hence, whatever aid the government may afford in lessening or preventing this tax, is an encouragement to agriculture.

Opinions of the French Economists considered.

It has been stated, that agriculture is a branch of industry, peculiarly adapted to the early stages of national existence, and that it is the employment, in which most nations at that period in their history are found engaged. The inquiry may arise,—How far it is expedient that communities advanced in wealth and engaged in other departments of industry, should still continue their agricultural pursuits? In other words, it may be asked, whether it should be left to capital and industry, to follow the rate of profits, and to be directed to different branches of production, just so far as is most advantageous to producers, or whether the public welfare is so much more concerned in the products of Agriculture, than in those of Manufactures and Commerce, that special efforts should be made to direct capital into the former channel.

It is known, that a sect of Political Economists formerly existed in France, and individuals in modern times hold nearly the same doctrines, which maintained, that Agriculture is the only source of national wealth. These Economists, for so by way of eminence they were called, allowed indeed that other departments of labor were advantageous to those engaged in them, that is, they gave them a support. And this, these writers maintained, was all the benefit derived from them, the same amount of value being consumed in the support of these laborers, as was produced by their labor.

A more extended view of the system of the Economists, may be found in Chapter 9, Book IV, of Smith's Wealth of Nations. Two statements fully disprove the leading proposition, on which this system is founded.

1. It is well known, that nations engaged extensively in manufactures and commerce, have made rapid and great advances in wealth; more so indeed, than some other nations, which have confined their industry to agriculture. England is an example of the former kind, and Poland of the latter. Now how is this fact consistent with the position, that no additions can be made to individual, or national wealth, from the labors of those engaged in manufactures and commerce?

2. Taking the Economists on their own grounds, their leading proposition may be shewn to be erroneous. They allow, that producers in manufactures and commerce are supported out of the gross amount of products, which are

the result of their labors. Now if this be the case, these branches of production are important sources of national wealth; for in determining the amount of national wealth at any time, we do not look at the net products but at the gross products. Indeed agricultural products, more than others, are immediately consumed in the support of producers. And there is evidently no reason for considering the accumulations and additions made to national capital, as resulting more from agricultural, than from other branches of production.

In modern times, there have been those, who though not fully adopting the doctrines of the Economists, have still maintained, that agricultural producers are to be ranked in the first class, and that those engaged in other branches of production are secondaries, and in some way dependent upon and sustained by, agricultural industry; and many, no doubt, have some general impressions of this kind, without any very definite opinions upon the subject.

In the introductory chapter, it was shown, that production is in its nature the same in agriculture, as in other departments of human industry. It must also be the case, that the average profits of capital and labor cannot be higher, when employed in agriculture, than when employed in manufactures and commerce. If it were so, the latter branches would be deserted for the former. How then are we to account for the impression, so general, of the superiority of agriculture? This question has in part been answered, in the statement made as to the nature of the wants supplied by agricultural products, which are of the most urgent class, and also of the fact, that the materials, about which other branches of production are employed, are derived from agriculture.

But there is also another circumstance, which tends to give rise to and cherish the same impression. Nations in their early state, and as they grow up to greatness, owe a large share of their increasing wealth to agricultural production. Here are the beginnings—the foundation, to a great degree, both of individual and national wealth. And this is to be accounted for in the following manner; in agriculture, more than in other branches of production, natural agency comes to the assistance of man—it does a larger share of the work. And here I must ask the reader to call to mind the distinction between natural agency, and other natural aids in the form of machinery, where man is the agent, and the natural aid the instrument by which he acts. It results then from the superiority of the assistance, rendered by nature in the first mentioned form, that the returns of capital and labor are greater in agricultural, than in manufacturing or commercial production ; and at this period of a nation's existence, there is nothing to balance this superiority of agriculture. But as the nation advances, and other branches of production are more fully introduced, the circumstances of the case become different. Division of labor and machinery come to the aid of production, and so much greater is the extent to which they are carried in Manufactures and Commerce, than in Agriculture, that they compensate, and more than compensate, for the superior advantages derived from natural agency in the latter branch.

And here another circumstance, tending to the same result, comes into operation. As nations become more populous, and it is necessary, that a larger amount of agricultural products should be furnished for the supply of the wants of the great national family, inferior soils must be cultivated,—those which yield a less abundant return to the capital and labor, employed in their cultivation. Thus the natural agency connected with agricultural production, becomes less efficient, and this cause, conspiring with the other causes just mentioned, brings about the result, that in a nation, in which the different branches of production are in combined and joint action, no larger amount of wealth is derived from Agriculture, than from Manufactures and Commerce. And hence, the impression we are considering, is without just foundation, though the circumstances, which have been mentioned, may account for its origin and prevalence.

Before leaving the subject of Agriculture, it may be mentioned, that the pleasantness of the employment in this branch of production, is such, as often leads individuals to prefer it, even when the profits it affords, are less than in other departments of industry. There is also a sense of security and independence, felt by the farmer, who supplies directly by his own labor a large proportion of his own wants, and who looks around upon his fields, yielding to him in rich abundance the necessaries of life. Especially does the landholder feel a higher sense of individual importance, and a deeper stake in the national welfare. But these, and other like considerations, are brought to view in another connexion.

CHAPTER IX.

Manufactures.

It has been stated, that the introduction of the mechanic arts in their more simple forms, must be of the same date with the first advances made in the cultivation of the earth ; for these advances cannot be made till the more common implements of husbandry are furnished. So too, when the products of agriculture become various and multiplied, the processes of manufactures are needed to adapt these products to the use of man. But when we speak of a manufacturing nation, or of Manufactures, as one of the great departments of national industry, we have in view a more advanced state of the manufacturing arts. We think of a community in which a large amount of industry and capital are thus employed, and which furnishes products of this class, not only for the supply of its own wants, but for foreign markets, and where too machinery is in extensive use, and large manufacturing establishments are scattered over the surface of the country.

Looking at manufactures in this light, I propose to state some circumstances favorable to the introduction and success of this department of national industry, and also to shew the effects of manufacturing establishments on the prosperity of the immediate neighborhood where they are located, and of this department of production on the welfare of the country generally. Some general views will in another chapter be taken of the expediency of measures, designed for the encouragement of manufactures.

Circumstances favorable to the introduction and success of Manufactures.

1. Territorial advantages. Some countries seem peculiarly adapted to become the abode of a manufacturing people. In return to agricultural labor, employed either in the cultivation of the soil, or in the working of mines, they furnish in rich abundance the raw materials, used in the most important branches of manufacturing production. They offer also to an uncommon extent, facilities for the construction of machinery and the employment of the aids of nature. Wood and metals of different kinds used in the mechanic arts, extensive forests and coal mines, to which has been added increased importance from the general use of steam power in manufactures, and more especially water power in the form of mill privileges, are to be ranked in this class. And further, so essential to success in manufactures is an extensive market, that we may place among territorial advantages favorable to this branch of production, navigable rivers, commodious harbors and other facilities for transportation.

Of these different classes of territorial advantages, the first mentioned is least essential, since the materials of most manufactured products may without difficulty be supplied from abroad. One of the staple manufactures of England is cotton cloth, yet her own territory does not furnish to any amount the materials of this texture. For this she is dependent on foreign nations, but the extent and enterprise of her commercial industry amply compensate for this deficiency.

2. Large amount of capital. A poor nation cannot be-

come to an extensive degree a manufacturing nation. A leading object in manufactures is to produce the largest amount at the least cost of production; and to effect this result, large and expensive establishments are needed. Much must be expended in the erection of buildings and in the construction of machinery. Large expenditures are also needed to put these establishments in successful operation. Great quantities of materials to be wrought up into manufactured products, must be kept on hand, and the wages of numerous laborers must be paid. And since, in some instances, a considerable time must elapse before returns from the sale of products are received, a proportionally large supply of capital must be provided.

In the United States, where individuals possessed of great wealth are rarely found, these expensive establishments are supported by joint-stock companies. By this arrangement, the necessary capital is provided, and our country is enabled to enter the lists as a successful competitor with older and richer nations. It is obvious, however, that it would not be practicable to effect an accumulation of capital in this way, in a country where there is a deficiency of capital, and where the price of it, or the rate of interest, is high. This unfavorable circumstance would so essentially affect the cost of production, that unless balanced by peculiar advantages in other respects, it would effectually prevent a nation from competing in foreign markets with other nations, in which the price of capital is less.

3. Low price of labor. After all that has been effected by labor-saving machines, labor still remains an important item in the cost of manufactured products. Hence a nation in which the price of labor is high, may on this ac-

count find it disadvantageous to engage extensively in manufactures. But it should be remembered, that the average price of manufacturing labor is far less, than of other kinds. This results from the simplicity and ease of many of its processes, which allow of their being performed by females and children. Were the average wages of manufacturers in the United States as high as that of mechanics, or even day laborers, it is not probable that our manufacturing establishments could be sustained. But instead of this, we find connected with these establishments a class of laborers, who otherwise would probably be without employment, and whose average wages, compared with the wages of other laborers, is low.

And here some importance may be attached to the circumstance, which is often noticed and mentioned, that there are found in nations certain characteristic traits, which seem to adapt them to manufacturing labor. Thus the inhabitants of some countries are more patient of toil and confinement; some have more ingenuity; some have the imitative principle more fully developed. However these national diversities may be accounted for, there is reason to think, that, to a greater or less degree, they exist and offer facilities for the successful introduction of manufactures into some countries, which are not found in others.

From the known connexion between population and wages, the inference will here readily be drawn, that for a nation to become a manufacturing nation, its population must be large. And this will generally be found to be the case. But the principles, which are concerned both in the proposition and in the exceptions to it, will be more fully brought to view, when treating on the influence of machinery on wages.

Three circumstances have now been mentioned as favorable to the introduction and success of manufactures,— territorial advantages, large national capital, and a low price of labor. Sometimes these favoring circumstances are found existing together, and then, especially if there be added the advantage of extensive foreign commerce, opening many and profitable markets for manufactured products, we may expect a nation to become to a great extent a manufacturing people. Such is the case with England. In other instances, some one or two of these favoring circumstances are found to an extent, which counterbalances deficiencies in the others. And such nations may engage advantageously in manufactures, especially, if this deficiency is one which may easily be supplied from abroad.

But should a nation be agitating the question, whether it be expedient to engage in manufactures in competition with other nations, there are other circumstances to be taken into the account, in addition to those now mentioned. I refer particularly to the skill of operatives and the possession of the market, or the course of trade. A nation which for many years has been engaged in manufactures, has those among its inhabitants, who are possessed of great skill and tact in this department of labor. Hence, not only more work will probably be done in the same time, but it will be executed in a superior manner. On the other hand, where manufactures have been lately introduced, some time must elapse, before those unaccustomed to manufacturing labor will execute with equal rapidity and perfection. And further, the manufactures of a nation frequently bear a character in foreign markets, arising from their superior quality, which gives them, and for some time will continue to give them, an advantage over the same class of products of another nation, even should those of the latter become equally good. Add to this, that where the course of trade has become established, those who conduct it, are always averse to changes, unless attended with important benefits.

Local effects of Manufactories.

The suddenness, with which manufacturing establishments spring up, and become imposing from their extent and influence on the surrounding country, causing what was before a quiet and obscure agricultural village to become the site of a thriving and populous town, or city, is often the subject of remark. We are almost ready to think, that the tales of ancient fables have become realities, and that other powers, than those of human industry, have been called into exercise. But on examination, we find, that these striking results are but the quickening influences of a great and sudden, and, as it may be termed, an unnatural outlay of capital. It may be useful, then, as developing the principles of our science, briefly to trace out some of the consequences, both immediate and remote, which are thus witnessed.

1. Labor of every kind is in requisition. A great work is to be done, and all are called upon to come and assist in its accomplishment. Full and profitable employment is given to common laborers and to mechanics of every class, not only to those previously located in the neigh-

borhood, but to those who in crowds rush in from abroad. With the increase of business and of population, professional labor comes more into demand. Physicians and lawyers find their services in more constant requisition, and the number of these unproductive laborers is increased. Indeed every member of the community who is disposed to work, finds a ready and profitable employment in which to engage. And it is in this constant and well paid demand for labor, more than in an advance of wages, that the genial effects of this new outlay of capital are felt by the laboring part of the population. It is true, that in some branches of labor there will often be an advance of wages, but this effect is prevented from being generally the case by the coming in of large numbers from abroad.

2. There is a sudden rise in the price of agricultural products. Provision must be made for the supply of the wants of the multitude thus collected together. Hence all the products of the farm are in demand, and as the nature of agricultural products is such, that they cannot be brought from a distance without having their price much increased by the cost of transportation, the products of this class raised in the neighborhood, will be sold at the same advance. Thus there will be a sudden rise in the price of agricultural products. And this advance of price will continue, till new land is brought under cultivation, and a supply is furnished, which shall meet the increased demand.

3. A sudden and great rise in the value of houses, lands, and whatever is included under the phrase—real estate. This effect is felt most strongly in the immediate vicinity of the manufactories. The great increase of the population creates a demand for houses, and leads to the erec-

tion of many new habitations, and as each one is desirous of a site for his buildings near the centre of business, land thus situated, is sold at a high price. A few months transform the waste and comparatively valueless pasture into the site of a populous city, and more is obtained for a single square rod, than was paid before for many acres. To the fortunate proprietors of these lands, there comes a sudden flow of wealth, like a lottery prize ; and they exchange the toils and the simple style of the farmer, for the anxieties and the luxuries of the wealthy capitalist.

But this rise in the value of land is not confined to the immediate vicinity of the new establishment. The effects of the increased demand for agricultural products and of their advanced price, is felt for miles around, and, as the lands of the farmer are brought nearer to a market for the products which he raises, he finds their value increased.

I have now stated the immediate results to a neighborhood, or village, of a large outlay of capital in the establishment of manufactories. But these hot-bed influences are of short continuance. Should we look in upon the same manufacturing town, or city, after five or ten years have elapsed, we might still find a thriving and industrious community ; but the demand for labor in the different occupations of life, and of the various kinds of agricultural products, is not greater perhaps, in proportion to the supply, than in other prosperous villages, in which no manufactories have been located. Some permanent salutary effects of the stimulus given to agricultural production, are indeed seen in the highly cultivated farms and rich fields of the surrounding country, and the high value of land in the immediate neighborhood still continues, though to the present proprietors there is little advance, perhaps none, on the prices they have paid. Business has returned to its usual channels, and except that there is a fuller and a quicker flow, the current of affairs goes onwards as before.

The statement which has been made, is where the consequences which follow from the establishment of manufactories, are of a salutary kind. In other instances, the stimulus given is far greater than is justified by the outlay of capital, or conducive to the interests of the community. There is a species of insanity, or wild adventure, which characterises every business transaction. The prices of real estate and of commodities generally are exorbitantly high, and laborers crowd in from every quarter.

But after a few months have elapsed, the *mania* is over —those who have made purchases of land and other objects of the nature of real estate, sell at a loss, and many individuals, both professional men and others, who had crowded to the new centre of business, expecting to find full and profitable employment, retire with disappointment and loss. And thus again, though their sudden rise has not been equally harmless and fertilizing, the swollen waters subside.

Advantages derived from Manufactures as a branch of national industry.

It is now proposed to extend the view, and to look at the benefits which arise to a nation from this branch of production. It is supposed in the statement here made, that in connexion with Agriculture and Commerce, Manufactures are in full and successful operation, and it is designed to point out the advantages derived from this mode of employing capital and industry.

1. Manufactures lead to the developement of the territorial advantages of a nation.

I have already, in this chapter, made mention of the territorial advantages favorable to the introduction of manufactures. Of one class of them—such as water-privileges and metals and woods used in the construction of machinery, no use, or a very limited one, will be made, where manufactures are not found. Indeed the existence of many of these natural aids to production within the limits of the nation, will be unknown; or if they are known to exist, no sufficiently strong motive will lead to their developement. Here and there, as the wants of the country require, a fine water-privilege will become the site of a common grist-mill, but in such instances there is perhaps a waste of water-power to ten times the amount of that which is improved. So, to a limited extent, metals and woods used in the arts, may be employed by mechanics and in rude manufactories, but no well directed, systematic efforts are made, to bring into use the mineral treasures of the country, or its other natural aids to production, used in manufactures. But now let different branches of manufacturing industry be introduced, and the influence in developing this class of territorial advantages is at once felt by the nation. Its water-privileges become valuable and are turned to good account;—its coal-mines and beds of iron and other ores are discovered, and made to yield their treasures as aids in the great work of production. Other materials used in the construction of machinery, are also sought after and made useful.

On the other class of territorial advantages—those which adapt the country to furnish the materials of which manufactures are composed, a similar effect is exerted. Some developement may have been made in furnishing supplies to other nations, but the existence of manufactures at home, leads to the production of a much larger amount of this class of agricultural products. At the same time perhaps that supplies continue to be furnished to foreign nations, an equal, or even larger amount, is required to meet the demands of home consumption.

The present state of England as to the developement of its territorial advantages, especially if contrasted with what in this respect is witnessed in other European nations, offers an illustration of the statements here made. Or we might even contrast what is seen at the present time in the United States, with the condition of the country thirty years ago. Either instance teaches an instructive lesson, as to the effects of manufactures on the developement of territorial advantages.

2. Manufactures offer profitable employment to the industry and capital of a country.

In the early periods of a nation's existence, full and profitable employment to its industry and capital will be found in agricultural labors, but as advances are made in wealth and population, its prosperity requires, that new modes of employing its productive resources should be opened. The different branches of manufactures offer these new kinds of employment, and that they are highly profitable to a nation, may be inferred from the following statements.

Manufactures allow of division of labor to a greater extent than other branches of industry. This was shewn to be the case in the preceding chapter on economical arrangements. It was also there stated, that division of labor tends, for different reasons there assigned, to render human industry more efficient, and to increase the amount of products. Hence then the inference is easily drawn, that manufactures offer profitable modes of employing industry and capital.

Labor saving machinery is used far more extensively in manufactures, than in other branches of production. This proposition is closely connected with the preceding, for it is division of labor, which, by dividing and rendering more simple the processes of production, leads to the invention and more extensive use of machinery. But employments which allow of the extensive use of machinery, are highly profitable. Here then is a second argument in support of our leading proposition.

Manufactures are profitable as a branch of national industry, since they call forth a larger amount of productive labor, than would otherwise exist. I refer particularly to the labor of women and children, who are seldom productively employed, except in some branch of manufactures. In every community also some are found in the class of laborers, who from the constitution of their minds, or their general habits, both of mind and body, seem particularly fitted to engage in manufacturing labor, and whose industry would otherwise be probably lost to the community. Both these circumstances have before been referred to, and they are of importance in the view now taken of them.

3. Manufactures exert a highly stimulating effect on other branches of national industry.

The stimulating effects of manufactories on agricultural production, was brought to view, when treating on the local influences of these establishments. Now what is true of a village or neighborhood, will to some extent hold true of a whole country, when manufactories are scattered over its surface, so far as its territorial advantages will allow of their establishment. The extension of manufactures, connected as it is with an increased demand for agricultural products and a consequent advance of their price, brings many tracts of land, which have before been left unimproved, into the proximity of a market, and causes them to be cultivated. It also leads those employed in agricultural pursuits to be more industrious and enterprising, and thus the stimulating effect of manufactures is felt in this branch of production.

Agricultural production will still further be stimulated by the demand for those products, which are the materials of manufactures. This, if it does not open a new field of agricultural industry, greatly extends those which before existed, and is an important source of revenue to the farmer. Such is the effect of woollen manufactures on the raising of sheep, and of cotton manufactures on the culture of cotton. It is true, as has been stated, that for products of this class a market may be found in foreign countries; and this may still continue to be the case, the domestic demand being superadded to the foreign. And here it may be remarked, that for agricultural products, a domestic market is generally preferred to a foreign one; but of this more will be said hereafter.

The stimulating effects of manufactures on commercial production are also obvious. Materials for manufactures are to be brought from abroad, or from different sections of the same country, or collected from the immediate neighborhood. Manufactured articles must also either be conveyed to foreign markets, or scattered about for home consumption. Thus, in different ways, new employment will be afforded to commercial industry and capital. Indeed, the general principle which relates to commercial production, might here be applied—that in proportion to the variety of products furnished by a nation, will be the extent of its commerce; since this variety both holds out an additional inducement to foreign customers, and increases the objects of home production for exportation to foreign markets.

Objections to Manufactures.

Of the objections made to manufactures, a part relate to the condition and interests of laborers in this department of industry; others are more closely connected with the general welfare and prosperity of the country. It is to the latter that I now propose to direct the attention.

There is a prevailing impression, that the prosperity of nations extensively engaged in manufactures is less sure and stable, than that of nations devoted to other branches of production. This impression, when the reasons of it are sought after, may be traced to the following sources;

1. It is supposed, that there is a strong tendency to excess, in the extent to which industry and capital are directed to this branch of production. This tendency is accounted for by the statement respecting the local effects of manufacturing establishments, which was made in a preceding part of this chapter. The sudden and striking prosperity of villages, in which manufactories are located, is known to all, and wherever, through the country, territorial advantages of a similar nature are found, it is natural,

that the desire of turning them to good account should be felt. Hence, in the common language of the country, the business is overdone. More manufactories are established, than the amount of capital in the nation, or the demand for products of this kind, will sustain, and thus losses and embarrassment follow.

It must be acknowledged, that what is here stated is sometimes witnessed and seen to be true. But it will be noticed, that these embarrassments and losses are connected with the first establishment of manufactures in a country, or, as it sometimes happens, with special encouragement given to this branch of national industry by the government of the country. Where manufactures have been fully introduced, and a regular course of business as to markets and amount of products is established, no inconveniences of this kind will attend them. So far then, there is ground for objection, not against the branch of production itself, but against some circumstances which attend its establishment in a country.

2. But it is said, that after manufactures have been introduced, and a regular course of business is established, there is a tendency to over-production and its consequent evils. And perhaps facts are appealed to in support of this assertion. Our attention is directed to the gluts, which not unfrequently occur in manufacturing nations, with the consequent depression of prices and other evils that follow in the same train.

In reply to this objection, it may be said, that over-production is not peculiar to Manufactures. It is seen both in Agriculture and Commerce. A year of scarcity as to the staple commodities of agriculture, is almost sure to be followed by a year of over-production of the same commodities. It is so in commerce; here it is called over-trading, and the effects which follow, are often more extensive and disastrous than in manufactures. But while over-production is found in other departments of national industry, there are two reasons, why the effects which attend it are especially noticed in manufactures. 1. From the extent to which competition is carried in some branches of manufactures, those who undertake and conduct these processes of production, are compelled to content themselves with a low rate of profits. A slight reduction of price on any article produced, is therefore soon felt. It falls at once below the cost of production, and as the amount concerned is large, important consequences follow to the producers. In other instances of over-production, as in agriculture, where the rate of interest is higher, the effects of a small reduction of price on any commodity, are not so soon felt, neither is the amount concerned so large. Hence the loss is easily sustained, and is balanced by the larger profits of another year. In commerce, also, the average rate of profits is higher, and calculations are made to meet those losses which may arise from variations of price. 2. Another reason, why over-production in manufactures attracts more attention, than in agriculture or commerce, is, that the number of those whose interests are immediately affected, is much larger. It is obvious, that when large numbers of those dependent on the fruits of their labor for daily support, are deprived of employment, the consequences must be severely felt and extensively known.

3. It is further objected to manufactures, that products of this kind are peculiarly liable to feel the influence of fashion, and that on this account their value will be sub-

ject to variation. Some kind of cloth, for example, at one time is fashionable. The demand for it is great, and the price high. The manufacturer adapts his outlay to meet this increased demand, but before the new and larger supply of cloth is in the market, the fashion changes —the price falls, and a consequent loss is sustained. And not only is there a loss on the products themselves, but perhaps to some extent on the machinery used in making them.

In reply to this statement, it is said, that the influence of fashion is felt but little on those products, which are of general consumption, and which are produced in large quantities. Fashion has more to do with luxuries, than with the common every day articles of life ; hence the rate of profits on the former class of products is higher, and thus provision is made for whatever losses may arise from this source. And further, when losses of this kind occur, they fall on commercial producers, no less than on manufacturers. Those employed in manufacturing, do not usually keep their products on hand a long time. They are compelled to make arrangements for quick returns of capital, and hence they lose perhaps only on what is in the process of production, when the change of fashion occurs. And in respect to losses on machinery, it is said, that what is thus thrown out of use, generally, with some modification, admits of being adapted to some other form of production ; and thus the loss arising from this source is small.

4. One other objection to manufactures, which is supposed to give support to the prevailing impression of the instability of this kind of property, remains to be considered. It is said, that a manufacturing nation is depend-

ent on foreign markets for the sale of its products, and that hence, in addition to the disturbing causes of price, which are found at home, and which apply in some measure to all branches of production, there is opened a new source of uncertainty and variation in the value of manufactured products. War may break out and hinder the operations of foreign commerce. The policy of nations abroad may change, and they may forbid the importation of manufactures. Other nations may enter the lists as competitors for these foreign markets, and become successful rivals. From either of these causes, or from others of a like nature, the sale of manufactured products may be prevented and their value affected.

A very general answer is all that can here be given to this objection. The influence of foreign markets here brought to view, is not confined to manufactures. An agricultural nation may be wont to look to foreign markets as a vent for its surplus products, and may therefore feel the effects of a war—of a change of foreign policy, or of the success of a rival competitor in the market. It is true, that in the case of agricultural products, other markets may perhaps be found with less difficulty, and the loss sustained on invested capital will also be less. A new direction is given to the productive energies of the country with less inconvenience and loss.

After all however it must be allowed, that nations extensively engaged in manufactures and dependent on foreign markets for the sale of their products, are peculiarly exposed to the disturbing influences which have been mentioned; and on this account capital thus vested, ought in some way to be indemnified for the risk that is incurred.

The question, how far the government of a country should assist in the introduction and support of manufactures, or, as it is usually stated, what encouragement should be given to domestic industry, has been much agitated, and is a leading inquiry in the science of Political Economy. This question here presents itself for our consideration, but since the manner of giving encouragement is connected with commerce, forming what is called the restrictive system, I have thought it best to defer the whole subject, until the nature of this remaining branch of national industry has been explained.

CHAPTER X.

Commerce.

Commercial industry includes two operations, which, though generally connected, are in themselves distinct. One is the buying and selling of commodities; the other their transportation. I speak of them as distinct operations, since one may be performed when the other is not. Commodities may have their value increased by the purchase and sale of them, while they remain undisturbed in the ware-house or granary. Their value may also be affected by transportation, when they are neither purchased nor sold. Usually however the two operations are united, and together constitute commercial production.

Some writers in Political Economy have been disposed to limit commercial production to transportation. They have maintained, that the only way in which value is added to products by commercial industry, is in conveying them from one place to another, and offering them to consumers under such circumstances as may suit their convenience. Such is the opinion of Say. But it is thought, that this is too limited a view of the nature of commercial production, and that it should be extended so as to include the purchase and sale of commodities. It is not meant by this assertion, that commodities increase in value, from the simple act of passing from the possession of one man into that of another. Neither is it supposed, as some seem to have thought, that in all transactions of a commercial nature, what one gains another loses. But it is meant, that in the existing economical arrangements of society, the very act, which is performed by the merchant, of standing between the producer and consumer, advancing to the former capital and receiving products in return, and then handing over these products to the latter, receiving back capital in return, is a transaction, which both facilitates the economical processes of the community, and adds value to the products in relation to which it is performed.

To establish this point, let us analyse the operation of buying and selling. Suppose a certain amount of manufactured products to be in a finished state and ready for delivery to the consumers. But the manufacturer is not able to find a market for them, and they remain on his hands for one month, during which time he is endeavoring to effect a sale. In this instance then, there is interest to be paid on capital, and also remuneration for oversight and labor, both of which are to be set down to the account of selling the commodities concerned. Again, here is a numerous family, whose daily consumption requires a supply of many products, both agricultural and manufactured, or a large manufacturing establishment, for which a supply of the raw material must be furnished. Suppose, now, that to furnish these supplies, various as they are in one case and large in the other, it were necessary in each instance to collect them from those by whom they are produced. How much time and labor and capital would thus be consumed!

Now it is for the performance of what in these supposed cases is done by the producer and the provider, that the merchant comes in with his capital and personal services, and takes upon himself the management and responsibility of the whole transaction. To the manufacturing producer, he advances payment for his products when ready for delivery, thus saving to him further interest on his capital and the labor and care of finding a purchaser. To the provider, either for the family or the manufactory, he comes, bringing into his neighborhood the very articles, both as to variety and amount, which are needed. Thus then an important service is rendered —a service that requires an outlay of capital and labor, and which, since it adds value to products, for the same products in the hands of consumers are worth more than in the hands of producers, may strictly be considered an act of production.

In respect to the other part of the process of commercial production, its nature is more easily understood. Every one is aware, that a commodity receives an accession of value by being brought to a market, or into the neighborhood of consumers. Indeed in respect to many commodities, a large proportion of their value results from transportation. It is also obvious, that in the work of transportation, human industry, capital in various forms, and the aids of nature, are called into exercise. Here too is division of labor. There is retail, wholesale, domestic and foreign commerce, each of which in its subdivisions and different operations, gives employment to numerous laborers. This part of commercial production admits also of the improved use of the aids of nature. Every year is offering labor-saving inventions of this kind in the form of railroads, railroad cars, steamboats, carriages &c.

We are then to understand by commerce both the purchase and sale of commodities, and their transportation, thus calling into action the different agents of production, and adding new value to the products of agriculture and manufactures.

Those circumstances in the nature and condition of man, which give rise to exchange and barter, were brought to view in a preceding chapter. Commerce, as a distinct form of industry, giving employment to capital and requiring a separate class of laborers, is of gradual growth, increasing with the advancement and enlargement of society. At first, perhaps, it is restricted to the exchange of the surplus products of the farm, but as new branches of industry, both agricultural and manufacturing, are introduced, and a greater variety and amount of products exist in the nation, it enlarges itself, and becomes established as a distinct system of production with its divisions and subdivisions. There are also, as in manufactures, territorial advantages, which conduce to the success and prosperity of this branch of production. Such are navigable rivers extending far into the interior of a country, commodious bays and harbors, and materials used in the construction of ships, and of other vehicles employed both in land and water carriage of commodities. A nation extensively engaged in commerce, must also possess a large productive capital. This is necessary, not only as capital is required for the conducting of commercial production itself, but as its existence is implied in the ample supply of agricultural and manufactured products which is the basis of commerce.

Divisions of Commercial Industry.

Commerce has been divided into retail and wholesale, and also into domestic and foreign trade. With the meaning of these terms all are familiar; and though the same leading principles apply to every branch of commercial production—to the pedlar with his merchandise upon his back, and to the opulent merchant whose warehouses are filled with the products of different climes, there are peculiar circumstances, which affect their application to these several divisions. I design therefore to consider separately, each of these leading branches of commercial production.

Retail Trade.

It is the business of the retailer, to bring the commodities in which he deals, into the immediate vicinity of consumers, and to offer them in such quantities and under such circumstances, as may suit their convenience. In a newly settled country, where the inhabitants are few and scattered over a wide extent of territory, the merchant with his wares upon his back, or in his travelling cart, visits every family. In other instances, fairs are held—

that is, on appointed days the merchants of the country congregate together in one place, and there expose their merchandise for sale ; and to this market the whole neighboring population resort for a supply of their wants. When a country has become more densely settled, the retailer locates himself in some village, or neighborhood. He there erects his storehouse, and supplying it with merchandise suited to the market, devotes himself to the business of buying and selling.

That important service is rendered to society by the retail merchant, may easily be shewn. "Unless," says Smith, "a capital was employed in breaking and dividing certain portions either of the rude or manufactured produce, into such small parcels as suit the occasional demands of those who want them, every man would be obliged to purchase a greater quantity of the goods he wanted, than his immediate occasions required. If there was no such trade as a butcher, for example, every man would be obliged to purchase a whole ox or a whole sheep at a time. This would generally be inconvenient to the rich, and much more so to the poor. If a poor workman was obliged to purchase a month's or six months' provisions at a time, a great part of the stock which he employs as a capital in the instruments of his trade, or in the furniture of his shop, and which yields him a revenue, he would be forced to place in that part of his stock which is reserved for immediate consumption, and which yields him no revenue. Nothing can be more convenient for such a person than to be able to purchase his subsistence from day to day, or even from hour to hour, as he wants it. He is thereby enabled to employ almost his whole stock as a capital. He is thus enabled to furnish work to a greater value, and the profit which he makes by it in this way, much more than compensates the additional price which the profit of the retailer imposes upon the goods."

A prejudice against retailers, which exists in the minds of some portions of the community, may here be noticed. It is often thought, that the profits of this branch of trade are exorbitantly high, and that in some way, retailers get the advantage of the common classes of consumers. But it is obvious, that there never can be any just ground for these impressions, except in those cases where a monopoly exists—that is, unless where some one engrosses the trade to himself to the exclusion of all others. Competition will ever place reasonable limits on commercial profits. No matter whether it respects the retail trade, or the wholesale, so long as nothing hinders any one who pleases from engaging in the business, the profits made cannot be exorbitantly high. If a dealer in any commodity asks an unreasonably high price for his merchandise, others engaged in the business will undersell him, and thus he will find himself obliged to lower his prices. And if he has monopolized the trade, no others in the community being employed as dealers in the same commodities, this will soon be known, and the lure of higher profits will lead others to engage in the same business. But it is to be remembered, that this statement is made on the supposition, that there is no interference on the part of the authorities of the country, or from any source—no privileged companies, no oppressive restrictions. Free, fair, open competition will always secure fair prices.

But there are other considerations, which relate more particularly to the retail trade. In this branch of commerce, much that is ordinarily looked upon as profits, is in fact a remuneration for labor. This is obvious in the case of the travelling retailer. In other instances, where a shop and other conveniences for retailing merchandise are provided, the expenses of the establishment, if not large compared with what is thus expended in other branches of production, are large in proportion to the amount of sales effected. Unless then the rate of profits be higher in proportion to the amount of business done, the expenses of conducting the business and the usual rate of profits, will not be obtained. It is right also, that consumers situated unfavorably to a market, should pay for the labor and expense incurred by those, who bring the commodities they need into their immediate neighborhood.

Wholesale trade.

The wholesale merchant, who is usually found in seaports and large cities, stands between the importer and producer on the one side, and the retailer on the other. His dealings are usually large in amount, requiring a large outlay of capital to be vested in the commodities bought and sold, and in accommodations for conducting his business. Much responsibility and constant attention are also required ; the state of the market must be narrowly watched and those supplies furnished which it requires. The rate of profits in this branch of commercial production is less than in the retail trade ; but the lower rate is compensated by the greater amount of business transacted, on which profits are received.

Some may be disposed to ask, whether there be economy in this part of the commercial arrangements of a country ?—whether the retailer should not rather look directly to the producer and the importer for his supplies? This in part is done by the retailer; and there is nothing to prevent his obtaining merchandise in this way to any extent he may find advantageous. Such however is the variety of commodities needed to meet the demands of his customers, that he often finds it for his interest to pay a small advance on their price to the wholesale merchant, rather than subject himself to the trouble and expense of collecting his supplies from different sources. Besides, by the wholesale trade, the importer and the home producer, especially the large manufacturer, having quick returns for their products, are relieved from the embarrassment and delay, which might otherwise attend their disposal, and thus assistance is given to different branches of production.

Another important service is also rendered by the wholesale trader to the community. When from over-trading, or from over-production, or from any cause, there is an excess of a commodity in the market, so that its price becomes reduced to the cost of its production, or below this cost, the wholesale merchant comes forward and buys up this excess at the reduced price, and thus prevents greater loss on the part of the producers and importers. What is thus purchased in a time of plenty at a reduced price, is kept on hand, till the price rises to its usual rate, or, as is sometimes the case, exceeds it. Thus the merchant is indemnified for the use of his capital, and for the trouble and risk of the transaction. At the same time consumers are benefited; for the price of the article as thus furnished, is lower than it otherwise would have been, since a deficiency of supply and a high price are almost sure to follow a glut of the market. This is called the trade of speculation, and though well founded prejudices sometimes exist against such as are called speculators, as the term is used to denote those who are unwisely adventurous and who often involve themselves and others in ruin, there is no ground for these prejudices, when the service that has been described is rendered to the community.

It is thus, that the wholesale merchant stands between the fluctuations of the market and the manufacturing and commercial interests of a country. He receives the first shock produced by these fluctuations, and if the impulse, though sudden and violent, soon ceases to be felt, its disturbing effects do not extend themselves to the agriculturist and manufacturer. These important branches of production are permitted to go on undisturbed, except in extraordinary cases.

Internal or domestic trade.

Internal trade, in distinction from foreign commerce, includes all commercial transactions of every kind carried on between the different members and the different sections of the same country, whether wholesale or retail. This is the most extended meaning of the term and the sense in which I here use it.

Internal trade, as thus defined, is absolutely essential to the prosperity of a community. It opens a vent for products, without which production cannot be conducted in the most profitable and successful manner, and is intimately connected with the economical arrangements of a nation. Corresponding to the utility of domestic trade is the amount of its extent in every country, far exceeding in most instances, as it is supposed, that of foreign commerce. Hence the importance, that every hindrance to its operations should be removed, and those measures adopted which may promote its advancement. In this view I remark,

1. No duties, imposts, or taxes in any form, should be laid on the operations of domestic trade.

In some countries a tax, or per centage, is paid to the civil or ecclesiastical authorities on all transfers of real estate. In other instances, large sums are collected under the name of licenses. Some European nations collect duties on merchandise passing from one province or department to another, and sometimes duties are levied by city governments. It is true, in all these cases the amount paid as duties, or taxes, is ultimately paid by the consumers, since it is added to the cost of production as the commodity enters the market. Still, as prices are thus raised, the demand for commodities decreases; and thus wherever taxes of the form specified are laid, they are hindrances to the operations of internal trade, and weights resting upon the productive energies of a country. They ought therefore to be removed. Buonaparte is said to have rendered important aid to internal trade during his reign, by abolishing the system of frontier duties, which previously existed among the European nations, and which has since been restored.

2. There should exist in every nation a convenient and safe currency as a medium of exchange.

The interests of internal trade require, that the circulating medium of a country should admit of the safe and easy transmission of values in the form of money from one section to another, however remote. It is also important, with reference to the same object, that the currency, so far as is practicable, should be of uniform value; but when the national territory is extensive, and many local banks are established, this desirable object cannot perhaps be fully effected.

But it is of still higher importance, that the currency should be sound. Whatever precautionary or supervisatory measures can be taken by the government of a country to secure this result, should be adopted. The breaking of a bank whose notes are in extensive circulation, causes much embarrassment and many vexatious losses through the community. It does much also to impair confidence in this part of the national currency, especially among the more numerous and less intelligent portion of the community, and thus often a check is given to its business transactions. The counterfeiting of money, when practised to a great extent, produces similar results. But as money is the subject of a distinct chapter, it is not necessary further to enlarge upon this topic.

3. Facilities should be furnished for the transportation of commodities.

Facilities for the transportation of commodities, which is an important part of commercial production, may be arranged in the two following classes; 1. The means of transportation, as ships, steamboats, wagons, horses and other beasts of burden. 2. Improvements of natural advantages for transportation. Such are harbors, breakwaters, docks, roads, railways, canals &c. In a country where such facilities are found, a highly favorable influence will be exerted on the interests of internal trade. Commodities in common use are brought into the vicinity of consumers, and are offered at such prices that most are able to purchase them, and thus the market is extended and the demand enlarged.

For improvements in the means of transportation, a community is generally indebted to the ingenuity of individuals. The present century furnishes many striking examples. Fulton's application of steam-power to navigation, has already been mentioned. Others have exercised their inventive powers in the modelling of ships and in the construction of carriages and railway cars. Improvements of this kind are of the same nature as labor-saving machines, and the same encouragement and protection should be extended to them, as to inventions in other departments of production.

Improvements of the other class are generally made under the direction and at the expense of the public authorities, excepting those instances, which from their nature allow of remuneration to individuals, or joint-stock companies, in the form of tolls, or duties of some kind. And since many of these works of internal improvement are attended with a large expenditure, and the benefits arising from them are not limited to any single portion of the community, it seems right, that a part of the public revenues should be directed into this channel.

4. A well sustained system of credit should be established.

In a large proportion of the commercial transactions constantly occurring in every trading community, some time intervenes between the purchase of an article and the payment for it. The individual consumer who receives from the retailer a supply of groceries and other articles consumed in his family, makes payments at stated times, every three or six months, as may be the custom, or as may have been agreed upon. So again the retailer receives his goods from the wholesale merchant on a like term of credit, as it is called. And perhaps, though this is not so commonly the case, the wholesale merchant has himself obtained his supplies from the producer, or importer, on credit; and thus the system of credit extends itself through every class of a trading community. Indeed the existence of this system in one class, to some degree creates a necessity for its introduction into others.

This system of credit is to be looked upon as simply a loan of capital. The seller consents to wait three or six months for payment of the price of a commodity, which he delivers over to the buyer. He thus advances to him for the time specified, capital to the value of the article sold, taking care to indemnify himself by a higher price, in which form he receives interest on his capital thus advanced.

The conveniences and advantages of this system of credit are the following; 1. It saves the necessity of keeping on hand an amount of funds required to meet the daily expenses of a family, or of a productive establishment of any kind, and thus it economises capital. 2. It is a convenient mode of loaning. What is thus loaned is in quantity and kind adapted to the wants of the borrower, and is in that form, in which it can be most easily furnished by the lender.

To balance these advantages, it is said, that by means of this system of credit, many are tempted to injudicious expenditures and enterprises, thus exposing themselves and others to losses and embarrassment. Indeed to this source are traced much of the over-trading and over-production, which result in the derangement of the market, and not unfrequently lead to failures and bankruptcies and their attendant evils. Upon the whole, however, the system of credit must be regarded as highly advantageous to domestic trade ; especially is this the case, when it is judiciously employed, and the debts thus contracted are engagements entered into in good faith. Whatever then tends to establish and secure a system of credit, is favorable to the interests of domestic trade. And there are two ways, in which this end may be promoted. 1. By legal enactments which assist in the collection of debts. 2. By supporting a high standard of moral obligation in the community. When the aid of law and of conscience are thus both brought in support of commercial credit, few instances of loss will occur, and those from providential and unavoidable causes.

Foreign trade.

A brief statement of the nature of Foreign Trade and of the basis on which it rests, was made in the chapter on Economical Arrangements. Further views on the same topics are found in connexion with the following exhibition of the advantages resulting from this source.

1. Foreign trade increases the variety of national supplies.

As the result of the economical arrangements and productive enterprise and effort which are found in nations of civilization and wealth, a large amount of commodities is produced, to be distributed among the individual producers and other members of the community. Of this gross amount of products, foreign commerce takes a portion and carries it abroad to other nations, receiving for it in exchange the products of foreign soils and climes. And then, when this substitution of these foreign commodities for domestic ones has been made, the gross amount of supplies is distributed to the different classes of the community. Thus the variety of commodities found in the nation becomes greater, and each individual is enabled to obtain on the most favorable terms and with little trouble, whatever his convenience and comfort and even his fancy may ask. Look at the table, the dress, and the furniture of even the common laborer, and how many articles are found, which are the products of foreign and distant countries! And when we enter the mansions of the rich, how much greater still is the proportion of these foreign products! For all this variety in the comforts and conveniences and luxuries of life, a nation is indebted to foreign commerce.

2. It increases the amount of national supplies.

This consequence results from foreign commerce as an important branch of national production, giving employment to a large amount of labor and capital. The outlay is in this case in the amount vested in merchandise exported, and in the expenses of transportation of home products to foreign markets, and then again in the purchase of foreign commodities and the expenses of the return voyage. And it is at the conclusion of the whole adventure, that we are to find its results in the excess of importations over exportations. This excess, in whatever form it may appear, constitutes the avails of commercial production—the returns of the labor and capital employed in this branch of national industry, and is an important addition to the amount of national supplies.

But perhaps these returns of commercial production are in the form of money, and it may be asked, whether in this case the preceding statement will hold correct? I answer, that if the merchant brings back the profits of his adventure in the form of money, it is because he finds it for his advantage so to do, that is, because this commodity is in higher demand at home, than other commodities found in the foreign market. Money as an article of trade, does not differ from other commodities. There is then in this case an addition made to the amount of national supplies, and in the form most needed by the nation.

Perhaps it will be said again, that the expenses of commercial production are an offset to all the increase of value effected by it, and that no addition is made to the amount of national supplies. Suppose this statement to be correct, and that importation returns to the country no more than had been sent abroad. Still as support is given to the large number employed in this branch of national industry, and interest paid on the capital thus invested, it is by no means unproductive. The same argument applies here, as was used when considering the system of the Economists. It is allowed that the gross amount of national products is increased, and it is to this gross amount, and not to the net products, that we look. But it is evident, that more than this is effected. If it be not so, why are capital and labor directed to commerce, when by employing them in agriculture, or manufactures, a return is not only received for the outlay, but the profits of the undertaking are added.

3. Foreign commerce exerts a highly stimulating influence on national production.

In support of this statement, a reference might be made to what was witnessed in Europe during the fifteenth and sixteenth centuries—especially to the effects which followed the discovery of America, and of the passage round the Cape of Good Hope. But historical facts on this subject are well known and have been often adduced. I shall therefore only offer a brief explanation of them.

It has been stated, that foreign commerce increases both the variety and amount of national products. It brings within the reach of every industrious individual, a liberal supply of those commodities, which, but for their commonness, would be ranked among the luxuries of life. In this way the style of living is raised and the number of human wants increased, and then to gratify this higher sense of enjoyment and these enlarged desires, more exertion must be made. Every consumer, who is at the same time a producer, feels a new stimulus to increase the amount of his own products, and thus, without doubt, large additions are made to the gross amount of national supplies.

But there is another way, in which this stimulating influence of foreign commerce is exerted. The facilities for transportation, and for effecting exchanges, thus afforded, bring the different nations of the earth into neighborhood with each other; and hence producers both in agriculture and manufactures, especially in the latter, make their calculations and arrangements, not only for the supply of their own country, but of other communities. Large investments are made in fixtures of various kinds, in machinery and other productive forms, and in many departments division of labor is carried to a minute extent. The consequences which follow, have been already stated.

The amount of products is increased—their price is diminished, and the effects of this diminution are seen in the enlarged demand, both for home consumption and for foreign markets. And by tracing still further the results which follow, which has been done in another place, it is seen, that the stimulating effects of foreign commerce extend themselves to every department of production.

4. Foreign commerce leads to the full developement of an important class of territorial advantages.

The territorial advantages here referred to, are materials used in the building of ships—timber, iron, hemp &c. but more especially an extended sea coast with commodious bays and harbors. Some use will be made of these advantages in domestic trade, but the more full developement of them is seen only in those countries, which are extensively engaged in foreign commerce. The commercial policy of the Chinese Empire at the present time, contrasted with that of most European nations, especially of England, is an example of the loss sustained by the neglect of this class of territorial advantages.

5. Foreign commerce offers a convenient mode of collecting a public revenue.

Many expenditures of the national government in commercial countries, are made for the support and protection of foreign commerce. In this list may be enumerated the building and outfits of national vessels—the erecting and support of light-houses on the coast—the salaries of those sent as ambassadors to foreign countries and other incidental expenses. Hence, there seems to be a propriety in collecting the revenue, out of which these expenses are to be met, from the same department of production. But it is here more particularly designed to bring to view the facilities offered in connexion with foreign commerce, for the apportionment and collection of a national revenue. By a wisely adjusted tariff system, high duties are laid on foreign luxuries brought into the country, while on commodities which constitute the more necessary articles of life, no duties are imposed, or those which are light. Hence, since in all cases duties are added to the price of the articles consumed, and of course paid by the consumers, the rich who make use of foreign luxuries, will be made to contribute largely in defraying the national expenses, leaving but a small part of the burden to be borne by the poorer classes of society. In this way, then, without the trouble of an apprisal, a tax is laid on property; and it may also be collected with less expense and trouble, than attend other forms of taxation. Perhaps the same results might be attained by some other method, but the facilities thus offered for apportioning and collecting a national revenue, are highly important.

6. Foreign commerce offers a convenient mode of assisting in the introduction of a new branch of domestic production.

There are two ways in which this assistance is given, —by the imposition of restrictive duties, and by the granting of bounties. When the duty laid upon any commodity of foreign production, is so high, that the importer cannot afford to pay it and offer the commodity for the price, at which it is furnished by the domestic producer, the duty thus imposed becomes restrictive. Or instead of imposing a restrictive duty on the foreign commodity, an allowance, or premium, is paid by the government of the country to the home producer, thus enabling him to sell his products, both in the domestic market and in foreign markets, at a lower price, than that of the foreign commodity. In this case, a bounty is said to be paid, and it is at once seen, that the effect on domestic production is the same, whether restrictive duties are imposed, or bounties given.

The commercial policy which is usually called the restrictive system, is made the subject of a distinct chapter. I shall therefore strictly limit the view here given, to the proposition which has been stated; and in relation to this, two inquiries arise; 1. What is the nature of the assistance thus given? 2. What is the nature of the instances, in which it may with propriety be extended?

The attempt to introduce a new branch of production into a country, is an experiment, which, if successful, will be a source of benefits to the community at large. It is reasonable then, that the expense and risk of the experiment should be borne by the community. And this is the result, which is effected by the imposition of restrictive duties and by bounties. If a bounty is paid, it is paid from the public revenue, which in some form of taxation has been collected from the individual members of the community. If restrictive duties are imposed, the amount of this duty is added to the price of the article, advancing its price beyond the rate at which it could otherwise have been afforded. These duties then are a tax on all consumers of the commodities on which they are laid, and as the commodities on which duties are thus paid, are usually articles of general consumption, the burden, as before, comes upon the community at large. It will also be the case, that the benefits of the experiment, if successful, will eventually accrue to those, by whom bounties and restrictive duties have been paid. For when the new branch of production, thus introduced, becomes established, it may be expected, that the products supplied will be furnished at a lower price, than that, at which foreign products of the same kind had previously been sold. From this statement, then, we learn the nature of restrictive duties and bounties.

Let us now direct our attention to the other inquiry proposed—the nature of the instances, in which this assistance may be extended. And here, I would refer to what has already been said on the order, in which the different branches of production naturally spring up in a country, first those of an agricultural kind, and afterwards of a manufacturing and commercial. We have seen, that the time will arrive in the progress of every nation, when the developement of its territorial advantages, and the profitable employment of its capital and industry, with other favoring circumstances, may require the introduction of new branches of production. Whenever, then, in respect to any branch of production not existing in the country, it is supposed, that this time has arrived, the attempt to introduce it should be made. And if, as will generally be the case when competition with other nations is to be met, this attempt may be attended with much expense, and be doubtful in its issue, but of general benefit to the community if successful, it is manifestly incumbent on the government of the country, to defray in some form from the public revenues, the charges of the experiment. And unless the attempt be prematurely and unwisely made, the branch of production thus introduced, will soon be able to sustain itself and prove advantageous to the public. Here then, it may be added, that if, after an experiment of this kind has been fairly made, it is found, that foreign products, burdened as they are with the cost of transportation and other incidental charges, can be afforded at a lower price, than those of home production, there is no reason, why the public should continue to be subjected to duties or bounties, for the support of this branch of domestic production.

That a branch of production may be introduced in the manner that has been stated, and in the end prove highly advantageous, is seen in the history of the manufacture of cotton fabrics in this country.

CHAPTER XI.

On the restrictive system.

In the history of Political Economy, different schools are found, attaching undue importance to each of the three great divisions of human industry. The doctrines of the Economists, who advocated the superiority of Agriculture, have been stated. A theory of earlier date, was that which bore the name of the Mercantile System. The basis of this system was the now exploded doctrine, that national wealth consists in money ; and the leading object which it proposed, was by commercial regulations to secure an increase of wealth, as thus defined. Hence, for many years the struggle among nations adopting this theory, was to secure what, by the supporters of this system, was denominated a favorable balance of trade. The meaning of this phrase and the reasoning on which this policy rests, may be learnt from the following statement ;

When the exports of a country exceed its imports, the balance will be received in money; and as money constitutes the wealth of a nation, the balance of trade will in this case be favorable. On the contrary, if the imports exceed the exports, this excess can have been obtained only in exchange for money sent abroad; in this case then, it was supposed that the national wealth was diminished, and the balance of trade was said to be unfavorable.

It is not a little singular, that this theory, once so generally adopted, and forming the basis of the commercial policy of the most powerful nations of the earth, is in direct opposition to facts and correct principles.

The other system to which reference has been made, was called the Manufacturing System. It had its origin in the state of society, and in the institutions of the feudal governments of Europe. In those troubled times, when the power of princes was often unsuccessfully resisted by the greater barons, the former, with the design of strengthening their cause, endeavored to conciliate the favor of the towns and cities which had sprung up in the country, and which were engaged in manufactures. Hence special privileges were granted to those towns and cities, pertaining to the branches of industry in which they were employed. The exportation of raw materials used in the manufactures established in the country, and also of breadstuff needed for the support of those thus employed, was forbidden on heavy penalties, and at the same time absolute prohibitions, or heavy duties, were laid on foreign manufactured products, to prevent their importation from abroad. This was called encouraging domestic industry, and other regulations relating to the same object, were adopted.

Such was the origin of the Manufacturing System, which was found to accord well, in the measures adopted for its support and furtherance, with the Mercantile. The same regulations,—the same restrictions and prohibitions, which were supposed to be advantageous in securing a favorable balance of trade, were also thought to afford the desired protection to domestic industry. Hence the two systems became blended together, and for many years the correctness of the principles on which they were founded, was unquestioned.*

The remains of these once celebrated systems of Political Economy, have come down to us in these later times under the form of tariff regulations, constituting what is usually called the restrictive system. And here we approach the much agitated question, how far it is expedient that a system of this kind should form the basis of national policy. On this question, which has divided public opinion in this country, a few simple propositions will now be advanced. This, it is conceived, is all that is required in an Elementary work on the science of Political Economy.

A restrictive system when fully adopted by any nation, is designed to effect the following results ;

1. To prevent the importation of foreign manufactures into the country.

2. To secure for its own manufactures a command of foreign markets.

3. To prevent the exportation of raw materials, used in those branches of manufacture which have become established.

---

*For a more full account of these systems I refer to Smith's Wealth of Nations, Book 4.

4. To encourage the importation of the same raw materials from abroad.

These results it seeks to effect in the following ways;

1. *By direct prohibitions.* By direct prohibitions, are meant laws relating to exports and imports, with heavy penalties attached to their violation.

2. *By prohibitory duties.* Suppose that broadcloth of a certain quality can be manufactured in England and sold in this country for five dollars per yard, while cloth of the same quality manufactured here, cannot be afforded under five dollars and a half. But to prevent the importation of this cloth, and thus give encouragement to domestic industry, a duty of seventy five cents per yard is imposed. In this way, then, the duty becomes prohibitory in its nature; for foreign manufacturers, when compelled to pay this duty, can no longer compete with our own manufacturers of the same class,—they cannot pay this duty, and sell their broadcloth for what it can be furnished in this country.

3. *By pecuniary bounties.* Suppose this same broadcloth to be sent to the markets of South America. Cloth of the same quality manufactured in England, is sold there for five dollars, but the manufacturer in this country cannot afford it under five dollars and a half. To counterbalance this advantage on the part of the English producer, the Government of the United States pays a bounty of seventy five cents per yard on broadcloths of this quality exported from the country. Thus, then, the American manufacturer is enabled to undersell the English, and obtain command of the foreign markets. This is an instance of a pecuniary bounty.

4. *By drawbacks.* A drawback is a tariff regulation,

by which the duties paid on any article are under certain circumstances paid back, or excepted. Suppose a duty of two and a half cents a pound to be laid on common brown sugar, to be repaid, or not required, on the sugar subjected to the refining process of manufacturing into loaf sugar. This would be an example of a drawback.

From this concise statement, the objects of a restrictive system and the methods adapted to effect these objects, may be learnt. I remark then,

1. That so far as a restrictive system is designed to effect a favorable balance of trade, it is based on erroneous principles.

It can hardly be necessary to offer any arguments in support of this proposition. The notion of a favorable balance of trade, is fully refuted by the generally received doctrines on the nature of money and of the operations of foreign commerce, found in works on the science of Political Economy at the present day. Still, it is unquestionably the case, that some nations are partially acting upon this doctrine, either from long established prejudices upon the subject, or from the difficulty of effecting alterations in what has become a part of a settled national policy.

2. So far as a restrictive system is designed to give special encouragement and support to any branch of production, as more profitable or more necessary to a country, than other branches, it rests on erroneous principles.

It is a favorite opinion with some, that certain modes of employing capital and labor are more profitable than others, or, at least, that there are some branches of production, which give more full and constant employment to capital and labor than others. Hence they are jealous of a course of trade, or any policy, which may give support to these branches of production in foreign countries, and are desirous, that the government of their own country may adopt such measures, as shall secure to its own citizens a monopoly of these more profitable modes of production. Perhaps also, these opinions are strengthened by the impression, that the products of these same branches are specially important, because of the urgent wants which they supply, or as they render a nation less dependent on other nations.

It will readily occur, that these opinions are in direct opposition to the explanation given of the nature of production in the first chapter of this work,—to the principles laid down on the subject of exchange in the chapter on Economical Arrangements, and also to what has been said on the manner, in which capital and labor are directed to different employments. Indeed they are opposed to most of the doctrines which have been advanced, and it might be sufficient to make some general references of this kind, to shew that they are regarded as erroneous. But besides this general reference, I shall endeavor to shew, by a brief statement of the opposite policy, that the course thus recommended, is not only unwise, but illiberal and narrow-minded.

Let us then first suppose a nation to be insulated—cut off from all intercourse with foreign nations, and dependent entirely on its own resources for the supply of its wants. The order in which the different branches of production would be introduced, and become established and enlarge themselves, has already been stated. The first efforts would no doubt be of an agricultural nature, accompanied with rude and simple attempts of a manufacturing kind. At a later period, domestic commerce, and manufactures with its extended division of labor and its various forms of machinery, would be found, each advancing with the increase in the abundance and variety of national products. In some instances, where experiments relating to the introduction of a new branch of production might be attended with risk as to success, or with unusual expense, and in which the advantages resulting would be of general benefit to the community, aid in some form might be extended from the public revenues, under the direction of the national government. But with these few exceptions, the productive energies of the country would be permitted to develope themselves, unaided, and in those forms, which the wants of the community might require. Each section would adapt itself to particular branches of industry, to an extent, and in a manner, most conducive to its own welfare and to the general good, free from all animosities and jealousies. Those portions, which from the superior fertility of their soil, or other favoring circumstances, might be best adapted to agricultural production, would thus employ the larger portion of their capital and labor. Other parts of the country, would for the same reason, and in like manner, become manufacturing sections, and others again, commercial. Such would be a brief outline of the economical arrangements and progress of a community, insulated and dependent entirely on its own resources ; and the happy results would be seen in the harmony of action, and the general prosperity of the whole nation ; each section contributing that aid, which it might be best fitted to furnish, and participating by mutual intercourse, in the peculiar advantages for production possessed by others.

And now, why may not the same principles and the

same policy, be applied with equally salutary results to the community of nations? The diversities as to territorial advantages and other productive resources, which exist in different sections of the same country, are found in different nations, and to a more marked extent. One nation possesses peculiar advantages for agricultural production, another for manufacturing, and a third for commercial. Why then should not these peculiar advantages be turned to the best account by each? It is not here meant, that a nation should limit its productive efforts to one branch, entirely excluding or neglecting others. This would be impracticable, or attended with much inconvenience in respect to different sections of the same country, and much more so, if attempted by different nations. All that is meant, is, that the larger share of the capital and labor of a nation, should be directed to those branches of production, in which, from territorial advantages, or other favoring circumstances, it is fitted to excel. Neither in this case, any more than in the former, ought the attempt, which may be made to introduce a new branch of production, to be regarded with jealous feelings and opposed. If in the progress of a nation, the time has arrived, when its resources and circumstances require, and justify, the introduction of any branch of production, not before existing, the attempt to introduce it, should be made. In this case, there will be competition between different nations, as there will between different sections of the same country, but it should be open, fair, and generous.

The policy now described, will at once be recognised, as that which has received the name of the free trade system, as opposed to the restrictive system, which forms the subject of our present enquiries. And there can be no doubt, that were this system fully adopted by the nations of the earth, the peace and happiness and prosperity of the human race would be promoted. Many jealousies and animosities, which now exist, would cease to be felt, and a fruitful source of wars and contentions would be removed. It would seem too that the very object, which the supporters of the opposite system propose to attain, would be secured, since the most profitable modes of employing capital and labor would be found. For what more advantageous course can be adopted, than that each nation should engage largely in those branches of production, to which its territorial advantages and other circumstances are best adapted.

Some perhaps will object to the system of free trade, that a nation thus becomes too dependent upon others,—that in the case of the breaking out of a war, or of any event, which might hinder or prevent the intercourse between nations, serious inconveniences and evils would arise. In answer, it may be said, that the exclusive attention of any nation is not supposed to be given to any one branch of production to the neglect of others. It must always and necessarily be the case, that a large proportion of the products consumed by a nation, must be furnished within its own limits. Especially is this true of most products of general consumption and primary importance. Hence, then, though in the case supposed inconveniences might arise, the consequences would not be so serious as is feared. There is also another view to be taken of this subject. Were the free trade system generally adopted by nations, as the basis of their commercial intercourse, it would present one of the most effectual checks to wars, that could be desired. For it would then be seen and felt, that no nation can engage in war, without cutting the sinews of its own strength, and bringing upon itself, as well as upon its enemy, the most serious losses and privations. Instead then of an objection to the free trade system, there is here found a strong argument in its favor.

But others object to the free trade system, that it is opposed to the generally received maxims of state policy, and that its adoption would require an entire revolution in the principles and modes of intercourse among nations. Allowing the correctness of this inference, it is evidently no argument against the system itself. A statement of this kind may shew, that a change of commercial policy might be attended with many difficulties, and should be made gradually, and with great caution, and this is all that it proves. To bring it forward against the system itself, would be to beg the question, for the very point at issue is, whether the generally received maxims of state policy, and the course of measures based upon them, be not selfish, narrowminded and injurious to the general good—such as should be discarded. But it may be the case, that the free trade system is not opposed to the soundest maxims of state policy, as is sometimes supposed. It may be but another, and a more distinct and sure way, of securing the most important of those results, which are the aim of those who oppose it. Indeed, the two systems differ from each other, not in respect to the end which is to be attained, but in the measures proposed for its attainment. The restrictive system is based on the doctrine, that the prosperity of a nation is to be promoted, by securing for it special privileges and advantages to the disparagement of other nations. On the contrary, the free trade system maintains, that all nations may advance together prosperously, and that the welfare of each will be promoted by that of others. Thus, while the former addresses itself to the selfish principles of our nature only, the latter makes its appeals both to the benevolent feelings, and to the desire felt by every nation for its own advancement.

But perhaps it may here be said, that the propriety of restrictive measures when designed to assist in the introduction of a new branch of production, has been admitted, and that the same measures should be continued, to give support and encouragement to the branches of production thus established, or to others equally important. To meet this statement, and make prominent the distinction in the two cases, I offer a third proposition.

3. So far as a restrictive system is designed to assist in the introduction and establishment of new branches of production, which, when thus introduced and established, are advantageous to the community,—or so far as it affords protection to any important branch of production existing in the country, against the attempts of foreign countries to break it down and destroy it,—or so far as it gives support to a branch of production necessary for the defence of a nation, it rests on sound principles, and should be adopted.

This proposition, it will be noticed, consists of three distinct parts, which are exceptions to the preceding proposition. These exceptions, one of which has already been considered, are stated together in this manner, because they rest on the same general principle which has before been partially exhibited. It is the following; All restrictive duties, bounties, prohibitions &c. that is, all the measures of the restrictive system, are to be looked upon in the same light as taxes—burdens imposed upon the inhabitants of a country for the public good. That such is the nature of these measures is inferred from the fact, that they are attended by an advance in the price of commodities, and this advance is an indirect tax on all consumers. Here then it is proposed to apply to this particular form of taxation, the same inquiries, as arise in relation to other taxes. Is the benefit to be secured such as to justify the imposition of the burden ? And it is the answer to this inquiry, which leads to the distinction between the case stated in the second proposition and the exceptions which make up the third. The distinction is as follows : A tax, or burden in the form of restrictive measures, may be imposed upon the public, to meet the expense of an experiment for the introduction of a new branch of production, or of affording protection to a branch already existing against an attempt to break it down,—or to support a branch essential to the public defence, because in each of these cases, the public will derive a benefit as an offset to the burden imposed. But a tax, or burden thus imposed, merely to give support or encouragement to a branch of production affording more profitable employment to capital and labor, or to secure for it undue advantages in foreign markets, is not to be justified from any advantages which are thus conferred upon the public. It may prove advantageous to those immediately concerned in the production of the favored commodities, but the consumers—the nation generally, instead of deriving any ultimate benefit, will be subjected to continued losses.

Let us now look more particularly, at the exceptions to the free trade system, which make up the third proposition. Of the first, enough has already been said in the preceding chapter. In respect to the second exception, which relates to protection against foreign aggressions, it may also be shown, that the interference of government is needed, and that aid thus extended will in the end prove advantageous to the whole community. To justify restrictive measures on this ground however, it is important, that the case should clearly be made out, to be one of aggression. If it be merely an attempt on the part of the foreign nation to introduce a branch of production, whose introduction is deemed to be required by the circumstances of the country, it should, as before stated, be met only by fair and generous competition. Any thing more than this, is itself of the nature of aggression. But that there are instances, in which it is the settled purpose of one country to break down a branch of production in another, and in which great sacrifices and many unfair practices are resorted to, for the accomplishment of this purpose, cannot be doubted. And it is to such cases, that the second part of the proposition is designed to apply. It is true, indeed, that the losses which follow successful attempts of this nature, will fall primarily and principally on producers. But since the breaking down of any established branch of production, which is furnishing its products at the lowest rate for which they can be afforded, will in the end, when foreign producers have obtained command of the market, be followed by an advance in the price of the same products, the public generally are interested in preventing this result. Instances of this kind then come under the general principle that has been stated.

The products referred to in the remaining part of our

proposition, are those articles used in war, with which it is deemed important, that every nation should be able to furnish itself without dependence on a foreign power. On this point, there is no difference of opinion : and until the time shall come, when the necessity of making provision for national defence shall cease, such branches of production may be protected and supported from their connexion with the national welfare.

CHAPTER XII.

On the different classes of Productive Laborers.

In preceding chapters, the attention has been directed to those economical arrangements found in society, which relate to production,—to human industry, the aids of nature and capital, the three agents by whose productive service the great work of supplying a nation's wants and increasing its wealth is carried forward,—and also to each of the leading departments of human industry, Agriculture, Manufactures and Commerce. And in the views which have been taken of these different subjects, I have been led to consider them for the most part as connected with the interests of the community. It is proposed in this chapter, to look at some of the employments and pursuits of different classes of productive laborers with reference to the interests of the trade, or profession, and of the individual laborer.

Day Laborers.

There are found in every community those who are denominated day laborers. Such are not usually confined to any particular department of labor, but their employments are various. They are assistants to others, performing such offices as may either directly help forward productive processes, or indirectly tend to this result, by enabling those employed as producers, to devote their time and efforts more exclusively to their work. Thus they become a sort of disposable force, which may be directed to any point, where there is need of additional aid. There are times, when the farmer can advantageously employ a larger number of laborers than usual,—it is haying season, or reaping season, and the favorable time will soon be past. So too in commercial production, there may be an unusual pressure of business—much must be accomplished within a few hours or days. In all such instances, there is found the convenience of having a class of men in the community, whose labor may receive any required direction, and who from the length of time for which they are usually engaged, and with reference to which their services are reckoned and paid, are called day laborers.

The situation of the day laborer is usually esteemed less eligible, than that of any other class in the community. His remuneration is small, often affording only a bare subsistence, with no opportunity of making accumulations and rising to a higher condition in life. But the principal disadvantage to which he is subjected, is the want of steady employment; this circumstance, to him who is dependent on his daily labor for his own support, and perhaps for the supply of the wants of his family, must be a source of much inconvenience. Not unfrequently also, injurious effects, arising from the want of employment, are felt by those, who are left to spend whole days without occupation. They become dispirited and indolent, perhaps intemperate and vicious.

That in every populous community large numbers are found in the class of day laborers, is not so much the result of choice on the part of laborers themselves, as of necessity. Many occupations require an outlay of capital, beyond the ability of most laborers to furnish, and in some nations, hindrances arise from the law of apprenticeships and other injurious regulations. But a few simple tools is all the capital the day laborer is expected to possess, and even these are sometimes furnished by his employers. The work performed by him, is also usually such as requires no uncommon skill, or knowledge, to execute it successfully. No preparatory training is required. Even the boy is enabled to turn his labor to account, and those whose necessities require immediate relief, at once find occupation and remuneration for their services.

Of the Mechanic.

It is often enjoined upon parents, whose children are to be dependent on their own labor for support, that they "put their sons to a trade." And those parents who have forethought, and whose circumstances will allow of it, are usually ready to follow this advice. A statement of some of the reasons, on which this advice is founded, will bring to view the comparative advantages of this species of labor.

1. *In this way the years of boyhood and of minority, are turned to the best account.* The apprentice to some mechanical employment, that of a house carpenter for example, is necessarily, while learning his trade, making acquisitions, which in after years are sources of profit to him. For when as a journeyman, or a masterworkman, he comes to the practice of his art, he will receive a remuneration for the knowledge and skill which he possesses. Thus the acquisitions of his early years become to him of the nature of capital, and he enters upon active life under more favorable circumstances, than he whose youth has been spent, either in idleness, or in the employments of common day labor.

2. *He who practises a trade, usually finds constant employment and receives high wages.* A skilful mechanic in a thriving community, rarely wants work; if he cannot find occupation in his own particular department of labor, he may engage in some kindred art, or in the common employments of day labor. Competition will also generally secure to him high wages, for inversely in proportion to the difficulty and expense of acquiring any art, or trade, will be the number of those practising it.

3. *He who learns a trade will probably acquire habits of industry.* Constancy of employment, especially in youth, may lead to this result. The mechanic also feels a peculiar interest in his work,—there is a call for ingenuity and a sense of reputation, which are favorable to the formation of habits of industry.

5. *The prospect of advancement is before the mechanic.* The apprentice becomes a journeyman, and if he is industrious, skilful, frugal and enterprising, he accumulates capital, and is enabled himself to undertake and conduct

work in his own department. He becomes a master workman, has others to assist him as apprentices and journeymen, and thus the way to competency, if not to wealth, is open to him.

Of the Manufacturer.

When we speak of the manufacturing laborer, we have in view those employed in large manufacturing establishments, in which division of labor and the free use of machinery have been extensively introduced.

This branch of labor recommends itself principally by its simplicity, and by the ease with which it is performed. As remarked in another place, it is often the mere watching and waiting upon machinery, which itself does all the work. Hence in this branch of industry employment is afforded to those of immature age, and to females, and thus the manufacturer not only receives a remuneration for his own labor, but for that of the different members of his family, for whose support he is bound to provide.

Full and constant employment is also usually furnished to the manufacturer. The outlay of capital in manufacturing establishments is generally large, and it is the interest of those on whose account the business is conducted, that the different processes should be rapidly executed, and succeed each other without delay. Hence, in these establishments, the laborer is employed as many hours and as constantly, as he can endure to labor.

The rewards of manufacturing labor are also generally higher, than are received by the same laborers in other departments of industry. The child earns a small amount, who would not probably in any other way earn any thing.

The female earns much more, than she could otherwise obtain, and as the remuneration of the manufacturer is generally dependent on the amount of work done, the skilful and industrious often acquire more than the average rate of wages.

But while some advantages are found in this department of labor, there is no one, against which stronger objections have been urged ; hence these objections require a distinct consideration.

1. It is said, that the manufacturer is more dependent on his employers, than other laborers. In the minute extent of division to which manufacturing labor is carried, the individual laborer is limited to the fractional part of a process of production. All the skill and knowledge which he possesses, extend to this single process, and his efforts are of avail only in connexion with others. When separated from his fellow laborers, "he is a mere adjective, without individual capacity, independence, or substantive importance." Thus, it is said, the manufacturer is completely in the power of his employers. They may reduce his wages, or require him to work more hours in the day, or impose upon him in any manner they see fit, and he has before him the alternative of submitting to these impositions or of being deprived of that employment, to which alone from his previous habits and acquirements he is fitted.

It must be acknowledged, that in those countries, where the laboring population is large, and where employment is found with difficulty, especially where injurious regulations exist pertaining to freedom of trades and apprenticeships, there will be some ground for this objection to manufacturing labor. Even here, however, the power of the master-manufacturer, or undertaker, over those employed by him, is not so great as it is often supposed to be. So excessive is the extent to which competition is carried in the manufacturing establishments of these countries, and so important is it from the large amount of capital employed, that the operations of these establishments should go forward without interruption, that employers are almost as much dependent on laborers, as the latter upon the former.

In our own country, or in any country where there is a demand for labor in its different departments, and where a laborer is permitted to change his occupation, as may suit his convenience or pleasure, this objection to manufacturing labor is little felt.

2. A second objection brought against manufacturing labor, is, that it is injurious in its effects on the mental habits and capabilities. It is said, that when a laborer is thus confined to one operation, which is repeated incessantly and with no variation, he becomes a mere machine, or rather the part of a machine. His mental powers, being left unoccupied, become torpid and enfeebled by inaction. Being also employed in this manner from early childhood, and enjoying no opportunities for acquiring knowledge, he becomes profoundly ignorant, and sinks low on the scale of intellectual being.

To the objection as thus stated, it is replied, that the evil effects enumerated, are not necessary consequences of being employed in manufacturing labor. They result rather from the extent, to which competition is carried in this department of production. Every master-manufacturer is endeavoring to bring his products to the market at a lower cost of production than others. It is for this end, that children of an immature age are kept employed many hours in the day, to the injury both of their health and of their education. It is on this account, also, that, through his whole life, the manufacturing laborer is pushed to a degree of effort and a constancy of employment, which leave him no time for the cultivation of his mind, and which are in other respects injurious to him. The objection then, that has been stated, is to be urged against the extent, to which competition is carried in manufacturing production, and not against the department of labor itself.

And further, in respect to the mind's being narrowed and enfeebled by being engaged in one simple manufacturing operation, it is said, that it can make no difference as to the mental culture and habits of the laborer, whether the part of the work performed by him consist of one simple act, incessantly repeated, or of two, or even three, simple acts thus repeated. In neither case is there a tendency to enlarge and strengthen the mind. It may also be added, that the more simple the task to be performed, and the more mechanical the manner in which it is executed, the greater will be the amount of leisure afforded, and the better the opportunity for profitable and improving reflection.

3. Another objection brought against the situation of the manufacturing laborer, is, that it is unfavorable to health and to morals. It is said, that the labor performed by the manufacturer is in many cases injurious, cramping the body, and not giving a free and healthy exercise to its different powers. Sometimes there is exposure to noxious gasses, to wet, and to unwholesome degrees of temperature. The state of the atmosphere in these establish-

ments is also not unfrequently unhealthy, the apartments of the laborers being crowded and badly ventilated. It is also said, that where large numbers are thus collected together, some of whom are corrupt in principle and in conduct, a bad moral influence is exerted. To support both these positions, appeals are made to facts. It is asserted, that of manufacturing laborers, a large proportion are sickly and short-lived, and that many are immoral.

That there is some validity in these objections to manufacturing labor, is generally allowed. At the same time however, it is maintained, that they exist in respect to other employments, besides manufactures. All kinds of labor requiring sedentary habits, are injurious to most constitutions, especially if pursued with great constancy and effort. There are also in other employments exposures to noxious gasses, to unfavorable temperatures and atmospheres, but in all instances of this kind, the risk incurred, is to be recompensed by a higher rate of wages. As to the frequent instances of sickness and mortality referred to, it should be remembered, that where population is condensed, such cases are more generally known and remarked upon.

To the other part of the objection we are considering, which relates to the immoral influences connected with manufacturing establishments, it is replied, that such influences are by no means necessarily attendant on the condition of the manufacturer. And if he is so situated as to be peculiarly exposed to temptations, which may lead him astray, influences of an opposite nature may also be brought to bear upon him with much effect; for where a population is condensed, they are in favorable circumstances to receive moral and religious instruction. As to the frequency, with which instances of immorality occur, in a crowded manufacturing population, the same remark may be made, as was suggested respecting cases of sickness and death. We have the impression, that they are frequent, because they occur within a very limited extent, and all come under our immediate observation.

In considering the replies, which have now been made to the objections brought against manufacturing labor, it will be noticed, that though they in some measure obviate these objections, they do not fully remove them. It may be true, that many of the unfavorable influences, both moral and physical, to which the manufacturing laborer is exposed, are not necessarily and in their nature connected with this form of human industry, yet if they are wont to attend upon it—if there is a strong tendency to that excessive competition, from which it is allowed many of the evils, which have been referred to, result, there is reason, why those who engage as laborers in this branch of industry, should guard against the temptations to which they are exposed, and why those appointed to watch over the welfare of the community, should adopt such measures on this subject as the public safety requires.

Of the Farmer.

In this country, the farmer is usually the owner of the soil which he cultivates, at least of the capital used in conducting his farm, and often of both. He works himself, employing others to assist him who are hired by the day, the week, or the month, as circumstances may render convenient. I propose then, in considering the interests of the agricultural laborer, to look at the farmer himself, viewing him not so much in his capacity of landholder, or capitalist, as in that of laborer.

And here, as this topic is one of common remark, it is unnecessary to do more, than make a simple enumeration of the advantages and disadvantages, pertaining to this branch of industry.

1. *It is a healthy employment.* The labors of the farm, which are performed for the most part in the open air, seem well adapted to the human frame and the human constitution, and there is generally more of health and of hardiness in this class of laborers, than in any other.

2. *It is a pleasant employment.* There is variety in its labors, and variety is always grateful. It is pleasant also to watch the progress of the fruits of the earth, and to assist in rearing and maturing them. It is permitted to the husbandman, says Cowley, "to see all his gardens and fields covered with the beauteous creations of his own industry; and to see, like God, that all his works are good."

3. *It is a moral employment.* The temptations to vicious indulgences, which offer themselves to the farmer, are far less numerous and urgent, than those which assail laborers in most other occupations of life. It would seem also, that he whose daily labors are in the midst of the works of God, and who receives the gifts of Providence direct from the hands of the Great Giver of every blessing, must be a religious, and of course a moral man.

4. *It is an employment, with which respect and influence are associated.* Though from the economical arrangements of society, the farmer is no less dependent on other classes of the community than these classes are upon him, it is apparently otherwise. He furnishes the

food, with which himself and other laborers are sustained. He furnishes also the materials of manufacturing and commercial labor. Thus every thing seems to originate with the farmer, and hence he regards his employment as one of great importance, and others accord to him the same estimation.

Of the objections made to agricultural labor, none are deserving of much consideration. It is sometimes said, that the labor of the farmer is hard work, and that there is much drudgery attending it. Others object to the lonesomeness of his situation—that there is little opportunity for the indulgence of the social feelings. Others again think that the gains of the farmer, though sure, are too slowly made ; they would have more of adventure and excitement. Of these and similar objections, it may be said, that they will arise, and the force of them will be felt, according to the characters and habits—the modes of thinking and feeling, which pertain to different individuals. Hence they do not here require a distinct and separate notice.

Of Commercial Laborers.

A division may be made of those in this department of production, including under one head such as are directly engaged in the purchase and sale of commodities, and under the other, those employed in the subordinate parts of commercial labor. In the former class, are to be ranked the retailer, the wholesale merchant, the exporter and importer. In the latter, are included clerks and those employed in the transportation of goods, as porters, draymen, sailors &c.

There is much in commercial pursuits to invite the attention of those who are entering on the business of life. In this department of production, the love of adventure, which is so deeply fixed in the human breast, is gratified. Instances are not unfrequently occurring, in which those who have started in life with small beginnings, become men of large possessions; and in the anticipations of youth, many are ready to mark out for themselves a course of life equally successful. The employments of the merchant are also exciting, especially as connected with the rise and fall of prices and the various fluctuations of the market.

But while many considerations allure the young and enterprising to commercial pursuits, the amount of capital which is needed, tends to limit the number of those who thus employ themselves. Skill and tact for business of this kind, and in some cases much knowledge, are also required. Add still further, the risk and responsibility incurred, for while some who engage in commercial pursuits make fortunes, others become bankrupts.

Of those who perform subordinate offices in the work of commercial production, many are job or day laborers, and the principles before stated apply to them. But there is one class of these subordinate laborers—the sailor—which requires a distinct consideration.

There are other inducements besides those of an economical kind, which lead many to encounter the hardships and toils of a sea-faring life. Curiosity is gratified in the opportunity presented of visiting different countries; and perhaps the dangers of the sea, as they call for a degree of hardihood and daring, are for these reasons more sought for by the young and adventurous. Economically considered, there is little to recommend this kind of employment. The remuneration of the sailor is apparently liberal, should all that he receives be looked upon in the light of wages; but if a fair deduction be made for the risks that he runs, and also for the injury sustained by his constitution from the fatigues and hardships, to which in times of peril and difficulty he is exposed, the amount left as wages becomes much reduced. Some time also must be spent, and many risks run, in acquiring the knowledge and skill of the accomplished sailor. On the other hand, it may be said, that though the labor of the sailor is at times difficult and severe, it is not so unremitted, as that of the farmer and manufacturer. There is also a prospect of advancement to the active and enterprising seaman, who obtains knowledge and skill in his employment, and whose character gives a title to confidence and trust. But of the thousands who enter on this pursuit, how few are there whose course is successful! How large a proportion are either swallowed up in the deep, or fall victims to the temptations that assail them! The efforts, which the humane and benevolent are now making to improve the condition of the sailor, leading him to become more provident, and rescuing him from the vices to which he is peculiarly exposed, are effecting much in making the situation of this portion of the community more eligible.

CHAPTER XIII.

On the different classes of Unproductive Laborers.

In the first chapter of this work, I have pointed out the distinction between productive and unproductive laborers, which, as there remarked, arises from the definition of the term production. It is there also said, that unproductive laborers constitute a highly serviceable and important portion of the community, supplying some of the most urgent wants of their fellowmen, and indirectly rendering efficient aid to the work of production itself. There is then in the term unproductive, as thus applied, nothing which is illiberal, or which is designed in any way to disparage those thus denominated.

In treating on the distribution of wealth, there will be opportunity for shewing in what manner unproductive laborers derive their revenue, receiving in return for the services they render, a portion of the gross amount of national products. I propose in this chapter, to offer a few general remarks on the nature of these employments, both as they are connected with the public welfare and with the interests of the laborers themselves.

The Physician.

The services rendered by the Physician relate to the preservation of health and of life;—they meet a class of wants, which in certain conditions, in which men are sometimes found, and in which they are ever liable to be found, become urgent. There is then in this case, as in the use of material products, the redressing of a want, and the individual to whom these services are rendered, finds his welfare and enjoyment essentially promoted.

The labors of the physician also indirectly aid in the work of production. The sick man cannot labor; his time is lost both to himself and to the public. He then, by whose instrumentality this sickness is removed, and the productive laborer is again enabled to perform his usual task, indirectly assists in the productive efforts of the community. Thus, in consequence of the services of the physician, more work is done and a greater amount of products raised. Hence, some have called physicians and other professional men, indirect productive laborers; and there is no objection to this phrase with the accompanying explanation.

And here I may be permitted to suggest, that this class of unproductive, or indirect productive laborers, might become still more serviceable to the public, if it constituted a part of their duty, to give directions and assistance for the preservation of health, as well as for its restoration when lost. Most of the diseases to which men are subject, are brought upon them by their own indiscretion and ignorance and folly; and without doubt, much might be done to prevent these unhappy results by the instructions and counsels of the intelligent and skilful physician, whose business it is, to investigate the laws of the human system, and to apply to practical purposes the knowledge thus acquired.

There are many inducements, by which individuals are led to engage in the study and practice of the healing art. The subjects, to which the attention is directed in a course of preparatory studies, embrace some of the most interesting departments of natural science, offering much to gratify curiosity and to inform and improve the mind. The practice of medicine also, though sometimes laborious, and attended with harassing cares and great responsibilities, has connected with it much that is grateful. It is pleasant to be the instrument of relieving distress, and the object of confidence and respect to those among whom we dwell; and such confidence and respect rest largely on the kind, faithful, and skilful physician. The average remuneration of the services of the physician is also ample and generous.

The Lawyer.

Laws are enacted by civil governments for the security of the property and persons of their subjects, and for the defence of the various rights which belong to the members of social communities. But laws thus enacted are necessarily general in their nature, and their application to particular cases is not unfrequently attended with doubt and difficulty. Hence the necessity of a class of men in the community, who may make the principles of law and the acts and statutes of legislative power, the subjects of their special attention and study, and thus be prepared to give counsel and assistance in the application of these principles and statutes to the transactions and events daily occurring. And those rendering this service evidently meet one class of wants, which to man in a social state, are highly important. In this case too, as in that of the physician, indirect assistance is furnished towards conducting the productive processes, which are carried forward in the community. Without the services rendered by the lawyer, men would with much difficulty associate together in combined action for the purposes of production, some furnishing capital, others natural agency, and others again labor. Transfers of property from one owner to another, would also be less easily and safely made. Hence it has been said, that he who by a legal instrument makes a man secure in the possession of the field which he cultivates, is a productive laborer, in the same sense, as he who assists in building the fence, by which the same field is enclosed. And it must be acknowledged, that if we look at the end to be attained, these acts are the same in their nature; but since the result of labor in one case becomes permanent in a material object, constituting a part of the wealth both of the individual and of the nation, while in the other case, there is no product possessing permanent value created, the ground of distinction before pointed out remains.

The study of the profession of law is usually accounted difficult and dry. Much however, in this respect, will depend on the constitution and previous habits of the mind. To some, the intellectual efforts it demands, and the inquiries to which it leads, are peculiarly grateful. But the practice of this profession is esteemed more alluring, as it offers much to awaken interest and create excitement. It leads also to competency and wealth; for while the average remuneration of legal services equals that of other professional laborers, there are not a few successful practitioners, who acquire large estates. The profession also opens in this country a prospect of preferment to places of public honor and trust, and sometimes of profit.

The moral and religious Teacher.

It was remarked in the introduction to this work, that man has other wants, than those pertaining to the body. These wants arise from his nature, and from the relations he sustains to the beings and objects around him. They relate to the cultivation of his moral and intellectual powers, to the enlargement of his knowledge, and to his instruction in what pertains to his duties and obligations. Hence there are classes of men in the community, whose employment it is to aid in the disciplining of these moral and intellectual powers, and in leading the mind to the different sources of knowledge; and it is one of these classes, which is had in view, when we speak of the moral and religious teacher.

Fully to appreciate the importance of the services rendered by this class of laborers, it would be necessary to trace their bearing on the whole of human existence, both in this life and in that which is to come. It might then be seen, that the individual, whose moral and religious interests are thus provided for, derives from those who thus minister to this class of his wants, the highest and most important benefits.

But Political Economy looks on this class of laborers with more especial reference to the public welfare; and in this view also, the service rendered and the influence exerted, are highly salutary and important. The necessity of good laws well enforced, that the economical arrangements and operations of a community may exist and be prosperously conducted, has been remarked upon in another place; and it may be added, that such laws owe their adoption and enforcement to public opinion. A law is nothing in a free community, if not thus sustained. But it is to moral and religious considerations, and to those who explain and enforce them, that we are to look for that influence, which, more than any other, forms this salutary public opinion, and gives to it its weight and binding power. Hence, the security and well ordered state of society, so important to its economical interests, are in no small degree to be ascribed to the services of its moral and religious teachers. And further, that men may be industrious and frugal, submitting to toil and self denial, they need to be urged forward and sustained by motives of great power and unceasing obligation ; and such, in a peculiar sense, are the motives adduced by the moral and religious teacher. Self interest offers strong stimulatives to exertion, but when a sense of duty comes in to lend its sanctions, there are wont to be more equable, and constant, and wisely directed efforts. Thus, then, moral and religious teachers become indirect assistants in the work of production, and it may be said, as was asserted of the physician and lawyer, that more labor is performed, and a greater amount of products obtained in the community, where they are found, than would otherwise be the case.

The professional studies and employments of the moral and religious teacher, to him whose mind is deeply imbued with moral and religious truths, are highly interesting and grateful. And such are left to find a large part of the reward of their services, in the satisfaction and peace of mind which result from doing good.

The Literary and Scientific Teacher.

Another class of professional laborers consists of those, who conduct the business of education in its different departments, thus increasing the enjoyments and usefulness of individuals, and advancing the interests of the community. By the services of those thus occupied, the way is opened to a distinct class of enjoyments, for to those whose minds have been expanded and strengthened by cultivation, and enriched by knowledge, and who have become men of refined literary taste, there are pleasures, with which the ignorant and uninstructed intermeddle not. The literary and scientific teacher also promotes in different ways, the economical interests of a community. By his assistance, scientific laborers, who, in another part of this work, are shewn to be productively employed, when applying the principles of science to the creating and perfecting of material products, are qualified for their work. It is his office also, to aid in preparing the different classes of professional laborers for the discharge of their several duties. And further, the general diffusion of intelligence, which has been shewn to be closely connected with the prosperity of nations, is promoted by those, who thus labor in the work of education.

In this country, the services rendered by the literary and scientific teacher, are at the present time more highly appreciated, and more generously rewarded, than at former periods. Those thus employed, are looked upon as constituting a distinct profession, the emoluments of which are equal to those of other professional laborers,—a rank and a remuneration, to which, whether we look at the nature of the services rendered, or at the bearing of these services on the welfare of the community, they seem richly entitled.

Of the public Functionary.

Under this head, are included all who in any way are employed in the administration of public affairs, whether as legislators, or as judicial, or as executive officers. The term also extends to those, whose services, both by sea and land, are required for the defence of a country. It is the business of the public functionary, to watch over the interests and conduct the concerns of civil society. Hence, as the security and happiness of a nation are closely connected with its civil institutions, and with the enactment and enforcement of wise and salutary laws, those thus employed may contribute much to the general welfare, and minister to an important class of human wants. And further, as the existence of the economical arrangements, and the undertaking and success of the productive processes of a community, are closely connected with the institutions of civil society, public functionaries become indirect productive assistants.

But here it is important to remark, that the number of those who thus do service for the public, should not be unnecessarily multiplied. If the machinery of civil society become too intricate, or be needlessly extended, this kind of service is obtained by the public at too dear a rate. For besides what is directly paid as a remuneration to public officers, a larger number, than is necessary, is taken from the productive classes of society; and thus, while the burden of supporting public functionaries becomes greater, the number of productive laborers, on whom this burden rests, is diminished. Probably also, the civil affairs of the community are less judiciously and efficiently managed.

The emoluments of public office are often large, in proportion to the remuneration of other services of a similar nature, and as stations of this kind are places of trust and of power, as well as of profit, they are usually sought with much eagerness. This is especially wont to be the case in those governments, where, either in theory or in practice, the voice which decides the amount of remuneration to be received, is that of public functionaries themselves, often with no check on the part of those, from whom the public revenues are derived.

Of Domestic Servants.

There remains one other class of the community, who according to the kind of labor they are called to perform, may be denominated productive, or unproductive laborers. I refer to domestic servants, some of whom are evidently employed in processes, by which material objects are adapted to the supply of human wants, while the services rendered by others receive a different direction. Thus the individual, on whom devolves the culinary processes of a domestic establishment, is a productive laborer, while the coachman and lacquey of the same establishment, are unproductive laborers.

Whether productively or unproductively employed, domestic servants constitute a highly useful class of the community, and contribute largely to the comfort and happiness of society. To some extent, also, they often become indirect assistants in production, since they set free from many cares and labors, those who are productively engaged, and who are thus left free to direct all their time and energies to their own appropriate employments.

The traits of character, which in this class of laborers are high recommendations, entitling those possessing them to confidence and a generous remuneration, are skill, and honesty, and fidelity. And it should ever be remembered, that kind and fair treatment on the part of those employing laborers to assist them in their domestic arrangements and processes, will ordinarily be met with activity and faithfulness on the part of those employed. A good master makes a good servant.

PART II.

DISTRIBUTION AND CONSUMPTION OF WEALTH.

CHAPTER I.

Distribution of Wealth.

The prosperity and happiness of nations are not always in proportion to their wealth. In some communities, where an abundance and variety of products are found, this supply is in the hands of a few, while multitudes—the mass of population, are poor and degraded. To him then, who is inquiring for the causes which are connected with the prosperity and welfare of nations, it is not enough to ask in what way a supply may be furnished for the wants of the great national family. He must also direct his attention to the manner, in which what is thus provided is distributed,—he must shew upon what principles and in what ways, this distribution may be so effected, as to promote the greatest good of the whole, and of each individual.

In looking at the early and more simple stages of society, few inquiries arise respecting the distribution of wealth. Indeed there is little wealth to be distributed. Each one, so far as he is able, makes provision for the supply of his own immediate wants, and small accumulations and few exchanges are effected. So far too as exchanges are made and producers seek a remuneration for their productive services, the basis of these exchanges and of this remuneration, is simply the amount of labor bestowed on each commodity. "If among a nation of hunters," says Smith, "it usually costs twice the labor to kill a beaver which it does to kill a deer, one beaver should naturally exchange for or be worth two deer. It is natural that what is usually the produce of two days' or two hours' labor, should be worth double of what is usually the produce of one day's or one hour's labor.

"If the one species of labor should be more severe than the other, some allowance will naturally be made for this superior hardship; and the produce of one hour's labor in the one way may frequently exchange for that of two hours' labor in the other.

"Or if the one species of labor requires an uncommon degree of dexterity and ingenuity, the esteem which men have for such talents will naturally give a value to their produce, superior to what would be due to the time employed about it. Such talents can seldom be acquired but in consequence of long application, and the superior value of their produce may frequently be no more than a reasonable compensation for the time and labor which must be spent in acquiring them. In the advanced state of society, allowances of this kind, for superior hardship and superior skill, are commonly made in the wages of labor; and something of the same kind must probably have taken place in its earliest and rudest period.

"In this state of things, the whole produce of labor belongs to the laborer; and the quantity of labor commonly employed in acquiring or producing any commodity, is the only circumstance which can regulate the quantity of labor which it ought commonly to purchase, command, or exchange for."

But our attention is to be directed to a more advanced state of society,—one in which few are engaged in making direct provision for the supply of their own wants, and where other agents than human industry, are extensively employed in the work of production. We look on a community, in which the basis on which wealth is distributed, has become more complicated, and where too new divisions and classifications of society have arisen, with mutual relations to each other and with distinct and separate interests and pursuits. Here then in connexion with the distribution of wealth, there opens to us a new and interesting field of inquiry.

One leading principle of great importance as connected with this part of the science of Political Economy, may here be stated and should be kept steadily in view. It is, that wealth should be left to flow in its own natural channels, unchecked and unimpeded. Wherever it is permitted thus to flow, its diffusion becomes most general and salutary ; for it is there, that its little streams are found on every hill-side, in every plain and valley, and the whole region is a well watered land. Under those governments then, where full protection and security are afforded to the rights of person and of property, and where no regulations or institutions exist, inconsistent with the free and natural distribution of wealth, the situation of the different members and classes of the community becomes most favorable. That there are many governments, even at the present day, whose subjects are not thus favorably situated, is well known. In many of the nations of Europe, the rights of primogeniture are recognised, and in connexion, the system of entails; and both these institutions are highly injurious to the best interests of society.* Peculiar privileges are also granted to some classes of the community to the disparagement of others; and thus, in connexion with a system of favoritism, the distinctions of society become more marked, and wealth is not only unequally, but unfairly distributed.

In the statements and reasonings which follow, none of these unfavorable influences are supposed to exist. We look on a community, in which wealth is left to diffuse itself in a manner, which is consistent with the rights of individuals and the principles of the social compact.

Economical arrangement for the distribution of Wealth.

Revenue is what accrues from productive service to those by whom this service is rendered. This productive service may be human labor, and then the returns for it are called wages. It may be rendered by capital, under some one of the numerous forms assumed by capital that it may become productive, and what thus accrues to the owner of this capital, if paid by another, is called interest; otherwise, the profits of capital. Or this productive service may be rendered by land, or some other natural agent, acting in concert with man and under his direction; in this case the revenue yielded to the proprietor of the land, or of other natural agency, if paid by another, is

* On the subject of primogeniture and entails, I would refer the student to an instructive passage in Smith's Wealth of Nations, Vol. I. page 272.

called rent, otherwise, the profits of natural agency. There is yet another kind of productive service, rendered by him who takes upon himself the arranging and conducting of some process of production, and on whom also rests the risk of its success. The returns to this kind of productive service are called the profits of the undertaking, or simply profits. Now it is to these four classes of the community, to the laborer, as wages—to the capitalist, as interest, or profits of capital—to the owner of land, or other natural agency, as rent, or profits of natural agency —and to the undertaker, as profits, that the gross amount of products in a nation are primarily apportioned; and this may be said to be the arrangement, which in an advanced and well ordered community, is established for the distribution of wealth.

It is to be noticed, that the distribution to be made is of the gross amount of products. What uses shall be made of the net products, that is of what remains to the producer after the expenses of production have been met, is a distinct inquiry, and will be considered when treating on the consumption of wealth. I here look at the sum total of whatever is obtained by productive service of every description in the community. It is true, that a portion of what is thus produced is directly consumed by the producer himself, but this portion, in an advanced state of society, is inconsiderable. We may then in theory consider all those engaged in production of every kind, as contributors to this gross amount of products, each one drawing out in return for the productive service rendered by him, that portion, to which he is entitled, and which is received under one of the four forms above stated.

This gross amount of national products is also said to

be primarily apportioned to producers; and this is the case. There is found in every community, a numerous class of unproductive laborers, and there are others, who neither labor nor furnish productive service in any form. These portions of the community, in common with producers, have wants to be supplied, and this supply must come from the gross amount of national products. Still it is true, that the returns of productive service accrue in the first instance to producers, and to them only. These producers give employment to unproductive laborers, and pay over to them in return for these services, a portion of their own revenues. Under some form also, as charity, or a poor tax, these productive classes of the community contribute for the support of those, who are to be ranked as paupers or idlers; and thus it is, that products are ultimately distributed to every member of the community.

Another explanatory remark requires attention. The laborer, the capitalist, the owner of natural agency and the undertaker, are spoken of as constituting distinct classes. To this in theory there can be no objection, but practically, the productive service pertaining to two or more of these classes, is often rendered by the same individual; and consequently the returns to this individual will include two or more of these different kinds of revenue. In agricultural production, the owner of the land is often the undertaker of the work, and perhaps furnishes the capital employed. His revenue will then be made up of rent, profits and interest. In other instances, as often occurs in manufactures and commerce, the same man is undertaker and capitalist. He then receives for his portion both profits and interest. But not unfrequently the classes are found entirely distinct. To illustrate this point, and also to exhibit more fully the economical arrangement which relates to the distribution of wealth, I shall now trace out this distribution in the case of different products.

One employed in the business of production has raised a crop of wheat, suppose 1000 bushels, which is valued at $1,00 per bushel. The wheat produced constitutes a part of the gross amount of national products, and its value in the form of money, we will suppose to be in the hands of the producer, to be divided among those, who have contributed any portion of productive service towards the raising of the crop. The producer is the owner neither of land nor of capital, nor has he taken any part in the labors of the farm. He is the undertaker—that is, he has planned, arranged and conducted the process. He went to the landlord, and for a stipulated sum obtained of him the use of land. He went to the capitalist, and by agreeing to pay the customary rate of interest he obtained capital. He collected laborers, contracting to pay them the usual wages of laborers thus employed. After thus securing the productive service in its different forms needed for the undertaking, he made further arrangements, and took upon himself the over-sight, and conduct, and risk of the whole adventure. And now that the returns are in his hands in the form of money, a distribution is easily made. The stipulated sum, which is the usual amount paid for the use of land of the same quality, is paid to the owner of land as rent; the usual rate of interest is given to the capitalist, for the capital employed, and the laborers receive their portion as wages. What remains of the $1000 belongs to the undertaker as the profits of the adventure.

Take now the example of a manufactured product—a piece of broadcloth. In this instance, the undertaker needs only the productive service of capital and labor. By means of the former, he furnishes himself with the raw material used in this fabric, and with machinery and whatever other helps are needed in conducting the process of production. And here, as before, when returns are received, a portion goes to the capitalist for the productive service of capital, another portion to the laborers as wages, and what remains as profits to the undertaker. But here it is to be noticed, that the principal material of which the broadcloth is composed, is itself an agricultural product, in the furnishing of which a distinct set of productive services have been called into action. So it is with other materials—the drugs used in dying the cloth ; these have been furnished by the productive service of capital and labor, perhaps of appropriated natural agency, and connected with their production, profits have been made by those who have undertaken and conducted it. A portion of the value then received in exchange for the broadcloth, and which is first divided among the laborers and capitalist and undertaker, by whose joint productive services the manufactured product is obtained, is subject to further distribution,—it goes to pay for the productive services of those, by whom the materials used in the manufactured product are furnished. This portion has perhaps been advanced to the producers of these materials, long before the product is in the hands of the consumer. To make these advances, is one part of the productive service rendered by the capital of the manufacturer. Thus it is, that eventually the value of the product is distributed, not only among those employed in its manufacture, but among those, who have furnished the materials of which it is made, or been in any way instrumental in its production.

In the statements which have been made, the returns for productive service are supposed to be made in the form of money. This is not necessarily the case; there may be a distribution of the products themselves in payment for this service. But it is usually found more convenient, both for those who pay, and for those who receive, that these transactions should be conducted by the help of a circulating medium. Soon, however, the money thus received as rent, or interest, or wages, or profits, is exchanged for such commodities, as the individuals receiving it need for the supply of their wants. Thus, in effect, each producer is contributing towards the gross amount of national products, and then, by means of the same productive service, drawing out in return some portion of these products.

But here the question presents itself, what determines the amount to be paid severally to the laborer, the capitalist, the owner of natural agency and the undertaker? In the cases stated, the usual rate is supposed to be paid; but on what principles, and in what manner, does a customary or usualrate become fixed? To this inquiry, and others connected with wages, interest, rent and profits, the attention will be directed in the following chapters.

CHAPTER II.

Wages.

No inquiries in Political Economy are of more practical importance, than those connected with the subject of wages. This results from the fact, that in respect to most commodities, labor is a principal item in the cost of their production, and also from a consideration of the large number in every community, whose interests are involved in these inquiries.

Before entering upon any discussion of the question proposed at the close of the last chapter, as applied to wages, I remark, that in these inquiries, labor is to be regarded as a commodity, the price of which is paid under the form of wages. It is also to be kept in mind, that it is the average price of common labor, with which we are here concerned. I mean the average price of that labor, which is employed in the common branches of production. In some employments the presence of peculiar circumstances so affects the price of labor as to raise it far above the average price of common labor. Of such instances, mention will be made hereafter.

Upon what then does the average rate of wages, or the price of the commodity—labor, depend? And here it is necessary to refer back to the principles, brought to view when treating on price. It was there stated, that the basis of price is the cost of production, while its temporary variations depend on the fluctuations of the market, or the varying influence of supply and demand. If then we look at labor as a commodity, and wish to determine its price, we have to apply the same principles, as are applicable in the case of other commodities. We must first direct our inquiries to the cost of its production, and then see, what influences of the nature of supply and demand affect, as it has been called in respect to other commodities, the cost price.

Viewing labor then as a commodity, what is the cost of its production? I answer, it is what in different communities is consumed in support of laborers and their families. Stating the same proposition under another form, I mean, that the point where there is a tendency of the rate of wages in every community to settle, is determined by what will furnish a support to the laborer and his family, according to the usual style of living in the community. As will be seen presently, supply and demand, and other causes may and will produce variations from this cost price, but it is to this point that the rate of wages tends in every community. Hence it will readily be inferred, that if the style of living which prevails among the laboring population in any country, is either raised or depressed, there will be a correspondent rise or fall in the cost price of labor. So too, if from any cause, the price of the necessaries of life should vary, increasing or diminishing the expenses of the laborer in sustaining himself and his family, a like variation will take place in the cost price of labor. This is seen in those countries, where machines, which have reduced the price of the common articles of life, have been extensively introduced.

But instead of stopping to illustrate and establish these two propositions, let us first look at the influences, which cause a variation from the cost price of labor. And here is brought to our view, what is usually considered the great regulating principle of the rate of wages—the rates between the productive capital of a country and its laboring population. It is the common theory of political economists, that as the amount of productive capital in a nation is large or small, in proportion to the number of laborers, the rate of wages will be high or low. The same proposition, with a slight modification, I would here advance, as expressing the disturbing influence of supply and demand on the cost price of labor. The modification, to which I refer, is, that instead of the whole amount of productive capital, we speak only of that part, which is so directed as to give employment to laborers. The importance of this limitation will be seen, when we look at those countries in which machinery is extensively used.

But it is necessary to be more explicit in the statement and application of this proposition. The demand in this case is the work to be done, and the supply is the number of laborers in the community, ready to undertake this work. By the work to be done, is meant the work, which some one proposes to accomplish, furnishing what is necessary to carry it forward. But capital is what is necessary that work may thus be undertaken and accomplished; and hence it is, that the demand for labor is said to depend on the amount of capital in a community, which is so directed as to give employment to laborers. If from any cause, the amount of this productive capital so directed, is diminished, there will be less work to be done, that is, there will be less demand for labor; and hence, if the laboring population continues the same, the ratio between the demand and supply will vary, and the price of labor will fall. So too, if the amount of capital, giving employment to laborers, remains the same, while from some cause there is a diminution in the number of laborers, the ratio between supply and demand will again be disturbed, and the price of labor will rise. And the converse of these propositions will also hold true. Thus in respect to the commodity—labor, there will be in every country a variation of its price, dependent on the ratio of supply and demand; and this variation will sometimes raise the cost price above the exchangeable price, and sometimes sink it below.

To illustrate and more fully exhibit these statements, I propose to look at the rate of wages in different countries.

In England, the average rate of wages is from twenty pence to two shillings per day. This probably is not far from the cost price of labor in that country, since at this rate, the laboring population can sustain itself, though few are able to make accumulations of capital, and thus rise into a higher class than that of laborers. Looking then at those causes which affect the cost price of labor, we find, that the style of living in England is a style of comfort and abundance, more so than in most neighboring nations. This high style of living has a tendency to raise the cost price of labor; but on the other hand, the price of many commodities used by the laborer, is lower in England, than in most other countries, and this is a counteracting cause, which brings down the cost price of labor. And here we may notice the effects on wages of machinery, when extensively used in a country. The productive capital of England is immense, and were the whole of it so directed as to give employment to laborers, the price of labor would at once rise above its cost price, and above the standard price in neighboring nations. For though the population of England is large, the amount of its whole productive capital in proportion to its population, far exceeds that of any other European nation. The tendency of machinery then, when extensively used, is to reduce the rate of wages. But this disadvantage to the laborer is counterbalanced by the reduction in the cost of many necessary commodities, which also attends the introduction of machinery. The same cause, which lowers the rate of wages, increases their value.

And in this connexion may be mentioned an advantage, which results to a nation from a low rate of wages when compared with other nations. Labor, as has been stated, is a principal item in the cost of production of many products. In those countries, then, where the rate of wages is low, other circumstances being equally favorable, products can be afforded at a lower rate than where the price of labor is higher. And when these nations come into competition in foreign markets, the advantage arising from this circumstance will be felt, since a low rate of wages will give a command of the market. Thus, while the condition of the laborer in England is no less favorable, than it would be with a higher rate of wages if attended with a higher price of the necessaries of life, the cause of production is advanced generally in the country by the low price of labor, which gives to the manufactures of that country an important advantage in foreign markets.

Look next at Ireland. Here the rate of wages is about six pence per day, and this its average rate is below the cost price of labor in that country; for the laboring population of Ireland cannot sustain itself. The style of living is not only reduced to the lowest point possible, but many die of famine, or are compelled to emigrate to other countries. Here then the effect of the principle of supply and demand is most fully felt. The population is dense, and the amount of productive capital giving employment to laborers, is small. The supply of the commodity—labor, far exceeds the demand for it, and its price is reduced.

Look next at the United States. Here the rate of wages is not far from seventy five cents per day. This is above the cost price, for laborers are not only able to support themselves, but large numbers are continually making accumulations of capital and rising from the class of laborers into that of capitalists. Here then the influence of supply and demand are felt; but it is to raise the exchangeable price of labor above its cost price, and not to reduce it below, as in the case of Ireland. It is true, that the productive capital of the United States is not so large, in proportion to its laboring population, as that of England, but a larger part of the capital is so directed as to give employment to laborers. It is true also, that the increase of population in this country is much greater than in England, and this tends to lower the rate of wages; but to counterbalance this greater rate of increase in the population, it should be remembered, that multitudes as just stated, are continually rising from the class of laborers into that of capitalists and land owners; and hence the increase in the class of laborers is not in proportion to the increase of population in the country. Thus it results, that though the style of living of the laboring population in the United States is high, still, as the demand for the commodity—labor is great in proportion to the supply, the rate of wages is higher than the cost price of labor, and higher than in any other country.

The statements and illustrations now given, are sufficient to explain most of the variations which occur in the rate of wages. But before leaving the subject, it may be well to trace out some further consequences, which result from the same causes. Look then first at the community, where, from a reduction in the cost of the necessaries of life, the value of wages has risen, their rate remaining the same. Here, probably, there will eventually follow an increase in the laboring population, for there is a tendency in population always to progress at the same rate with the means of support. But as this result cannot follow till after some years have elapsed, in the mean time the style of living among laborers will be improved; and as men are not prone to reduce their style of living further than is absolutely necessary, some permanent improvement will probably result. Hence, no doubt it is, that in most modern nations the condition of the laboring population has of late years been advancing. The rate of wages has perhaps remained the same, but their value has been increased, and there is a more general enjoyment of the comforts and conveniences of life.

Look next at a community, in which from some cause the style of living is reduced. This reduction may also be attended with an increase of population, especially where the rate of wages continues the same. But generally, a reduction in the style of living is followed by a correspondent fall in the rate of wages. It is always the aim of those who undertake processes of production, and thus are the immediate agents in giving employment to laborers, to reduce wages to the lowest point to which they can be brought, since in this way, the amount of what remains to the undertaker as profits becomes larger. Hence, if the laboring population consent to a reduction in the style of living, it is usually followed by a lower rate of wages. But here it should be noticed, that there is a limit, beyond which it ceases to be for the interest of the undertaker to effect a reduction in the price of labor. For unless the laborer is able to support himself, and to rear up a family, soon the numbers of the laboring population will be diminished, and then, the supply of labor becoming less than the demand, the price will rise. Hence it follows, that it is not for the advantage of any part of the community, that the rate of wages should fall below the cost price of labor—that is, below what is necessary to support in health and comfort the laborer and his family.

And here perhaps it may be well to allude to some of those causes, which lead to variations in the ratio between productive capital and the laboring population in different countries, and thus affect the rate of wages. With this object in view, I offer the following historical illustrations.

We are told, that in the reign of Louis XIV, the opinion prevailed in France, that the laboring classes are benefited by the profuse consumption of commodities. Hence, at that period, the rich indulged in extravagance and dissipation of every kind. Estates, which had been accumulating for many years, were wasted in a few months. But in a short time, the ruinous effects of this course became too obvious to be unnoticed or mistaken. The want of capital was severely felt in different branches of production, many profitable employments were abandoned, and general ruin and poverty threatened the country. The laboring population, who, it had been supposed, would derive benefit from this profusion, found themselves deprived of their usual employment. The supply of labor far exceeded the demand, and the consequence was a reduction of its price.

The plague, which prevailed in London in 1665, is said to have swept off 90,000 inhabitants of that city in a single year ; and a large proportion of this number were laborers. This diminution of the laboring population was immediately followed by a rise of wages. The supply of labor fell short of the demand, and though Parliament, by passing an act for the regulation of wages, endeavored to keep them at the former rate, it was a vain attempt.

About the year 1500, Vasquez de Gama discovered the passage round the Cape of Good Hope, thus opening a new route to the East Indies. The consequences of this important event, and of the discovery of America made about the same time, were immediately felt by all the nations of Europe. A new stimulus was given to every branch of production, and wealth in overflowing streams poured in upon the nations. An important advance was at once made in the condition of laborers. The demand for labor became much greater than before the rate of wages fell, and at the same time, from a reduction in the price of commodities, their value was increased.

Other examples of the same nature, connected with wars, civil revolutions and commotions, and illustrative of the same principle, are found in the history of almost every people.

But there is another circumstance of equal or greater importance to the prosperity of the laborer, than a high rate of wages, or their high value arising from a low price of the necessaries of life. I refer to the opportunity enjoyed by him for the profitable investment of his savings. Where this is the case, the laborer sees constantly before him the prospect of improving his condition, and of rising into a higher class in society, and hence he is led both to more vigorous efforts and to greater frugality. It is on this account that the condition of laborers in the United States is more favorable, than in any other part of the world. Hence, also, the importance of Savings Banks and other similar institutions to the laboring part of a community, might be inferred. But to this topic allusion is made in another place.

Besides the variations in the rate and value of wages which have now been brought to view, there are others arising from a different source, and which, in distinction from the former, are called nominal variations. I refer to those changes in the rate of labor, which are connected with alterations in the value of the circulating medium. And here the same principles are applicable to the price of labor, as have been applied to other commodities. If a depreciation takes place in the value of money, the price of commodities rises, and on the other hand, if the value of money becomes greater, the price of commodities falls. But if the same rise or fall be made in the price of labor, as is made in the price of other commodities, it is evident, that though the rate of wages may vary, their value remains unaltered, and the condition of the laborer is in no way affected; and hence the variation is said to be nominal. Sometimes however it happens, when a depreciation occurs in the value of money, that the rate of wages will continue the same; at least some time will elapse, before the rate of wages becomes adapted to the variation in the value of money. In this case inconvenience and loss arise to the laborer.

And here I remark, that fluctuations in the rate of wages, from whatever source they may arise, are generally injurious to the interests of the laboring population. If there is a sudden depression, the consequent privations and embarrassments are immediately and severely felt. If, on the other hand, there is a sudden but temporary rise, though the laborer finds himself in possession of more ample supplies for a while, the effects which ultimately follow are usually injurious. Either his habits of industry are relaxed, or his style of living is raised to a point where it cannot be sustained, and the reduction of it which follows, is both mortifying and embarrassing. It may then be considered as a settled principle, that the condition of the laborer is most favorable, so far as it depends on the rate of wages, in those communities, where the price of labor continues about the same, with no sudden and temporary fluctuations. Especially is this the case, where the progress of society in arts and wealth is attended with a gradual advancement in the value of wages.

The principles stated in this chapter, are designed to apply to the average rate of the wages of common laborers —those engaged in the ordinary employments of life. There are instances of variation from this average rate already alluded to, and which arise from different circumstances. Some of these circumstances will now be stated.

Skill and talent. For the successful performance of some kinds of labor, a long apprenticeship, or course of previous training is required, which is necessarily attended with expense. A portion of capital thus becomes permanently vested in the laborer himself, and the higher remuneration which he receives for his services, may be looked upon as paid in part for the use of the capital thus vested.

A watchmaker, for example, or any artist, expects on this account to receive higher wages, than a common day laborer. In other instances, the success of the laborer depends on the possession of some peculiar natural endowment, as in the case of the portrait or historical painter, or of the musician. We may look upon such endowments as natural agency of a peculiar kind, of which there is a limited supply. And thus, a part of what is paid under the name of wages, is in fact a remuneration for the use of this peculiar natural agency.

Constancy of employment. In some kinds of work, a laborer can be employed but a part of his time. Hence he expects to receive higher wages for the time during which he is engaged. In cold climates, a mason cannot work at his trade in the winter season, and hence his wages are higher, than those of other mechanics engaged in similar employments. Hence too job-work is paid at higher rates, than when men are steadily employed.

Trust and responsibility. When men are engaged in employments, in which there is much difficulty, or in which a large amount of property is entrusted to their care, and its safety and right management depend on their fidelity and success, their wages are enhanced by this trust and responsibility. It is in part on this account, that the wages of the master of a vessel so much exceed those of any one of his crew.

Numerous other circumstances lead to the same result. Some employments are dangerous,—some are noisome and unpleasant,—some are looked upon as degrading. In these several instances, the remuneration received by the laborer for his services, is greater than the average rate of wages.

On population as connected with Political Economy.

From the statements found in this Chapter, we may learn in what manner the subject of population is connected with Political Economy. It has been said, that the supply of the commodity—labor, will depend on the number of laborers in a community ready to engage in any work of production. The tendency then of an excess of population, must be to diminish the rate of wages, while at the same time, perhaps, from the great demand for the necessaries of life, the value of the small sum received by the laborer is also reduced. Hence poverty and suffering ensue, and population is said to press upon the means of subsistence. And here some political economists, basing their speculations on the different ratio of increase of the means of subsistence, on the one hand, and of population when unchecked on the other, have maintained, that every advancing nation, and indeed the whole human race, is destined to the same disastrous results. The time, say they, will come, when more will be born into the world than can be sustained, and long before that point is reached, the privations and sufferings of men must be great. Indeed they seem to look upon diseases, famine, wars, and other evils which men bring upon themselves by their own rash and vicious indulgencies, as retarding causes in the progress of society to its wretched destination. Other remedies, however, of a more humane and elevated kind, are proposed by this school of political economists. For this purpose they recommend what they term moral checks, including under this term whatever tends to make men more considerate, and to lead them to a more just and enlarged sense of the relative duties of life. Education, as it enlightens the mind and extends its views, and at the same time matures the judgment, is especially enjoined.

Others who have turned their attention to this subject, look to different sources for the prevention or remedy of the evils of an excessive population. Some have maintained, that from the nature of production, every one, however populous the world may become, will be able to sustain himself. Production, say they, is the creation of utility, and it is this utility which is the basis of value. Every one then who is willing to bring productive service of any kind into action, will in return receive what may be required for his support. He will thus draw out for himself some portion of the gross national products. Others look for a remedy in the indefinite extent, to which the accumulation of productive capital may be carried. It is capital, say they, which is the basis of demand for labor, and since capital is unlimited in its extent, it can never be exceeded by the supply. Productive employment will then always be furnished for those disposed to labor.

Whatever opinion may be entertained respecting the speculations of writers on this subject, the following positions may be maintained.

1. The period when the surface of the earth shall be so covered with inhabitants, that population will equal the means of subsistence, is so distant, and all calculations and reasonings relating to this state of things so indefinite and shadowy, that the whole subject is one of no practical importance.

2. Most of the evils which are wont to be ascribed to an excess of population, may be traced to some existing abuses of civil institutions, or to some unwise neglect of

nations to avail themselves of the productive resources within their power. Most of the nations of Europe afford examples of the former kind; China is an instance of the latter.

These propositions are not meant to undervalue the importance of moral checks, or of any measures which are designed and fitted to improve the condition of men, and remove the evils and abuses to which they are exposed. They are merely designed to afford a reason for omitting the further consideration of the question proposed.

CHAPTER III.

Interest, or profits of capital.

Our attention is now to be directed to interest, or that portion of the gross amount of national products, which in the distribution made to producers, is assigned to the capitalist, as the remuneration of the productive service of capital. Of the nature of capital, the different forms which it assumes in the processes of production, and its various uses, I have before treated; and thus the way has been prepared for understanding the nature of interest, and the principles by which its rate is determined.

It is a common impression, and one that needs to be corrected, that interest is a sum of money paid for the use of money. But though for the convenience of those receiving the loan, and the facility of computation, capital is more frequently loaned and interest paid in the form of money than in other forms, neither of these circumstances is essential to the transaction. Capital may be loaned in any of the various forms which it assumes, and it is for the use of capital, and not of money merely, that interest is paid. Interest also is not unfrequently paid in kind, that is, in some portion of the products obtained from the productive service of the capital loaned.

Another remark also requires attention. In the statement of the distribution of wealth to different classes of producers, interest is defined as the remuneration for the use of capital, paid by some one employing it to the owner or capitalist, and thus interest is the same as the profits of capital. But as the term is generally used, it includes not only the remuneration given for the use of capital, but the premium of insurance, for the risk incurred by the lender of receiving again the principal, or capital lent. Hence it is, that in some nations both in ancient and modern times, the rate of interest has been enormously high. Hence, also, the fact, that capital loaned to be employed in branches of production particularly exposed to loss, bears a higher interest, than when no unusual risk is incurred. Thus we are told, that in Athens the usual interest on capital employed in navigation was 60 per cent. But of this per centage, it is supposed by Say, that not more than three or four per cent was paid as a remuneration for the use of capital. The remaining part was a premium of insurance. It is to be noticed then, that in the inquiries on which it is now proposed to enter, relating to the different causes which affect the rate of interest, I look only at what is paid as a remuneration for the use of capital; so that the term interest, as here used, expresses the same as the profits of capital. The rate of interest then is the price paid for the productive service of capital.

Upon what causes then does the rate of interest depend? In answering this question, we are not, as in determining the rate of wages, to ascertain the cost price, and then to explain the variations from this cost price on the principle of supply and demand. Still, there is in this case that which corresponds to the cost price,—a price, which is looked upon in usual circumstances as a fair equivalent for the productive service of capital as employed in the common branches of production, and from which variations are made, as those circumstances occur which require them. Our first inquiry then relates to this original, or primary price, or equivalent for the productive service of capital. Afterwards, the causes which tend to variations from the original price will be brought to view.

For some years after the first settlement of a country, the practice of loaning capital is not introduced. So far as capital is accumulated and made productive, it is usually employed by the capitalist himself, who is also perhaps a laborer, and thus receives what in other circumstances is paid as wages, interest and profits. But now let us suppose, that the individual who has thus accumulated capital, instead of employing his capital himself, entrusts it to another person to be productively employed, and contracts to give in return to him who thus makes it productive, a moiety of what remains after the capital which has been productively consumed, is replaced, and the wages of labor and other charges have been paid,—that is, a moiety of the net profits. In this case, then, the profits of the undertaker are united with the profits of capital, and an equal division is made; and in this way, the amount received by the capitalist as a remuneration for the use of his capital is determined. Soon, however, it is found a preferable arrangement, that he who employs capital, instead of becoming an agent for the owner, should himself bear the responsibility, and have the entire control and direction of the business in which he is engaged. He receives then the capital to be thus employed as a loan, contracting to return it, with an equivalent for its use, at a specified time. And now, in determining this equivalent, the parties interested are governed by what was before paid as the proportion of the capitalist. It is in this way, I apprehend, that the original price paid for the use of capital, or the rate of interest, becomes established; for we find it historically true, that allowing for what is paid as a premium of insurance, and for the influence of other causes of variation, the rate of interest in most countries is about the same, as the profits of those who undertake and conduct processes of production. This is the case in the early periods of national existence, when profits are large, and the rate of interest high, and there is also a gradual reduction of both, as nations become older and more wealthy.

Supposing the usual rate of interest in any country to have become established in the manner that has been stated, we are now to look at those causes, which lead to variations in this usual rate. And here, just as in the variations in the exchangeable price of commodities, the influence of supply and demand is felt. Whenever, from any cause, the supply of capital to be loaned exceeds the demand, the rate of interest will fall; and when the reverse occurs, it will rise. Our attention must then be directed to whatever affects the relative supply and demand of capital. And here it becomes important to state when capital is in the market, constituting a supply, and also, on the other hand, what is meant by a demand. Capital is in the market, when it is in those forms, which admit of its being transferred to others to be employed in processes of production, and when also those holding it, are disposed to yield to others possession of it as a loan. There is a demand for capital, so far as individuals are to be found, who are disposed to receive it and able to offer satisfactory security for its return with the usual remuneration for its use.

The causes, which through the medium of the relative demand and supply of capital affect the rate of interest, are numerous and various, being connected both with national prosperity and adversity. Instead of enumerating these causes, I offer the following statement of principles with a few illustrations.

1. Advances in national prosperity, by increasing the supply of capital in proportion to the demand, tend to diminish the rate of interest.

2. Advances in national prosperity, by increasing the demand for capital in proportion to the supply, tend to raise the rate of interest.

3. Adverse circumstances in the condition of a nation, by reducing the amount of productive capital, thus diminishing the supply in proportion to the demand, may lead to a higher rate of interest.

4. Adverse circumstances in the condition of a nation, by diminishing the demand for productive capital in proportion to the supply, may be followed by a lower rate of interest.

An illustration of the first and second of these principles, is found in the economical history of many nations. In the early stages of national existence, the productive energies of the community are usually brought into vigorous action, and, as simple and frugal habits of living prevail, large accumulations of capital are rapidly made. And as a nation becomes older, if its prosperity continue, accumulations of capital will continue to be made, not so great perhaps as at first, because of the larger proportion of revenues which are unproductively spent. Thus, then, from the increase of capital in every prosperous nation, there will be a constant tendency to a reduction of the rate of interest. And if, as it sometimes occurs, there are seasons of unusual prosperity, in which rapid advances are made in the accumulation of capital, there will be a corresponding tendency to a lower rate of interest. But now let us look at the counteracting influences, which arise from the same source. In prosperous nations, frequent discoveries and inventions are made in the different branches of production, which offer new forms of investing productive capital; and thus a demand arises for a portion of the gradually accumulating supply. Enterprise is continually leading to new branches of business, and ingenuity is devising new and improved modes of production. Agricultural industry is enlarging its domains, bringing new tracts of land under cultivation, and rendering more fertile those already subdued. Manufactures, in their various forms, are furnishing new articles of convenience and luxury, or offering at a diminished price and in greater abundance, those before in use. Commercial industry also is employed in the discovery of new countries, and in openng new and profitable markets. Thus, in connexion with national prosperity, an enlarged demand for capital is continually arising. And hence it is, that for many years, during the most thriving and vigorous portion of a nation's existence, when large accumulations of capital are made, little, if any, depreciation of the rate of interest is witnessed. The larger supply is all absorbed by the increased demand.

So far the causes, which through the influence of relative supply and demand affect the rate of interest, are connected with national prosperity. Let us now look at the effects of adverse circumstances in the condition of a country. By these adverse circumstances I have particular reference to those events and circumstances, which either prove destructive to capital already existing, or prevent its further accumulation. War with its desolating and withering influence, may sweep over a land, laying waste its fields, its manufactures, its workshops and its shipping, consuming and destroying productive capital, wherever, and in whatever forms it may be found. At other times, the same destroyer of national prosperity may be drawing out and sending abroad, in the form of subsidies to foreign armies, that which is designed to give nourishment and support to industry and enterprise at home. But while war thus destroys and exhausts the resources of a nation, other more secret causes may be at work, undermining its greatness. Of this nature, are intemperance and luxurious indulgences of every form. Sometimes also a prevailing propensity to wild and foolish speculation and adventure, will drain off a portion of a nation's capital from its more useful employment, proving ruinous to those more immediately concerned, and injurious to the public welfare. Now it is easily seen, that these adverse circumstances in the condition of a nation, as they lead to the destruction of capital already existing, and also prevent its further accumulation, must diminish the supply of it in the market; and thus, should the de-mand continue the same, the rate of interest will rise. But these same adverse circumstances may also eventually produce the oposite effect; by diminishing the demand for capital, they may lead to a depression in the rate of interest. For while war destroys and consumes the productive capital of nations, it also draws off many of their inhabitants from the industrious occupations, in which they had been previously engaged. Many laborers it also cuts down and brings to a premature grave. Intemperance too, and other vicious indulgences, impair the energies, and prove injurious to the enterprizing and industrious habits of the laboring population. Other adverse circumstances, connected with the civil polity of a country and the administration of public affairs, lead to the same results. Where there is a want of confidence in the national government, either as to its stability or as to the wisdom of its measures, leading capitalists to feel insecure in their investments, or those engaged in different processes of production, to fear, lest by some change of public measures they may be subjected to disappointment and loss in their enterprises,—such want of confidence will tend to diminish the demand for capital. Undertakers and laborers will be less ready to engage in the adventures and labors of production, and instead of a progress in national wealth, the movement will be retrograde. All these adverse circumstances then, and others of a like nature, as they tend to diminish the demand for capital in proportion to the supply, will lead to a fall in the rate of interest.

From this statement of the different causes which affect the rate of interest, it will be readily seen, that here is no ground, on which conclusions can be made respecting the prosperity of nations. We have seen, that the same results follow from directly opposite causes. The rate of interest may be lower because a nation has advanced in prosperity and wealth;—its fall may also be the sign of national impoverishment and decay. Again, the rate of interest may rise because the capital of a country has been wasted and its resources exhausted by war, or by vicious indulgencies and ruinous speculations. It may rise also as a nation becomes more prosperous and thriving.

Another inference which we are led to make, and which is supported by facts, is, that these counteracting and conflicting causes will so operate, that the variation of the rate of interest during a long period—a century or more, will be inconsiderable. Some of the causes mentioned, or others of a like nature, may produce a temporary elevation or depression, but except a very gradual diminution which attends the advancing age of the nation, no perceptible and abiding change is effected. Such is the usual course of events. The discovery of a new country, the opening of a new market, or the introduction of a new and important branch of production, or any important event of rare occurrence, will be followed by unusual consequences.

Ought the rate of interest to be fixed by legal enactments?

The inference stated in the last paragraph, leads us at once to the conclusion, that such interference on the part of the government of a country is unnecessary. If, in the usual course of things, the average rate of interest will remain unaltered for many years, it would seem, that this is sufficient reason, why the government of a country need not interfere in its regulation. But the principle, on which the decision of the proposed question should be based, is the following;—that every member of the community has an undoubted right to make use of his own property for his own advantage, provided, that in so using it he does no injury to others and to the public good. We have seen, that the productive service of capital is worth more, and when left to itself bears a higher price at one time than at another. Now who shall reap the benefit of this advance in its value. No one certainly has a fairer claim to it than the capitalist, and to deprive him of this advantage by law, is an unwarranted infringement on his right of property, unless it can be shewn, that the public good requires that such restrictions should be imposed. And here in fact is the point at issue.

The laws of usury prohibit the capitalist from receiving more for the productive service of his capital, than a prescribed rate of interest. They do not, and they cannot, secure to him this amount. Of course, such laws are for the benefit of the borrower only. Indeed it is their professed design to secure the borrower against extortion on the part of the lender. Hence they are defended on the ground, that the public good requires, that in the case of the loan of capital, the exception, stated in the last paragraph, to the great principle of the right of use of property, should take effect. To support this position, some striking cases are usually brought forward. Suppose, it is said, a young spendthrift would anticipate his patrimony. He goes to the money lender, and by the offer of extravagant interest obtains large sums, which are soon squandered in vicious indulgencies. And thus, when this heir perhaps of a rich and ancient family succeeds to his ancestral estate, he is broken down in his constitution and impoverished in his fortune, which has gone to be added to the heaps of some sordid miser. Or suppose some young adventurer of sanguine temperament, full of wild schemes and half formed plans of business, to be just entering upon his career. He feels at once the necessity of capital, of which perhaps he is himself destitute. He too has recourse to the money lender, and to effect his purpose, makes to him proposals of a rate of interest, three or four times larger than the ordinary profits of business will enable him to pay. But this course of rash and foolish adventure is soon run, while ruinous consequences result to the adventurer himself, and to others, whom, perhaps by the aid of the capital thus obtained, he has duped. The public too is injured, in what is thus done to impair credit and to disturb the regular and prosperous course of business transactions. And while all this evil has been sustained, the avaricious capitalist alone has been benefitted. Spider like, he has taken care so to spread out his net, that the rash animal buzzing about him, shall become his prey.

Another case is supposed. Here is an individual who is industrious and enterprising. He is skilful in conducting his business, and his calculations and plans are cautiously and judiciously made. But he has been unfortunate—has been subjected to unexpected losses, and is threatened with bankruptcy and ruin. Still his affairs are not so desperate but that they might be retrieved. Could he obtain a loan of capital at the usual rate, his insolvency might be prevented, and he might be enabled to provide for himself and his family. In this desperate state of his affairs, he resorts to the money lender with an offer of extravagant interest, and though the day of his ruin may for a short time be deferred, it is made doubly sure.

By these and similar statements, designed to shew, that the public good requires, that such extortion with its ruinous consequences to those immediately concerned, should be prevented, the policy of laws regulating the rate of interest is supported. The case is thought to be made out, that there is reason for a departure from the principle, which it is allowed ought to be recognised in the use of property.

On the other side of the question, it is said, that allowing the suppositions made to be correct, and that such instances of extortion occasionally occur, they do not justify a violation of the rights of property. The profligate minor would probably waste his estate a few years later, should he be prevented from so doing in his minority. And the rash adventurer would no doubt find some other way, in which he might run his career of folly, should that which has been described be closed to him. And as to the unfortunate individual whose affairs are embarrassed, it will ordinarily be the case, that if he is an honest man and his fortunes are not desperate, he will find those who will assist him on fair and honorable terms. If they are desperate, it is no object to defer his bankruptcy.

It is further said, that laws regulating interest are injurious to those they are professedly designed to benefit, since they increase the difficulties of obtaining loans when urgently needed. Those bent on dissipation and extravagance, and determined to obtain loans at any rate, will find no difficulty in evading the laws, while the fact that such laws exist, furnishes some pretext to the extortioner for the course which he adopts. He knows, that as a violater of law he is liable to penalties, and looks upon a part of what he receives under the name of interest, as of the nature of insurance for the risk that he runs. As to the unfortunate individual who is threatened with bankruptcy, it is far better for him, that he should be left to obtain assistance on the most favorable terms he can find. He may be obliged to pay more than the usual rate, but such may be his circumstances, that a loan thus obtained may be advantageous to him. Thus it would be for the benefit of the borrower and of the community, that no laws should exist upon the subject, but that the rate of interest should be determined by the barterings of the market, in the same manner as the price of commodities generally becomes fixed. In extraordinary cases—when the capital loaned is destined to be employed in some unusually hazardous branch of business, or when the borrower is in embarrassed circumstances, and on this account the lender is exposed to loss, something more than the usual rate of interest may be paid, not strictly as higher interest, but as a premium of insurance. And as in this case such transactions would be open and fair, no ground of complaint would be found. Still there would be a necessity, that some rules should exist for the adjustment of interest claims on debts long due, and where no terms had been agreed upon by the parties concerned. Such cases would often occur in the settling of estates, and in the balancing of long standing accounts. But for all such cases, the laws might provide, and yet leave free the rate of interest in the common business transactions of the community.

On Stocks and Stock-jobbing.

There is a mode of loaning capital, which differs in some respects from the usual transactions of this nature between individuals. It is loaning to some public body —the authorities of a country, or a city, on the condition and with the expectation, that the securities given for repayment of what is thus loaned may be transferred to others, and thus become what is termed negotiable. In some cases also, there is no expectation on the part of the capitalist of ever receiving again the principal, or what is thus advanced as a loan. Public securities of this nature are called stocks, and in countries where capital is abundant, trading in stocks, or stock-jobbing, often becomes an important branch of business.

Loans in this form are preferred by capitalists, 1. Because of the safety of the investment. The public faith is pledged for the redemption of securities of this nature; and though in some instances failures have occurred, capital is thought more safe when thus loaned, than when it is in the hands of private individuals. 2. Another recommendation of this form of loaning capital is, that what is thus loaned continues to be disposable property. He who loans to an individual, usually places his property loaned, for a time at least, out of his own control. But stocks are ever in the market, and the owner of them may at any time realize their value in the currency of the country. 3. A third circumstance which recommends public securities to large capitalists, is the magnitude of the transaction and the permanency of the investment. He who has his hundreds of thousands or his millions to loan, is thus relieved from much perplexity and labor.

From these considerations, capitalists are usually willing to receive a lower rate of interest on investments in the form of stocks, than on what is loaned on private security. And some maintain, that important advantages arise to a government from its being indebted in this way to the rich and influential members of a community, since such individuals thus become strongly interested in its support. On this account it is sometimes said, that a national debt is a national blessing. England, whose debt is now immense, is supposed to owe the permanency of her institutions and the stability of her government, in no small degree, to this source.

The variations in the value of stocks, on which the stock-jobbing business is based, arise from the various causes, which affect the stability of governments and the prosperity of nations. The breaking out of a revolution, or any event, which brings a cloud over the prospects of a country and threatens it with coming evils, lowers the price of its stocks. Again, the dawning of a brighter day, in which quiet and security and national prosperity are looked for, is followed by a corresponding improvement of public securities. All these indications are early seen and calculated upon by the stock-jobber, and serve as the basis of transactions in the stock market.

Important advantages arise to nations from these transactions in those times of difficulty, when it becomes necessary to provide for national defence. Formerly, when the liberties of a people, or even their existence, were threatened by a foreign foe, the reigning power was compelled to resort to violent and often injurious measures, to obtain the means of self defence. Private property to a great extent ceased to be respected,—great inroads were made on the capital of the nation, and serious injury done to its economical interests. Now, the exigences of these occasions are met by a loan, and the revenues of the nation for future years, are pledged for the payment of what is thus obtained for its defence in the hour of its need. It must however be allowed, that at the same time an attending evil has arisen, since these increased facilities for obtaining the needed supplies of a time of war, have enabled the ambitious and the restless, to embroil the nations under their sway in expensive and useless wars.

CHAPTER IV.

Rent, or the profits of natural agency.

That natural agency may become the property of individuals, so far as its nature will admit of appropriation, and consulting the interests of society, may be thus appropriated, was shewn in the chapter on Economical Arrangements. With this proposition, another is closely connected—that the owners of natural agency are entitled to a remuneration for its productive service. Hence, in the distribution of the gross amount of national products, a portion is assigned to the owner of land and other natural agents; and our inquiries in the present chapter relate to the principles, on which this amount is determined.

What is received by the owners of natural agency in return for its productive service, may be termed the profits of natural agency; but if, as is often the case, another individual is permitted to make use of this productive service for his own benefit, the remuneration made to the owner, is paid under the name of Rent. Hence, as in the case of interest and the profits of capital, rent and the profits of natural agency, are to be looked upon as the same in their nature and amount. I shall therefore, as it is more usual to speak of rent than of the profits of natural agency, make use of the former term in the present chapter.

It will be noticed also, that I treat principally of the rent of land. I do so, because other kinds of natural agency are comparatively of small importance, and the principles applicable to land are of general application. I have too in view, when treating of the rent of lands, the rent of corn lands, or lands used in raising the common agricultural products of the country.

And here I would call the attention to the distinction, made in the first chapter of this work, between natural agency and the aids of nature. In the latter case, where it is meant, that the properties of material objects are made subservient by human ingenuity and skill to the work of production, the return for the productive service of these aids of nature, is in the form of interest, or the profits of capital,—that is, the objects in which these properties, thus made useful, are found, are among the different objects, or forms which capital assumes, that it may become productive. Hence, as in the case of other forms of invested capital, the remuneration for productive service becomes, as before stated, the profits of capital. But in instances where the phrase natural agency is applied, the productive service is rendered directly by the natural agent itself, and the remuneration for this productive service is rent, or the profits of natural agency.

To illustrate this distinction, we may look at a steam engine. In this complicated piece of machinery, the aids of nature are under various forms called into use. Thus the properties of the different metals and woods employed in constructing the machine, and of the fire and water used in generating the steam, are all distinct instances of the aids of nature, made subservient to the purposes of production by the ingenuity and labor of man. But so far as those aids of nature can be appropriated, or any returns be made to their owners for the productive service rendered, it is only as the different objects in which these properties are found, can be appropriated. Hence, then, as before stated, the objects in which these useful properties are found become objects of value,—forms in which capital is invested, and the remuneration made for the service rendered, is the return for the service of capital. But now look at a tract of land, which either itself by a spontaneous effort yields products useful to man, or under human guidance and skill yields similar products, but in greater abundance and of superior quality. Here is natural agency—a distinct species of productive service claiming for itself its own remuneration, and which is rendered under the name of rent.

But here instances may occur to some, in which capital is exchanged for land. An individual, who receives an inheritance in the form of money, gives it in exchange for a farm. Hence it may be thought, that as his capital has now assumed the form of land, the return received for the productive service of his farm, should be included under the head of the profits of capital. But here it is to be remembered, that the capital, which in the form of money has been given in exchange for land, still exists in its original form in the hands of the individual to whom it was paid, or of some other one who has received it from him, and, if productively employed, yields interest, or the profits of capital. So too the land which has been purchased, yielded to its former possessor a return for its productive service under the form of rent, and it continues to yield the same return, and under the same name, to its new owner. There is then in the community the same amount of capital paying interest, and of natural agency paying rent, as before, the ownership of each being changed.

And here I remark incidentally, that individuals are often found, making the exchange of money, or capital in other forms, for land, even when the revenue received as rent from the land thus purchased, falls short of what is received as interest on the capital given in exchange for it. They are willing to receive a smaller revenue, either on account of the greater security of property in the form of land, or of the pleasure found in the conducting of a farm, or of the greater respect and consideration, which in most countries are attached to landholders.

After these preliminary remarks, we are prepared to enter on the examination of the principles, on which the amount to be paid as rent, or a remuneration for the productive service of land or other natural agency, is determined.

In newly settled countries, where are found rich and extensive tracts of land, with few to occupy and cultivate them, and where most of the inhabitants are themselves agricultural producers, furnishing supplies of this class for their own wants, though land may be appropriated, no rents will be paid. Soon however, this ceases to be the case ; rents will be paid, and as the community continues to make progress in numbers and in wealth, both the amount of land paying rent will become greater, and the rate of rents will advance, till eventually, no land is found within the territorial limits of the nation, for which rent is not demanded and received. But as during this progress some lands yield a rent to their owners, while others do not, the question arises, what leads to this difference ? I answer, that rent will be paid on those lands from which the returns received are sufficient to pay the expenses of their cultivation and to leave a surplus. The expenses of cultivation include both the outlay of capital and labor and the usual profits of the undertaker. Land which does not pay the expenses of cultivation, will of course be left uncultivated. Land which pays these expenses and nothing more, will not be cultivated, unless the owner, from motives of convenience, is willing to forego remuneration for the productive service of his land ; of course it can pay no rent. But, as before said, land yielding a return, which both pays the expenses of cultivation and leaves a surplus as a remuneration for the productive service of natural agency, will be cultivated; and if occupied and made productive by any other person than its owner, will enable him who thus occupies and possesses it, to pay a rent for its use. Here then we see what it is which lays the foundation of rent; it is the surplus which remains to the cultivator of land, after the usual expenses. Evidently then, in order to determine the rate of rent, we have in the first place to look at the circumstances, which in different cases will affect this surplus, and cause it to vary both in its amount and its value.

And first let us suppose, that rent is paid to the owner of land in the form of agricultural products. In this case, then, our inquiry respecting the rate of rent, assumes the following form: What proportional part of the agricultural products obtained by the cultivation of any tract of land, is to be assigned as a surplus for the payment of rent? And here, I know of no better way of stating the question, than by resorting to the language of Arithmetic. Let us then call the total amount of products obtained, the *minuend*,—the deduction, to meet the outlay of cultivation and the usual profits of agricultural production, the *subtrahend*, and the surplus, or proportional part of the products respecting which we inquire, the *remainder*. Now then it is evident, that whatever causes affect the minuend, making it either greater or less, will affect the remainder in a corresponding manner and degree. So again, whatever causes affect the subtrahend, making it greater or less, will in like manner as before, affect the remainder. We are then, in order to determine the amount of the proportional part of products, which forms the remainder, or surplus, or rent in kind of any tract of land, to look, 1. At the causes which affect the total amount of agricultural products obtained from the land, and 2. At those causes, which affect the outlay of its cultivation and the usual rate of agricultural profits. And at these causes, I now propose to look.

Upon what, then, does the total amount of products obtained from the cultivation of land depend? I answer, primarily and principally upon the fertility of the soil, whether this fertility be original, or whether it arise in part from the more permanent improvements of cultivation. Hence no doubt it is, that in newly settled countries, the first rents are paid for the productive service of the most fertile tracts of land. And so, ever afterwards, those lands yielding the largest returns will continue to pay the highest rents, unless other circumstances hereafter to be mentioned, prevent.

And here I remark, that improvements of the soil which are of a permanent kind, after they have once been made, and the capital and labor thus expended have become united with the land, are ever after looked upon as of the nature of natural agency; and accordingly a rent is paid for them. Thus a tract of land, which this year yields only sufficient to meet the expenses of its cultivation, with no surplus for rent, may in a subsequent year, from the permanent amelioration and improvement of its soil, yield a large surplus, and of course pay a corresponding rent. The permanent improvements made upon it, raise it into the rank of superior soils, and its owner is thus enabled to obtain a rent for land, which otherwise would have yielded no rent.

We are now to look at those causes, which affect the *subtrahend*, as the case has been stated. And here the amount of outlay, both of labor and capital, which is required for the cultivation of the land whose rate of rent we are considering, is to be taken into the account. Some tracts of land are far more easily cultivated than others. The labor necessary to obtain from them the annual crop, and the amount of dressings and other annual improvements, are both less than are required by other tracts. Of two farms of the same number of acres, employed in raising the same kind of agricultural products, and yielding the same total amount, one may be cultivated at an expense less by one third, than is required for the cultivation of the other. It is evident then, that in this case the remainder, or surplus, which is to be paid as rent, will vary.

Let us now suppose equal amounts of products to be received from two equally fertile tracts of land, and also that the amount of labor and of capital required for their cultivation is the same, but that either wages, or the rate of interest paid for the capital employed, or both these items in the cost of production, are for some reason higher in one case than in the other. Here again is another cause, which will affect the surplus, or remainder; for if the price, either of labor or of capital, be higher, a larger proportion of the total amount of products will be required for the payment of these items, and of course the surplus remaining will to a corresponding extent become less. This case is to be carefully distinguished from the preceding. In the former case, the amount of labor and capital required for the cultivation of the two tracts of land, was supposed to vary, the price of labor and of capital remaining the same. In the latter, the variation is in the price of labor and capital, the amount of each required being the same.

There yet remains one other statement to be made. What is deducted from the whole amount to meet the outlay of capital and labor, is first received in the form of agricultural products. But to pay the wages of laborers and the interest of capital, it must be sold. But it may be, that the price of agricultural products is less in the region where one of these tracts of land is situated, than in the neighborhood of the other. Here, then, supposing the total amount of products in the two cases to be the same, and also that both the amount and the price of labor and capital, required for the cultivation of the two tracts of land, are the same, there still is ground for a difference in the surplus, arising from a difference in the price of agricultural products.

To bring the different circumstances which have now been enumerated into one view, I offer the following illustration ;

A. and B. are two landholders, who possess tracts of land of the same number of acres, situated in neighboring towns. We will suppose the land of each to be occupied by tenants, and to be used in raising the same kinds of agricultural products, on the condition, that the rent to be paid in both cases, is the surplus, which remains, after the expenses of cultivation and the usual profits of farming have been deducted from the total amount of products raised. The following are circumstances, which may cause a variation in the amount of this surplus.

1. Owing to a difference in the fertility of the two tracts of land, the total amount of products obtained from one of them may be greater than that received from the other.

2. The cultivation of one farm may be easier and less

expensive, than the cultivation of the other, requiring less labor and capital.

3. Supposing the amount of labor and of capital required in the two cases, to be the same, the rate of wages or of interest may vary.

4. There may be a difference in the price obtained for the portion of the agricultural products, sold to meet the expenses of cultivation.

It has been shewn, that each of these four circumstances may lead to a variation in the surplus, which is to be paid as rent. I should also add, that should there be any difference in the profits of agricultural production in the two towns, here will be another circumstance leading to the same result. But ordinarily, it will be the case, that in the same neighborhood, the profits of the same branch of industry will not vary.

In the statements which have been made, it has been supposed, that the remuneration made for the productive service of land, is a certain proportional part of the products raised by him, who occupies and cultivates the land. But rent is more frequently paid in the form of money. Here then we are still further to take into the account those circumstances, which affect the price of agricultural products; for if the price of commodities is high, the surplus, which is appropriated for the payment of rent, will be sold for a larger sum. On the contrary, if the price of agricultural products is low, the rent, if paid in money, must to a corresponding degree be reduced.

The price of agricultural products is determined by the same principles, as regulate the price of other commodities; and these principles have already been brought to view in the former part of this work. But there is one circumstance pertaining to agricultural products, which in this connexion requires a distinct consideration. I refer to their vicinity to a market. Products of this class are for the most part bulky and some of them perishable. Hence they are with difficulty and with much expense transported to a distance, so that from this cause their price, or value when exchanged for money, will be much affected. This consideration, it will be remembered, has already come to view, as one of the circumstances, determining the surplus, or remainder, which itself is rent, if rent be paid in kind. It is again to be regarded, now that this surplus is to be exchanged for money, with which the payment of rent is to be made.

The circumstance then of proximity to a market, becomes of leading importance among those causes, which determine the rate of rent. Such is the result to which we are led by our reasonings, and this result is fully corroborated by facts. It is well known that a farm in the neighborhood of a sea-port town, or any populous city, is rented at a much higher rate, than a farm of equal extent and fertility in the interior of the country, far removed from a market. Hence also it is, that the opening of a canal, or a railway, connecting a part of the interior of a country with its principal towns, affects the rate of rent throughout the whole region in which it is located. And still further, it is on this account, that the rate of rent is sometimes affected by the kind of agricultural product, to the raising of which a farm is adapted. Thus a tract of land in the interior of a country, which is well adapted to the raising of sheep, may yield a small rent to its proprietor, when other lands in the same neighborhood better suited to the raising of grain, will pay no rent.

I have now only to add to all the other circumstances, which have been mentioned as affecting the rate of rent, the influence of supply and demand. But it will here be noticed, that the rate of rent thus far considered, is what may be called the natural price of the productive service of land,—what corresponds to the cost-price, as this term is applied to other commodities. So far then as supply and demand produce variations from this natural price, he who takes a lease of the land, gives more or less than he can afford to give, paying the expenses of cultivation and retaining for himself the usual profits of agricultural production. Hence then it will be inferred, that the effect of supply and demand on the rate of rents, will be restricted to narrow limits, especially so far as this influence tends to raise the rate of rents; for in proportion as the profits of agricultural production are thus raised, the motive to take leases of land and engage in this department of production, is diminished. I will merely add on this topic, that by supply, is meant the amount of land, which land-holders are willing to lease to others on fair and reasonable terms, and by demand, the applications for land to be thus occupied and cultivated.

CHAPTER V.

Profits of the Undertaker.

Of the several portions, into which the gross products of a nation are primarily distributed, one yet remains to be considered—the profits of the undertaker, or manager. The term profits, is applied to the returns yielded both to the landholder and the capitalist for the productive service of land and capital. Thus we speak of the profits of land, and also of the profits of capital. But when the word profits is used alone, it is to be understood as denoting the profits of the undertaker. If the same individual, who undertakes and manages a process of production, is the owner of the capital, or of the land employed, then the profits of the undertaker will be united with the profits of the capitalist, or of the landholder. But, as is sometimes the case, if the undertaker possesses neither capital nor land, but obtains both from others, paying interest and rent, then the portion which he receives becomes distinct, being the remuneration for the productive service which he renders.

If now we look at the nature of the productive service thus rendered by the undertaker, we find that it is labor of a peculiar kind and accompanied with varying degrees of responsibility or trust. In considering then the remuneration made for this kind of productive service, we are naturally led to direct our attention to the two particulars mentioned—the labor and the responsibility. But so far as profits include a remuneration for labor, we are in determining the rate of profits to be guided by the same general principles as regulate the wages of common labor. And here, to learn the modifications and exceptions of these principles, we may look at the influence of supply and demand, more especially at those causes, which limit the supply and thus tend to raise the price of this species of labor. The most important of the causes are the following; 1. The undertaker must be able to furnish from his own resources, or to obtain from others on his good credit, the capital which he needs. To do this, he must either possess property himself, or sustain a reputation for intelligence, good management and honesty. This circumstance tends in no small degree to limit the supply. 2. There is further needed to constitute a good undertaker, a combination of qualities, rarely found united in the same individual. He should possess an unusual share of foresight and calculation, that his plans may be well laid. He must also exhibit perseverance and constancy of purpose in carrying his plans into execution. Often too he is called upon to superintend and direct the efforts of others, and to execute this office well, he needs both discretion and decision of character. There is required also, to conduct some branches of production successfully, much knowledge, both of the state of the world generally, and of the details of particular employments and pursuits. Now all these various requisites tend to limit the supply, and consequently to raise the rate of the remuneration of this species of productive service; and were there no other circumstances to be taken into the account, this limitation of the supply, would alone lead to an important difference between the wages of the common laborer and of the undertaker.

We are next to look at the responsibility which rests upon the undertaker. This responsibilty is often great, arising in part from the amount of property concerned, and in part from the risk of success; and it is thought reasonable, that a remuneration should be received for its assumption, proportional to its greatness. But in this case, from the nature of the circumstances to be regarded, it is difficult by the application of any principles, to measure the influence which will be exerted on the rate of profits; still the effects of this cause are recognised and deemed important. Here, indeed, is one principal ground of distinction between the rate of profits in different branches of production. Thus the labor of the agricultural undertaker is usually more toilsome and longer continued, than that of the commercial undertaker, but if, as is usually the case, the amount concerned and the risk run, be much greater in the latter instance than in the former, the profits will be proportionally higher.

CHAPTER VI.

Fees and Salaries.

In the preceding chapters, the attention has been directed to the distribution of wealth among the different classes of productive laborers, in the form of wages, interest, rent and profits. This may be regarded as its primary distribution. It is still further apportioned out to other classes of the community, who, though unproductively employed, as that term has been defined, are still contributing to the enjoyments and prosperity of the nation. These unproductive classes receive a remuneration for their services, under the name of fees, salary, and sometimes the more general term compensation; and it is proposed, in this chapter, to consider the further distribution of wealth, as it is affected in these different ways.

Of Fees.

By a fee, is meant a recompense for services rendered, the amount of which is either determined by law, or by the agreement of those interested. It is in this form, that the revenues of lawyers and physicians are received, and also of some public functionaries.

Legal Fees. The compensation of most public functionaries, and in some instances of lawyers, is fixed by statute. The services thus rendered are acts of civil power, and those who render them are to be regarded as agents, by whose instrumentality the authority of the State is brought to the aid of individuals in their private transactions. Hence the propriety of determining their compensation by law, and hence also a portion of what is thus received, usually goes under some form into the public treasury. It is also obvious, that this course is not only reasonable and just on the part of the government, but beneficial to those, by whom these public agents are employed and paid. For otherwise, since services of this nature are by law made absolutely essential in many instances, it would be in the power of those by whom they are performed, to make exorbitant exactions of their employers. I refer in this remark to conveyances, writs and other legal instruments.

In determining the amount of legal fees in different cases, the government is accustomed to take into consideration the nature of the service rendered, as it is difficult or easy—the responsibility incurred, and the time occupied. Reference is also had to constancy of employment ;—for an occasional service the fee is higher, than for one of more frequent recurrence, especially, if for the performance of this occasional service it be necessary to support an expensive establishm nt, or to refrain from other employments. The rate of legal fees, will also be affected to some extent by the prevailing style and expenses of living, in different sections and parts of the country.

Customary Fees. In by far the greater number of instances, the fees of professional men are determined by custom, that is, by a rate of compensation, which is the common or prevailing remuneration of similar services in the neighborhood, or through the same section of the country. Thus, though the fees of lawyers and physicians in the city and in the country, or in the remote parts of the same national territory, may differ, an average rate is in each instance found, and such are called customary fees.

The principles, on which the amount of the customary fees of professional services is determined, are evidently the same, as relate to the wages of productive laborers ;—we are to look at the cost of production, and at the modifying influences of supply and demand. But the cost of production in this case, relates not only to the expenses of living ; it includes also the time and capital expended by professional men, preparatory to the services which they render. It should also be remembered, that the permanency of the investment is in this case dependent on the continuance of life; and hence, the rate of interest to be received, should be calculated on the principles of life annuities.

The risk of success is another circumstance, which is taken into account in determining the average compensation of professional services. Of those who enter on this course of life, some fail to acquire the confidence of the public, and to find employment adequate to their support. The want of mental capacity, or some peculiarity, either in the constitution of their minds or in their habits, disqualifies them for rendering the services required, and they are compelled to abandon the undertaking with the loss of their time and capital. This risk of success then, entitles those who succeed to a higher remuneration.

Extra Fees. Individuals in the different professions are accustomed to receive extra fees, as a remuneration for their services—that is, a compensation over and above the customary rate; and it is well understood, that the compensation in such cases is for services of a superior order. What is thus paid in excess of the customary fee, may either be looked upon as a gratuity on the part of him by whom it is paid, evincing his confidence in the superior powers and attainments of the individual employed by him, or as the higher price of a commodity, arising from its limited supply; since the services of one who is distinguished as a lawyer, or physician, will be in extensive demand, and thus the price of such services will be enhanced by competition.

It is evidently for the public good, that the services of professional men should in this way be left to command any price, which those making use of them are disposed and able to pay. Were it otherwise, the strong motive, which now exists to make those attainments and acquire that superiority, which it is highly important to the public should be found among its professional laborers, would be wanting. It is also generally the case, that this superiority has been attained by many years of painful and strenuous effort, and perhaps of a large outlay of capital, or it is the result of much experience—the long practice of a profession, and by one, who has been gifted by nature with more than ordinary powers. In this view, then, there is a well founded claim for higher compensation.

What has now been said on the subject of fees, may tend to remove a prevailing impression, that the services of professional men receive an extravagant compensation. So far as the rate of fees is fixed by statute, if they are too high, it is manifestly the fault of the government; for the fee thus paid is of the nature of a tax imposed by the government on its subjects. So far as the rate of fees is customary, it rests on the same principles, by which the wages of productive laborers are determined. So far as fees are above the customary rate, they are a gratuity, which it is for the advantage both of the public and of those more immediately interested, should be given. In neither case, then, is there ground of complaint. It is further to be considered, that if some professional men acquire wealth by their labors; many remain poor, and not a few are compelled to abandon the course of life, they have attempted to pursue. In this view of the subject, the average compensation of professional labor is far from being extravagant. Besides, it is to be remembered, that what is paid to the lawyer, or the physician, for a service rendered in five or ten minutes, perhaps only a few words of advice, is not simply a remuneration for the time and effort required to give this advice, but for what it has cost to attain the knowledge and skill, necessary to give it, and for the responsibility, which is in this way assumed.

Salaries.

A salary is a fixed compensation for labor, paid at stated periods. It implies a stipulation on the one part to render certain services, and on the other, to pay in a form and at times specified, a certain amount of value. If, in the agreement thus made, nothing is said of the form in which the salary is to be paid, it is understood to be in the currency of the country. Sometimes also the times of payment are not specified, but are left to be regulated by the prevailing custom, which may be to pay annually, semi-annually or quarterly.

And here it may be asked, why in certain instances the services of professional men are remunerated in this form, while in other cases a fee or daily compensation is given? The ground of distinction is, that where a salary is paid, the services thus remunerated are rendered to the public, or to some associated portions of it, and in other instances to an individual. It is true that the public, and the society thus receiving the services of the professional laborer, is made up of individuals, who are thus benefitted in their individual capacity, still he who is thus employed, ministers to the whole community, and each one avails himself, so far as he pleases, of the assistance afforded. Thus the teacher of a school, or of a religious society, is in the employment of the whole school, or society ; still, it is as individuals, that the members of these communities derive benefit from their services.

In looking at the nature of this mode of remunerating professional services, it will be seen, that it is in the stipulation to pay a definite sum at stated periods, more than in any other respect, that it differs from remuneration in other forms. At least, the principles on which the amount of salary is determined, are the same. There is a reference to the cost of production, that is, to the expenses of living in the style, which prevails in similar classes of the community. The expenses of education, including the outlay both of time and capital in preparing to render the services specified, are also taken into the account, and the return for this outlay is calculated on the principles of a life annuity. In particular instances also, great endowments and uncommon attainments command a salary which exceeds the usual rate.

The principal advantages which arise from this form of compensation, are the following ; On the part of the employers, it gives a command over the services of those employed by them for an extended, perhaps an unlimited period, which in many instances it is highly important to acquire. On the other hand, it enables those who are thus remunerated, to make their calculations and arrangements, both as to their means of support, and the employment of their time and the direction of their energies, with greater definiteness and certainty. The public also are benefitted, for when men have before them stations of usefulness and of competency, if not of affluence, to which they may aspire, they are led to make greater efforts and seek higher attainments, than would otherwise be the case; and thus, whether those thus remunerated are public officers, or professional laborers, the community is more ably and faithfully served.

But with these advantages of salaries, some disadvantages are also connected. When a stipulated sum is to be paid year after year, inconveniences sometimes arise, either from changes in the circumstances of contracting parties, or from variations in the value of the compensation; and these inconveniences may affect both those by whom a salary is paid and by whom it is received. Sometimes, those bound to the payment of a salary, become unable to fulfil their engagements without embarrassment and loss. On the other hand, those to whom payment in this form is made, find that their calculations as to the expense of living have been erroneous, and that the amount which they receive is inadequate to their support. In such cases, the happiness and usefulness of those concerned may require, that the agreements, thus entered into, should mutually be given up, and new arrangements made.

It is sometimes stipulated, that salaries shall be paid, in whole, or in part, in other commodities than money. In judging of the expediency of arrangements of this nature, we may apply the principles stated in the former part of this work on the subject of price. If the commodity, in which it is stipulated that payment shall be made, be one of prime necessity, as wheat, or any other agricultural product in general use, the value of the compensation, though subject to occasional variations, will remain nearly the same for many years. If the commodity be of a different kind—an article of luxury, either manufactured or agricultural, the changes of value will be greater and more permanent. Of this we have an example in the celebrated case of the Virginia clergy against their parishioners. The latter had stipulated to pay the salaries of the former in tobacco ; but it was found, after a few years, that the value of this commodity had become greater, and it was contended, on the part of the parishioners, that they were bound only to the payment of an equivalent of the price of tobacco, at the time the contract was made. And here, it may be noticed, that the value of salaries thus payable in agricultural products, will generally increase.

But at the present day, salary contracts are generally paid in the circulating medium of the country ; hence variations in the value of salaries arise from alterations in the relative value of money and other commodities, or, which is the same thing, from changes in the price of commodities. I have incidentally referred to this subject in a preceding chapter, and shall here briefly state and apply two propositions, the correctness of which has before been shewn. 1. Money from variations in the cost of its production,—from its comparative plenty and scarceness at different periods, and also from the changes of its denominations, is subject to fluctuations of value, so that, supposing the value of other commodities to remain the same, their price, as affected by variations in the value of money, will alter. 2. The value of those commodities which supply the common wants of life, is ever subject to changes, so that, supposing the absolute value of money to remain the same, its relative value to other commodities, and of course the price of these commodities, will be continually fluctuating. Now, as the value of any fixed compensation will evidently depend on the price of articles for which it is exchanged, it is evident, that here is an inconvenience, to which those who receive their income in the form of salary, must ever be subject. Sometimes, the different causes of variation in value which have been stated, will counteract each other, and then the change will be slight; in other instances, they conspire to produce the same result, and thus essentially raise or depress the value of salaries. And here it may be remarked, that in the progress of society, there is ever a tendency to higher prices of the more common and essential commodities of life, the demand becoming greater in proportion to the supply as population increases. There is also a tendency in the progress of a nation to a higher and more expensive style of living.

Whenever, in the different ways now stated, the price of commodities has varied, or other facts and circumstances have occurred, which essentially affect the value of a fixed compensation, the principles, on which the contract was originally formed, evidently justify and require, that a corresponding alteration in the salary should be made. Sometimes, indeed, the amount of salary to be received is based upon the price of the common articles of domestic consumption, and it is stipulated, that a rise in the prices of these commodities shall be followed by a corresponding increase of salary; and where no stipulation of this kind is expressed, it is still evidently implied.

It is often objected to salaries, that those who receive a fixed compensation will cease to feel any strong motive to effort and improvement. The incumbent of an office, it is said, is aware, that his support is secured to him independently of the manner in which his services are rendered, and may on this account become remiss; or if negligence is not found, no higher attainments, or increased ability, are sought. The force of this objection is to some extent acknowledged, but it may be hoped, that in most instances, some higher and better motive will come in to take the place of that which has been removed. There are also in many cases prospects of preferment. Still, perhaps, it might be advisable, wherever it is practicable, to let the amount of compensation depend in part on the success and ability, with which services are rendered. At the same time care should be taken, lest the increased effort thus secured, be attended with less fidelity.

The professional laborers who receive a compensation in the form of salary, are principally moral and religious, and literary and scientific teachers. In some departments of the civil service also, a remuneration is made in this form, especially, where it is deemed important, to raise those thus employed above all considerations of private interest. Hence judges, and the most responsible executive officers, receive salaries. And not unfrequently the situation of such is rendered still more independent, by the stipulations, that their salaries shall not be diminished during the tenure of office, which is usually for good behaviour ; and sometimes, when the term of office is limited, that they shall neither be increased nor diminished. There has of late been a tendency in this country, to multiply the instances, in which public services are remunerated by salaries. Thus, in many of our counties, sheriffs and clerks of courts, who formerly have derived their income from fees, now receive a fixed compensation, or at least are limited as to the amount which they are permitted to receive. It is designed in this way, to make it for the interest of this class of public officers, to exert their influence for the prevention of crime and of criminal prosecutions. Perhaps also the purity and permanency of our civil institutions, would be made more safe, if a limit were thus fixed to the compensation of public officers of every grade and description, since in this way the struggles for office, so dangerous to the State, would be less frequent and violent.

It was remarked, that a remuneration for the services of unproductive laborers, is sometimes made under the general name of compensation, or pay. I here have particular reference to legislators, and to other instances, where service is rendered on some special occasions, and for short periods, as in the case of commissioners and referees. Military services are also remunerated in this manner. But as the principles which apply in these instances, do not essentially differ from those already stated, it is not necessary to enlarge upon this topic.

CHAPTER VII.

Consumption of Wealth.

Production was defined in the first chapter of this work, to be the process of adapting material products to the wants of men. Objects thus adapted acquire properties, which make them articles of exchangeable value, thus constituting the wealth of individuals and of the nation. Now Consumption, in the most general use of the term, is the opposite of Production ;—it is the destruction of objects of value, or of the properties on which their value depends. Sometimes objects of value perish, or decay. They are then figuratively said to be consumed by time. In other instances, such objects of value are destroyed by violence, either accidental or designed ; and then they are said to be lost, or wantonly consumed. In other cases, again, such objects are used for the supply of the wants of the community, and thus consumption becomes the consummation of the original purpose of the producer,—the commodity adapted to meet the wants of men, is made to meet these wants. There is yet another way, in which material objects of value are said to be consumed,—it is when their destruction is a part of the process of production. Thus indigo, and other articles used in the dyeing of clothes, lose the form which they have in commerce, and become united with other materials which constitute the texture of the cloth. Of these different kinds of consumption, the last is generally styled productive consumption, from the circumstance just mentioned,—that their consumption is a part of a process of production. It will be noticed, that in these instances there is no consumption of value,—the same value existing under a new form. Perhaps, then, productive consumption might with some propriety be considered, as merely that transformation of capital, which has before been shewn to be a part of the process of production. In the other cases mentioned, the consumption is called unproductive.

But while the term consumption, in its most general sense, is thus applied to the destruction of material objects, or of the properties of these objects on which their value depends, it also denotes the appropriation, both of individual and of national revenues, to their different uses. In this signification of the term, and such is the use of it which is now to be considered, it applies simply to the value of objects, without any reference to the objects themselves.

To illustrate this distinction, and shew more fully the meaning of the word consumption, as it is applied to the appropriation of revenue, I offer the following example: A farmer raises a hundred bushels of grain, which is a part of his annual revenue. Now we might apply the word consumption to denote the use made of this grain, as in the form of bread it affords sustenance to the different members of the community, thus supplying an urgent want. Here consumption is opposed to production, and relates simply to the destruction, or final disposition made of products. But we will now suppose the hundred bushels of grain to be sold, and that the value of it in the form of money, is in the hands of the farmer. Here, again, as we look at the uses made of this money, we apply the word consumption, not in the sense of the destruction of material objects, or of their properties, but as it indicates the appropriation of individual revenue to its different uses. Thus a part of this revenue would probably be expended in the purchase of groceries, or of some article of clothing, or of furniture; another portion may be given to the lawyer, or to the physician, or to the instructor, in return for their services; another may be appropriated to the payment of taxes for the support of civil government, and for other objects of general interest. Some portion also may be spent in amusements, or may be given away in charity, according to the habits and character of the individual. There may yet remain another portion, to take the form of productive capital, and thus be accumulated for the increase both of individual and of national wealth. In these several ways, the proceeds, that is the value of the hundred bushels of wheat, are expended, and thus this portion of the farmer's revenue is consumed.

Now it is in the last mentioned application of the term, as it denotes the appropriation of revenue to different uses, that the subject of consumption here presents itself to our notice; and I propose in the following sections, to consider some of the different ways in which revenue may be employed.

1. *Of that portion of individual revenue which is appropriated to the supply of animal wants.*

The first and leading object of most who are either engaged in the business of production, or who render what have been called unproductive services to the community; is to obtain a supply of their animal wants; and to this object a large portion of their revenue is usually devoted. Indeed, by many, the whole amount of their income is thus necessarily employed, excepting perhaps some small share, reserved for the payment of taxes and other unavoidable expenses. Of these wants, the first class embraces food, shelter, clothing, fuel,—those articles which are essential to existence. Then come the comforts and conveniences of civilized life—the artificial wants of men, which by indulgence soon become real wants.

When a portion of individual revenue is thus apportioned to the wants of its possessor, it is not necessarily implied, that the objects themselves thus appropriated, or the value of them, immediately cease to exist. It is often otherwise. An article of furniture may contribute to the comfort or convenience of its possessor, and thus supply an animal want, and still may continue to exist for many years. The consumption of the object itself thus appropriated may be gradual, still, as a final disposition is made of the portion of revenue thus expended, this portion of revenue is said to be consumed.

In reference to that portion of individual revenue, which is thus apportioned to the supply of animal wants, Political Economy enjoins moderation in the use of the comforts and enjoyments of life. It says to the man of limited income, that his expenditures of this class should be proportioned to his revenue, so that a share may remain for the supply of other wants, and, if practicable, some portion be kept in reserve to take the form of productive capital, and thus become provision for the future. And to enforce this counsel, it points to the improved condition of him, who devotes a portion of his income to the supply of his mental and moral wants; it also exhibits on the one hand the certain ruin of that man, who lives beyond his income, and the advancing prosperity of him, who in the practice of frugality, makes continual additions to his productive capital. To men of affluence, it allows a freer use of the comforts of life, but at the same time it enjoins, that they be not wasteful. They are told, that as the laws and institutions of society make them secure in their possessions, they are to make returns for benefits thus received, by the employment of their revenues, and the exerting of their influence in those ways, which may conduce to the public good; and in this connexion, they are reminded of the influence of their example on the less favored classes of society.

In some nations sumptuary laws have been enacted, but the expediency and wisdom of such measures are more than doubtful. From the nature of the case it is difficult, if not impracticable, to fix on any limits to advantageous consumption of the kind we are considering, to decide where necessaries end and where luxuries begin. It is evident, that the expenditures of each member of the community, should bear a proportion to his income and to his condition in society, and what in one individual may be proper and advantageous consumption, in another might be improper and disadvantageous. Hence the difficulty of framing laws, which shall be applicable to individuals thus differing in their situation and circumstances. But there is another important objection to all restrictions of this nature. It deprives society of its most active stimulus to exertion. Men need ever to have before them the prospect of advancement,—of greater abundance and of higher enjoyments. It is thus, that they are led to become industrious, and to shake off that indolence and lethargy, to which they are so strongly inclined. Even a taste for luxuries may become in this way highly beneficial to the community.

But on the other hand, the impression, which has sometimes prevailed, that the wasteful extravagance of the rich is to be encouraged, on the ground, that in this way more full employment is furnished to the laboring classes of society, is to be guarded against, as unfounded and hurtful. On this point, neither encouragement nor restraint is needed. Set men free, on the one hand from the restrictions of legal statutes, and on the other, from the influence of erroneous opinions, and those results, will be secured, which are most beneficial to the individual and to the community.

2. *Of that portion of individual revenue, which is appropriated to the payment of public taxes.*

Taxes are requisitions made by the government of a country, or by local authorities, for the support of civil and municipal institutions, and for other objects of general interest. Every member of a community, who participates in the benefits arising from the association, is bound by this consideration and by other principles pertaining to the social compact, to contribute his share towards the support of the common burdens; and it is in the form of a tax, that this contribution is usually made.

Civil government is regarded by the political economist as strictly an economical arrangement; it is a mode of securing to each individual objects of the highest importance to his welfare. Security of person and of property are prominent among these benefits, and were individual members of a community to attempt the attainment of these objects, each one for himself, this course, if practicable, would evidently be far more expensive. The same remark applies to other objects, for the attainment of which the revenues of a nation are consumed—to what is expended in public works, in education, and in support of the poor. All these object are thus effected in the most economical manner.

Hence, then, it should be felt, that though taxation is a burden, it is a necessary burden, and that for what is thus expended, a full equivalent is received. At least this will be the case, where taxes are judiciously and impartially laid and collected, and the revenue thus derived is wisely expended. The expenditure of public revenue will form the subject of the next chapter. I propose in this place, to bring to view some of those principles, which relate to the assessment and collection of taxes.

Adam Smith, when treating on the subject of taxation, in his Wealth of Nations, has stated four general principles, by the application of which, the fairness and expediency of all measures of this nature may be tested. I shall here introduce what he has said on this subject, with some abridgement, and then apply the principles stated, to the system of taxation in our own country.

"I. The subjects of every state ought to contribute towards the support of the government, as nearly as possible, in proportion to their respective abilities; that is, in proportion to the revenue which they respectively enjoy under the protection of the state. The expense of government to the individuals of a great nation, is like the expense of management to the joint tenants of a great estate, who are all obliged to contribute in proportion to their respective interests in the estate. In the observation or neglect of this maxim consists, what is called the equality or inequality of taxation.

"II. The tax which each individual is bound to pay ought to be certain, and not arbitrary. The time of payment, the manner of payment, the quantity to be paid, ought all to be clear and plain to the contributor, and to every other person. The certainty of what each individual ought to pay is, in taxation, a matter of so great importance, that a very considerable degree of inequality, it appears, I believe, from the experience of all nations, is not near so great an evil as a very small degree of uncertainty.

"III. Every tax ought to be levied at the time, or in the manner, in which it is most likely to be convenient for the contributor to pay it. A tax upon the rent of land or of houses, payable at the same term at which such rents are usually paid, is levied at the time when it is most likely to be convenient for the contributor to pay; or, when he is most likely to have wherewithal to pay. Taxes upon such consumable goods as are articles of luxury, are all finally paid by the consumer, and generally in a manner that is very convenient for him. He pays them by little and little, as he has occasion to buy the goods. As he is at liberty too, either to buy, or not to buy, as he pleases, it must be his own fault if he suffers any considerable inconveniency from such taxes.

"IV. Every tax ought to be so contrived as both to take out and to keep out of the pockets of the people as little as possible, over and above what it brings into the public treasury of the state. A tax may either take out or keep out of the pockets of the people a great deal more than it brings into the public treasury, in the four following ways. First, the levying of it may require a great number of officers, whose salaries may eat up the greater part of the produce of the tax, and whose perquisites may impose another additional tax upon the people. Secondly, it may obstruct the industry of the people, and discourage them from applying to certain branches of business, which might give maintenance and employment to great multitudes. While it obliges the people to pay, it may thus diminish, or perhaps destroy, some of the funds which might enable them more easily to do so. Thirdly, by the forfeitures and other penalties which those unfortunate individuals incur who attempt unsuccessfully to evade the tax, it may frequently ruin them, and thereby put an end to the benefit which the community might have received from the employment of their capitals. An injudicious tax offers a great temptation to smuggling. But the penalties of smuggling must rise in proportion to the temptation. The law, contrary to all the ordinary principles of justice, first creates the temptation, and then punishes those who yield to it; and it commonly enhances the punishment too in proportion to the very circumstance which ought certainly to alleviate it, the temptation to commit the crime. Fourthly, by subjecting the people to the frequent visits and the odious examination of the tax-gatherers, it may expose them to much unnecessary trouble, vexation, and oppression; and though vexation is not, strictly speaking, expense, it is certainly equivalent to the expense at which every man would be willing ro redeem himself from it. It is in some one or other of these four different ways that taxes are frequently so much more burdensome to the people than they are beneficial to the sovereign."

Of the different taxes in the United States, the first and most prominent distinction is into direct and indirect. Direct taxes, of which there are several forms, are assessments upon individuals, based generally on their supposed ability to pay. Indirect taxes are duties on articles of consumption, which enhance their price, and thus fall upon consumers.

Different kinds of Direct Taxes.

Capitation Tax. A capitation, or, as it is more frequently called in this country, a poll tax, is an assessment on individuals without reference to their property. In England, and France, and other countries where distinctions of rank are known, a poll tax is assessed on the ground of these distinctions, those in each class of society paying the same amount. Thus, dukes, earls, marquises, and others, pay a poll tax, each in proportion to his grade. In our own country, where distinctions of rank are unknown, a poll tax is the same in amount on all male members of the community, who are not on account of age, or by some disability, excused by law.*

Tax on real and personal estate. Though in making out tax lists it is usual to mark the distinction between real and personal property, and also to enumerate different classes of objects, as lands, houses, bank-stock, navigation &c., these distinctions are made, merely with reference to the convenience of the valuation of property and the assessment of taxes, without any regard to a difference in the rate of taxation, grounded on the kind of property. For it is usual, after ascertaining in this way the total amount of property in the town, county, or State, as the case may be, to apportion the whole amount to be raised on the value of the property in the possession of each individual.

Tax on income. Another form of taxation, which is recognised in our statute books, though not extensively adopted in practice, is a tax on income. The law in reference to this tax usually provides, that the different professions and employments in life shall be subject to a tax, proportional to the income derived from them. In the application of this law, however, taxes on income are

---

* In assessing a poll tax, it is customary to proportion $\frac{1}{6}$ or $\frac{1}{8}$ of the whole amount to be raised on those subject by law to the payment of this tax, and if the sum assessed on individuals exceeds an amount prescribed by statute, and which is usually a small sum—one, or two dollars, the proportion of the whole tax to be raised in this form is diminished.

usually limited to professional men, especially to those whose compensation is paid in the form of salary.

Taxes on income are usually regarded with dislike, and the apportioning of them is attended with difficulty. It is difficult, except in the case of those who receive a fixed and known compensation, to ascertain the amount of income, and if this tax be limited to one class of the community, while others escape whose situation and employment are similar, there are grounds of complaint. Besides, it is to some extent a tax upon industry, and thus manifestly injurious to the interests of the public. It would also be necessary, in order to its equal apportionment, to take into the account the style of living, and the necessary expenditures of the different classes of society.

Indirect Taxes.

Indirect taxes bear different names, as duties, customs, excises, imposts, but under these different names, the same thing in its nature is denoted—a tax levied on commodities and paid by consumers.

The adjustment of indirect taxes, or the forming of a tariff list, prescribing the amount to be paid on different commodities, is often attended with difficulty, especially, as in this manner the interests of different classes of the community, and of different sections of a country, are liable to be variously affected. On this ground, objections are sometimes made to indirect taxation ; but the difficulties which arise from this source, when duties are levied with no other object than a collection of a revenue, are less, than those often attendant on the assessment and collection of direct taxes.

Objections are also made to indirect taxes as expensive in their collection; but where due economy is introduced into this department of the public service, this ground of objection is also removed

On the other hand, there are important advantages, which attend this form of taxation. What is thus paid is usually paid with little inconvenience and uneasiness. Indeed many are not aware, that they are paying a tax, when for their own use they purchase some article on which a duty has been laid, augmenting its price; or, if aware of it, the inducement to obtain the article is so strong, that the additional price, arising from the tax, is not felt to be an objection. Taxes are also thus paid in small sums, and according to the ability of the payer at the time.

Another circumstance before alluded to, which recommends indirect taxation, is, that it enables the government to exert an influence on consumption, favorable to the economical and the moral interest of the community.

I have thus mentioned the different taxes, that are imposed by the public authorities in this country, and which taken together, constitute the system of taxation here found. If now we apply to this system the principles, of A. Smith, it will be seen, that it is probably the best, that under existing circumstances can be adopted.

1. It secures, so far as is practicable, an equal and impartial distribution of the public burdens. Should each different kind of taxation that has been mentioned, be separately considered, objections would be seen to exist. The poll tax, which assesses an equal amount on all whether rich or poor, if it were the only tax imposed, would obviously be unfair. A tax levied on the amount of proper-

ty, both real and personal, in the possession of individuals, would not always correspond with their ability to pay, or their obligations to support public burdens, as determined by other considerations. A tax on income also, is unequal, since it looks only at the amount received, without reference to the necessary expenditures of the individual, in the situation in which he is placed, and which are evidently, much larger in some instances than in others. So too, in respect to indirect taxation, if it were the only form adopted, it would throw upon some a large proportion of the expenses of the community, while others would be left untaxed ; for while one part of the community are consumers to a large amount of foreign commodities, on which indirect taxes are collected, another part almost entirely dispense with their use. But now when the whole system of taxation is applied in its different parts, these inequalities are all remedied. He who bears too large a share of the burden in one form, has less to bear in another, and he who escapes one kind of taxation, is brought in to pay his due proportion in another kind, and thus an equal distribution is effected. Such at least is the tendency of our present system of taxation ; but it is obvious, that no general principles and regulations can be adopted on this subject, which in their application will not require exceptions to be made. Much also must evidently depend on the fairness and impartiality of those, by whom the business of assessing and collecting taxes is conducted.

If now we look at the second point mentioned by A. Smith—the definiteness of taxation as to time and manner of payment and the amount to be paid, this also is well secured by our present system. The principles and rules observed in the assessment of direct taxes are generally known and understood, and the time and manner of payments described. Every tax-payer is not only distinctly informed of the amount of his taxes, but, excepting the tax on income, which is left to the arbitrary decision of those by whom it is imposed, is permitted to know by what calculations this amount is determined. It is the case too, that those by whom direct taxes are assessed, are usually selected from among the people, and by their own choice, which offers a security that this assessment will be fairly and impartially made. Ways of obtaining redress are also open to those who consider themselves aggrieved. In regard to indirect taxes, the duties on each article thus subjected to taxation, are fixed by law, and made known; and every one is left to become a consumer of commodities thus taxed, to any extent which he pleases.

The third point to be considered, relates to the time and circumstances of payment. And here, as has been before mentioned, is one of the principal advantages attendant on indirect taxation, since what is thus collected is paid in small sums, and its payment is not felt to be an inconvenience; perhaps it is unknown, or not regarded by the payer. It is also usually so arranged in respect to direct taxes, that the amount assessed is known some weeks or months before the tax is collected, and thus the payer is left to suit his own convenience in the time and circumstances of payment.

The remaining particular relates to the expense and other circumstances, attending the collection of taxes, and also to the influence of different taxes on the industry and general interests of the community.

Perhaps no plan could be devised, to essentially diminish the expenses incurred in the collection of taxes in this country. As our Government is constituted, there are manifest advantages in the arrangement, by which the National and State authorities derive their revenues in different ways, and hence the expediency of supporting establishments for both direct and indirect taxation. And both are so conducted, that there is ground of complaint, neither as to the expenses of collection, nor any unnecessary trouble and vexation. At the present time, also, the burden of taxation in this country is too light to offer temptations to the evasion of taxes, or in any way to affect unfavorably the interests of the community. Every individual, therefore, is bound to pay his proportion of the public expenses cheerfully and promptly, knowing and feeling, that he receives in return an ample remuneration, in the civil rights and immunities, which he enjoys, and in the peace and security in which he lives.

Of that portion of individual revenue which is appropriated to the payment of unproductive laborers, to amusements and to charities.

That a part of the revenue of the sick man may wisely be appropriated to the payment of the physician, by whose advice and assistance health is restored, no one can doubt. So too, he, whose rights of property or person are endangered, or who needs aid in the transfer of property, or any legal act of a similar nature, applies to the lawyer for assistance, and can afford to remunerate him for the services thus rendered. And in most instances, there is no danger, that an undue proportion of individual revenue will be devoted to these objects. Now and then, a splenetic or a litigious man is found, who thus impoverishes himself, but such evils usually work their own cure.

Other services, for the remuneration of which individual revenue is expended, relate to education, and to moral and religious instruction. On the importance of these objects, as they are connected both with the happiness of individuals and the welfare of communities, incidental remarks have already been made. It has also been shewn, that such services have an indirect bearing on the economical interests of society. The general remark may here be added, with particular reference to education, that so far as the portion of revenue thus consumed, is given for aid in preparing for the more able and skilful discharge of the business of life, it becomes productive capital well invested ;—so far as it furnishes gratification to the natural thirst of man for knowledge, or leads to the enlargement and improvement of the mental powers, it is highly conducive to individual enjoyment.

Amusements. By some individuals a portion of their revenue is expended in amusements ; and the public good requires, on principles before stated, that the prospect of gratifications of this kind should be before men, as a motive to exertion. It also requires, that those amusements should be chosen, which are strictly consistent with purity of morals. And in this injunction, it looks at the tendency of the gratification. If from accompanying circumstances and associations, the indulgence, though in itself innocent, leads to evil, it is to be shunned. It is on this ground, that theatrical entertainments, and other amusements of a similar nature, are condemned.

There is also a class of amusements, which from their effects on both the economical and moral interests of individuals and of society, are deserving of particular reprehension. I refer to gambling in all its forms—at the bowling-green, the card table, or the lottery office. Whether we look at the passions indulged in these employments, or at the waste of time and property incurred, or at the ruin and misery, which so generally follow in their train, we see abundant reason, why they should be regarded as opposed to the best interests of society. It will also be noticed, that the transfers of property thus effected, are by no means advantageous, but, on the contrary, often place it at the disposal of those, who waste and squander it.

The most rational amusements are evidently those, which unite usefulness with pleasure,—either promoting the happiness of others, and thus gratifying the benevolent feelings, or adding to the stores of practical and valuable knowledge.

Charities. "Ye have the poor always with you," said our divine teacher, and whether we regard the sympathies of our nature, the constitution of civil society, or the general principles of moral obligation, we find abundant reason for the exercise of the charitable feelings. Every one, according to his ability, is bound to minister to the wants of the necessitous around him, and hence every one is bound to appropriate to this object some portion of his revenue.

The most interesting question, which presents itself on this subject to the Political Economist, relates to the manner in which relief is afforded, whether it shall be extended by the hand of individuals, or by public institutions and agents. But this topic will present itself in the following chapter.

CHAPTER VIII.

National expenditure.

Nations in their capacity as public bodies, receive a revenue and possess and consume wealth. It will be noticed, however, that what is thus received and held and used by the public authorities of a country, in behalf of the nation, is to be distinguished from national wealth, as that term has been defined. Hence the term public property is sometimes applied to the former, and the wealth thus held is said to belong to the government.

Public property may consist of all the different articles which constitute wealth. National revenues also, though generally received in money, may be paid in any form, suited to the convenience of those from whom they are received and of the government.

National revenues are derived from different sources, principally from taxation. An income is sometimes derived from the sale of public lands, and in some instances governments engage in processes of production. The second of these sources, it is evident, must soon be exhausted, especially as the policy of every nation requires, that its territory should be possessed and cultivated by individual proprietors. As to the third, it is ever found, that attempts of this kind are unwisely made, the expense of their management generally equalling, if not exceeding, the revenue derived from them. It is then, principally, to direct and indirect taxes, that nations look for their public revenues. And as this subject has already received attention, our inquiries in the present chapter will relate to the different ways, in which the revenues of a nation are expended.

The consumption of a nation is principally in the payment of the services of its functionaries in the civil, judicial and military departments. Some portion is also expended in public works, in education, and in affording relief to the destitute. These different modes of expenditure will now receive a distinct and brief consideration.

Of that portion of national revenue, which is expended in defraying the charges of civil and judicial administration.

The nature of the services rendered by public functionaries, and also the general principles which apply to the remuneration of these services, whether in the form of fees or salaries, have been considered in preceding chapters. One or two topics only of a general nature here require attention.

Economy requires, that the remuneration of public functionaries in the civil and judicial departments of public service, should be sufficiently high, to command the best talents in the community. Most of the duties to be performed are important, and some of them reponsible and difficult, requiring great integrity and skill ; and the public can well afford to offer the lure of a high compensation to those, who possess the necessary qualities, making it for their interest to engage in the service of the State.

On the other hand it should be remembered, that if the

compensation of public officers very far exceeds that of those, who are engaged in other similar employments in life, violent and dangerous struggles for office will arise, and very probably the places of trust and power will be filled by ambitious and corrupt men, who are altogether inadequate to the discharge of the duties of their stations. In some nations, there are public functionaries, who receive no other compensation for their services, than the honor and power attached to office. It is so with members of parliament in England. The principal argument adduced in support of this plan, is, that in this way security is obtained against venal influence, since those only will be employed in the public service, who from their ample fortunes are raised above all mercenary considerations. On the other hand, it is objected, that integrity and skill in conducting public affairs are not necessarily connected with great wealth, and that hence, from the incompetency of those employed, an arrangement which may be deemed economical, may eventually prove most expensive to the nation. Neither are men of large fortunes entirely insensible to venal and corrupt influences. The love of wealth and the desire for its attainment, often increase with its possession. It is also said, that the public safety may forbid, that the great influence which attaches itself to wealth, should in this way be augmented by the power of office.

Another remark connected with expenditures in support of public officers, merits attention. It relates to the fondness for show and parade, which exists in some communities, and the expectation, that those in office will gratify these desires. But it should be remembered that the expense of every kind of display made by those in office is ultimately borne by the community, since in this way the necessity of a higher remuneration is created. Every gratification then of the expectation of parade and show in public officers, is at the expense of those who are indulged, and is generally dearly paid for.

Of that portion of the public revenue which is appropriated to defray the charges of wars and of Military and Naval establishments.

From the prevailing sentiments and practices on the subject of war, it becomes necessary, that some provision should be made by nations, for their defence against foreign aggressions, and for the enforcement of their rights, and to this object no inconsiderable portion of the revenues of a nation are devoted.

The expenses connected with war are not limited to seasons of actual warfare, but embrace also the support of what is called a peace establishment, which includes military equipments and armaments, and also the pay of a professional soldiery. There are different arguments, by which the necessity and expediency of this arrangement are defended. It is thought to be more economical, and in other ways conducive to the public interest, thus to support a hired soldiery, than that those engaged in the productive employments of life, should be subject to interruption in their labors, and be exposed to the temptations and hardships and dangers of a military life. War too has become an art, and success in conducting it depends much on the perfection, to which this art is carried in a country; hence the necessity, that a professional soldiery should be trained and prepared for this department of public service. And further, the old maxim is adduced, that the best security for peace is a state of full preparation for war. If indeed this last argument were well founded, it would be wise to make large expenditures in support of a peace establishment; but it is to be feared, that a state of preparation for war and a desire for active service on the part of those trained to the art, have too often led nations to subject themselves to this greatest of national curses.

But the support of a peace establishment is an inconsiderable portion of the charges, incurred in this department of national expenditure. The consumption of wealth in a protracted war, is immense. If the contest is supported abroad, the expenses of conducting the war are much increased by the charges of transportation, and the difficulty of furnishing supplies to troops in a foreign land. If the scene of warfare is at home, the devastation and losses to which a country is thus exposed, are to be added to other expenses. The statistics of modern warfare furnish many and striking facts on this point.

No practice exists among nations, on which the political economist is compelled to look with more full and entire disapprobation, than that of war. Cases may indeed sometimes occur, in which the charges thus incurred, are justified in view of the benefits which result; but such cases are rare, and perhaps in all instances, the necessity of resorting to measures of this kind might be prevented. There are also other and more weighty objections to a state of warfare, which though indirectly connected with the economy of nations, it belongs rather to the department of ethics to exhibit and enforce. In many points of view, it is most desirable, that this practice, which is the scourge and disgrace of the human race, may speedily be done away, and those who are engaged in attempts to effect this important result, should receive the encouragement and support of every philanthropist.

Of that portion of the public revenue, which is expended in the erection of public buildings and in internal improvements.

The preservation of the national property and the conducting of public business, make it necessary, that many buildings should be erected at the public cost; and in the erection of these edifices, not only is utility to be consulted, but taste and national pride may also be gratified. Still, there should obviously be a correspondence in these expenditures to the resources and ability of the nation. And what is expended in this manner more than is necessary to meet the wants of the community, may be looked upon as designed to promote the advancement of the fine arts in the nation, and to strengthen the love of country.

Of the necessity and expediency of national expenditures for internal improvements, different opinions prevail. On the one side, it is maintained, that there are works of great national importance, which can be undertaken and carried forward in no other way. It is further added, that the resulting advantages are so widely and generally diffused, that the expense thus incurred, ought in justice to be borne by the whole community. On the other hand, it is said, that great difficulties and objections are connected with the disbursement of the public revenues in this form. Internal improvements, from their nature, must be local, and hence they are sources of sectional jealousies and contentions. There are also temptations to abuses and corruption, which arise from the opportunities thus offered to the ambitious and designing, to effect their selfish purposes and aims. Economy also requires, that so far as is practicable, a different policy should be pursued, since all public works are carried on at a much higher charge, than those which are conducted by private individuals.

Could some plan be adopted, which might obviate these objections, important benefits would obviously arise to a nation, from the portion of its revenues thus employed.

Of that portion of public revenue, which is appropriated to the relief of the poor.

It is customary in most nations, to make provision by law for the relief of the poor; and for this end, a system is adopted, under the direction of the public authorities, for the collection of revenues to be thus expended, and for their distribution among those who need relief. That some provision of this kind is needed, may be learnt from the following statement;

Justice requires it. Those, who either from events over which man has no control, or from their own vices, have become poor, will be found in every community. But, if it be left entirely to individuals to afford relief to the destitute, this burden will devolve wholly on those of humane and generous feelings, while others, on whom the obligation to assist is equally binding, will contribute nothing to this object.

Humanity also requires it. Unless some system for administering relief be adopted, and provision be made, to which in extreme cases all may apply with certainty of assistance, there is reason to fear, that some may perish from want. At least, instances of great privations and suffering would be far more frequent.

Economy requires it. The same amount, given by a judicious and well ordered system of distribution to those who reside under the same roof, and sit at the same table, under the supervision of the same overseer and provider, affords both more effectual relief, and to a greater number of individuals, than when gratuitously distributed. In this way, also, a favorable opportunity is afforded of benefiting the poor in other respects. They may be encouraged and aided in their efforts to supply their own wants, and led to form habits of industry and frugality. And further, they may be brought under those moral and religious influences, which are peculiarly needed for their consolation, and for the reformation of any vicious habits, which may have been contracted.

In opposition to this view, it is said that, to make provision by law for the support of the poor, presents the exercise of those generous and humane feelings, which should be indulged, and strengthened, and also that relief thus extended is wont to be received without any emotions of gratitude. Those who administer it, are oppressive and overbearing, those to whom it is given, claim it as a right, instead of thankfully receiving it as a charity.

It is replied to this objection, that to make provision by law for the support of the poor, will neither prevent the opportunity or necessity of private charity. Cases will often present themselves in every neighborhood, in which the generous and humane feelings of the heart may be indulged. The manner of administering public relief may also be such, as to be free from the abuses referred to. It need not render the situation of a pauper desirable, and still it may afford comfort and effectual assistance. But this leads me to notice another, and the principal objection to public charity.

I refer to the statement, so often made on this subject in connexion with the poor law system of England, that to make provision by law for the support of the poor encourages improvidence and idleness. It is indeed true, that the poor rates of England are a heavy burden upon the inhabitants of that country, and also, that much inconsiderateness and profligacy and idleness, are found in the lower classes of her population. But it is by no means a sure inference, that the pauperism and other evils found in that nation, are to be traced to her system of poor laws. Some of them are without doubt to be attributed to other abuses, connected with the institutions of the country and the management of public affairs, especially with the extent, to which her restrictive measures, and her oppressive direct taxation have been carried. Neither, if it be true that England by her pauper system makes her own poor, does it necessarily follow, that in other countries a system may not be adopted, which shall not be attended with these unhappy results.

The existing arrangements in the United States for the relief of the poor, are thought to combine as many advantages, and to be as little open to objection, as any which can be devised. There is an equal distribution of the burden;—effectual relief is provided, and at the same time those moral influences are brought to bear upon the poor, which may lead to the improvement of their characters and condition. Moral reform is also effecting much for the diminution of pauperism in the United States. Whether in the progress of this nation, the plan now adopted shall be found insufficient or become subject to abuses, time will shew.

Of that part of the national revenue, which is appropriated to Education.

A nation is evidently interested in the cultivation of the sciences, and the general diffusion of knowledge, within its limits. In different parts of this work, it has been shewn, that the former is intimately connected with the developement and improved use of the aids of nature in the different branches of production, and thus with the supply of human wants. The latter also, as it makes the laboring classes of a community more skilful and intelligent in their labors, and leads them more fully to understand the relations and duties of life, and to appreciate more highly their rights and privileges, is conducive to the national quietness and prosperity.

But here the question arises, how far it becomes necessary, that for securing these important results public assistance should be given? In respect to many branches of education, it is evident, that the interests of individuals, as connected with their success in the different employments and pursuits in life, will lead to their cultivation. Still, even in these instances, it may be economy on the part of a nation, to furnish at the public charge facilities and helps for professional education. But there are other cases, in which study and research are highly useful and important to the community, while no correspondent benefit results to the individual, who is engaged in these pursuits. It is so with the man of science, who investigates and developes those laws of the natural world, and those principles in science, which, when thus discovered and made known, are applied to important practical and profitable uses, from which however the discoverer receives no pecuniary benefit. In this view, then, since the public is so deeply interested in the labors of scientific men, there is reason, why public aid and encouragement should be extended to all who are thus employed.

If too we look at the other result, which, it is evidently important to the community should be secured—the general diffusion of knowledge, the reasons, which shew the necessity and expediency of public aid, are obvious. A large portion of the less wealthy classes of society are unable to provide instruction for their children in the common branches of education. Their revenue is barely sufficient to meet their more pressing and daily wants. Others, who are able to furnish the means of education to their children, do not appreciate its importance, and neglect it. In such cases, the general good evidently requires, that some portion of the public revenues should be directed to the support of schools, in which the poor, free of all charge and expense, may be taught the rudiments of knowledge.

It is thus, then, in the highest and lowest departments of education, that the necessity of public assistance is most urgently felt; and this aid may be extended both in encouraging and rewarding those who are employed in this work, and in offering facilities and helps for the acquisition and diffusion of knowledge. Hence then we may infer the utility and importance of the common school system of New England, by which the rich are made to contribute for the education of the poor, and by which, also, the school room with all its privileges, becomes accessible to the humblest child in the community.

But in addition to this view, which exhibits the importance of education to the national welfare, from its connexion with scientific discoveries, and the general diffusion of knowledge, it may be remarked, that whatever pertains to the cultivation and improvement of the mental powers, to the increase of knowledge, and to the gratification of the taste, is intimately connected with national prosperity and happiness. And that portion of revenue, whether private or public, which is thus expended, if it may not strictly be regarded as a productive investment of capital, is a rational and highminded consumption of wealth.

END.